The End of College Football

The End of College Football

*On the Human Cost of an
All-American Game*

Nathan Kalman-Lamb and Derek Silva

The University of North Carolina Press CHAPEL HILL

Set in Merope Basic by Westchester Publishing Services
Manufactured in the United States of America

Library of Congress Cataloging-in-Publication Data
Names: Kalman-Lamb, Nathan, 1983– author. | Silva, Derek M. D., author.
Title: The end of college football : on the human cost of an all-American game /
    Nathan Kalman-Lamb and Derek Silva.
Description: Chapel Hill : The University of North Carolina Press, 2024. |
    Includes bibliographical references and index.
Identifiers: LCCN 2024020850 | ISBN 9781469683454 (cloth ; alk. paper) |
    ISBN 9781469683461 (pbk. ; alk. paper) | ISBN 9781469683478 (epub) |
    ISBN 9781469683485 (pdf)
Subjects: LCSH: Football—Economic aspects—United States. | Football—
    Social aspects—United States. | College athletes—United States. |
    Exploitation. | College sports—United States—Management. | United
    States—Race relations. | BISAC: SPORTS & RECREATION / Cultural &
    Social Aspects | SPORTS & RECREATION / History
Classification: LCC GV956.4 .K35 2024 | DDC 796.332/63—dc23/eng/20240610
LC record available at https://lccn.loc.gov/2024020850

Cover art: Black football field, iStock.com/peshkov.

To Elizabeth and Avery,
For a world that doesn't require human sacrifice.

Contents

Tables

Preface

As Canadian fans preoccupied with college sport who became scholars of athletic labor at high-revenue NCAA Division I schools, we occupy an insider-outsider status that produces an unusual lens for grappling with the contradictions of a fundamentally exploitative and yet deeply naturalized political economy—big-time US college football.[1] We follow Dorothy Smith's vital injunction that sociologists cannot "claim to constitute an objective knowledge independent of the sociologist's situation," which is to say that "sociological inquiry is necessarily a social relation."[2] The sociologist can never be a neutral social scientist. Rather, researchers' positionalities always act on the object(s) of research. The point is to understand how and why, and that is what we unpack here in the interests of transparency, accuracy, and basic morality.

NATHAN: YOU MIGHT THINK THAT a Canadian child born and raised in Toronto by parents who attended Canadian colleges would have passing interest in US interuniversity athletics. But you would be wrong. My father attended university in Windsor, just a few dozen miles from Ann Arbor. He adopted the University of Michigan through the convenience of geography and an appetite for the meaning offered by the spectatorship of a sport he once played. I inherited the affiliation as readily as I learned from him to love sport itself. We were Michigan fans. My Saturday afternoons in the fall, like those of many of my kindred spirits across the border, centered around a game that fueled my vicarious fantasies for a week or left me in an absurdly exaggerated and yet undeniably authentic state of grief, disgust, or rage. I accumulated Michigan Christmas tree ornaments, miniature footballs, hoodies, basketball shorts, and a Charles Woodson jersey. But the entire landscape fascinated me. I had a Miami Hurricanes hat and UMASS (University of Massachusetts Amherst) basketball shorts. March Madness was my most sacred holiday.

It would probably be neat and tidy to say that I imported this college sport-loving subjectivity when I was hired to teach about inequality and athletics at Duke University, but it would not be truthful. By that point I had already become a scholar of sport, labor, race, and inequality. Although I retained affective investments in elements of college sport that I will probably never shake, they were locked in a constant internal dialectic with my more rational assessments of the harms inherent to high-performance spectator sport. And yet, coming to Duke was a learning experience, in part because I view the institution as the best of what college sport can be—resource rich and attentive to the academic needs of athletes—but nevertheless fundamentally exploitative to its very core. At Duke, I taught writing seminar classes on labor, inequality, and sport to first-year students. These classes were filled with athletes who comprise a disproportionately large segment of Duke's undergraduate population. As a consequence, the class, at times, felt like a consciousness-raising exercise about college sport, particularly in its summer iterations offered almost entirely to meet the eligibility requirements of incoming athletes compelled to play at school if they were going to spend a summer working on sport. Yet my consciousness was raised as much as theirs during classes and office hours where athletes shared details of their—to me—scandalous experiences of mistreatment in the course of athletic labor. It was the banal that struck me as much as the exceptional: athletes barely able to keep their eyes open in class, games that took them away from school throughout the week, team summer camp counselor responsibilities that forced them to spend all day outside working for free or a pittance under the merciless North Carolina sun. This book explores the structural necessity of all these forms of exploitation, but it is informed by the daily experience of teaching and thinking at a Power Five (now Power Four) university, often with campus athletic workers.

I have now worked in universities for more than fifteen years in a variety of roles—graduate student, teaching assistant, and adjunct—and I have been on strike for many months in these roles over two labor actions. I have also been a non-tenure-track faculty member without a union, a non-tenure-track faculty member with a union, and a tenure-track faculty member with a union. In all of these roles I have experienced the varying forms of precarity and exploitation that define higher education today, and also the remarkable capacity for solidarity to challenge and contest those dynamics through labor organization. It is these experiences that shape my reading of higher education and the role of campus athletic work in that political economy.

DEREK: MY OWN FANDOM was conditioned by a youthful obsession with the commodity spectacle of sport in all its manifest forms. Being a sports fan was a key performance of my identity through my formative childhood-to-teen years, and a growing part of that was the consumption of the college athletic spectacle.

We were, like many Canadians, a hockey family. Not until my early teen years did I begin to pay attention to college athletics. This period of my life represents the pinnacle of the 'uncritical consumerist' stage of my relationship with US collegiate athletics—unabashed, unapologetic, and routine consumption in as many forms as possible. The emotive draw to US collegiate athletics perhaps reached a climax when I was applying to PhD programs. I made a concerted effort to include several programs at 'top' research-intensive universities that also had well-known athletic departments.

When I first arrived at the University of South Carolina as a PhD student, college athletics intoxicated me. I intentionally avoided turning my sociological imagination toward sport because I did not want to ruin it. I saw how Donna Haraway interrogated the companion relationship between people and dogs—thus forcing me to question the relationship with my own—and it made me think about other parasocial connections I relied on in everyday life.[3]

I mostly continued as an uncritical consumer of US college athletics during my first year at South Carolina, attending all kinds of athletic events and readily and willingly participating in the US college athletic culture I had craved from afar. It was exciting, fun, entertaining, and social at a time when I was in a new country without any tangible relationships. I consumed the college athletics brand with very little thought about the labor on which it was built or the questionable ethical characteristics fundamental to collegiate athletics. I was a hypocrite, and I sort of knew it.

This ethical exchange intensified as I began teaching introductory sociology and sections of sociology of sport, where I interacted with huge proportions of so-called student-athletes (a concept we reject in favor of the more appropriate 'campus athletic workers'). In a series of troubling events, I started to see the hypocrisy I suppressed; the warts not only became clairvoyant, they became inescapable.

The initial instance occurred while I was teaching one of my first sports sociology courses. I was up late completing a paper for one of my required courses. It was well past midnight, and I thought I should get some sleep because I had an early class to teach. The Gamecocks were playing an away game, which I had on the TV while I worked. I knew some of the players were in my early morning class, and I wondered, how will these athletes get to class tomorrow? I went to sleep without giving it much more thought. The next morning those very same athletes who were finishing an out-of-state match past midnight the night before showed up for my early morning class.

The next incident happened one fall morning after teaching a class, when a burly man from the athletics department—middle aged, appearing over six feet tall, and likely over three hundred pounds—approached me as I left the classroom. The conversation began with a pleasant exchange before quickly getting to the point. "I want to talk to you about one of our players who's in your class," he said. "I understand he isn't doing very well, and I wanted to ask you how we can support him better to ensure he improves." "I am one of the coaches," he continued, "and I am just here to make sure [campus athletic worker's name] improves in your course." Growing tired of my opaque responses, he said, "I'm not sure you understand me, Derek, [the student] needs to pass your course and we need to figure out a way to make it happen." I shrugged and decided it was time to exit. I opened the office door, side-shuffled inside, and attempted to close it quickly. The man reached out and stopped the door from shutting. He stepped inside, closed the door, and used his hand to keep it closed. "We're not done, Derek," he said aggressively. "What will we do to make sure [the student] is able to play? I care about him passing. That's all." As he said this, he scanned the shared office, seemingly puzzled by the four desks, each with a separate computer, sectioned off with a bookshelf. "Oh, you're like a graduate student or contract teacher or something? No problem. I'll go have a chat with some of your superiors. Have a great day." He opened the door and left, but I couldn't shake the feeling of fear and anxiety for months.

This interaction fundamentally changed my perception of college athletics. For the first time I experienced the pressures surrounding college football, the power of athletic departments, and the antipathy and contempt that at least some athletic department staff hold for academics. This moment represented the death of the 'uncritical consumer' stage of my college sport fandom and marked a turning point in my academic career where ignoring sport, sporting culture, and sports-related phenomena was no longer possible.

WE WOULD BE REMISS in not acknowledging the ways in which our identities as cis white men inform this book. While these positions confer forms of privilege, power, and opportunity both within the academy and at large, and are part of the explanation for why we can coproduce this book in the first place or occupy the roles we hold and have held in the university, they are also relevant to our relationship to this research project. Given the prevalence of hegemonic masculinity in the world of elite football, our own presentation of heteronormative masculinity helped facilitate our interlocutions with the former college football players we interviewed. Yet it is also true that our whiteness may have been a complicating factor in conversations with Black players, who, given experiences within the plantation dynamics of higher education and college football, had every reason to be mistrustful of white people in positions of power/authority. We believe this factor was mitigated to a meaningful degree by a reputation we developed during and prior to our research through public writing that involved work with Black athletes that was highly critical of the racism ubiquitous in the world of college football. This unquestionably built some measure of trust. At the same time, we would be naive if we imagined our interview participants did not feel at least some (highly rational) misgivings about sharing with us. Because of this, the experiences of racism in the academy and college football for former players are likely worse even than what we depict in this book.

To be sure, the world of college football is a dynamic place. Over the last few years, we have seen (and continue to see) numerous shifts in the ways college athletes are exploited for their work. At the time of interviewing for and writing this book, for example, the men's basketball team Dartmouth had not yet voted on unionization, the Power Five conferences still existed as such (prior to the recent geographically convoluted consolidation to a Power Four), and the National Labor Relations Board was still only urging athletes to consider unionization efforts. None of the athletes interviewed for this book experienced unionization and few enjoyed the emergence of remuneration for Name, Image, and Likeness (NIL). The reader will note that we speak at length about some of these seemingly familiar concepts as if they have not and do not undergo periods of flux and change. While we hold that it is important to note this caveat, we also acknowledge that the lived experiences of those we interviewed for this book reflect a world of college sport that may not be entirely recognizable today—and those realities are both empirically and theoretically valid. In fact, these experiences provide a useful framework for understanding how and why even as the political economy of college football undergoes seemingly radical flux, a throughline of exploitation and extraction remains a guiding imperative for those empowered to oversee that change.

While neither of us are free from our own hypocrisies in our evolving relationship with US college sport, we believe that our participation in college academic and athletic systems has given us a unique position as observers and interlocutors of the realities of everyday life for campus athletic workers. We write as people intimately familiar with the pleasures and customs of college football and with its dynamics within the Power Five (at time of writing) university. At the same time, we approach the sport with a strange sort of anthropological distance. We are Canadians (although we eschew the nation as a form of personal identification), so we are also well acquainted with a system of higher education that does not fetishize the athletic nor privilege it within the university. We like to think that we approach this project as insider-outsiders, a position that allows us to see the same thing as everyone else, but perhaps just a little more askew. We invite the reader to approach college football from the same angle.

Acknowledgments

By far the most important acknowledgment of this book goes to all the former college football players who generously shared their time and stories with us. Those stories are the substance of this book, and it is for them and all their colleagues that we wrote it.

Portions of Chapter 1 were published in a slightly different form open access in the journal *Critical Sociology* as "'Play'-ing College Football: Campus Athletic Worker Experiences of Exploitation," *Association for Critical Sociology* 50, nos. 4–5 (2024): 863–82, DOI: https://doi.org/10.1177/08969205231208036, and are used with permission.

We also want to thank everyone who contributed directly to the production of the book. Thank you to our research assistant Melissa Elliott for their help with transcription and to Jessica Newman for her excellent editorial contributions that undoubtedly improved the general readability of the manuscript. Huge thanks, too, to Chen Chen for his generous reading of the manuscript, and to Jules Boykoff, who provided incredibly supportive and substantive feedback that has helped make this book the best version of itself that it can be—and also for years of friendship, support, and solidarity that mean more to us than he can possibly know. We quite literally would not have been able to accomplish this project without the aid of UNC's fabulous senior editor Lucas Church, who first raised the prospect of the book with Nathan prepandemic in 2019 and helped shepherd (and edit!) it to its current iteration, despite being confronted with a document twice the promised length.

Although it was perhaps the most urgent possible demonstration of the necessity of this project, the COVID-19 pandemic very nearly ended it. Nathan is incredibly grateful to Derek for agreeing to be a partner in the book. Without the collaboration, it would have been impossible. More than that, it is unfathomable to imagine a more ideal collaborator.

Finally, we have nothing but enormous appreciation for our families, who enable and sustain all of the work we do. This book is for Jen and Elizabeth, and for Ali and Avery.

The End of College Football

Introduction

Exploitation and Harm in the Ivory Tower and on the Gridiron

Imagine it's a hot summer day in the Southwest—sunny, not a cloud in the sky, dry, and about 108 degrees. You're a student at the university, and you also play on the football team. You woke up at 4:30 a.m. for an early morning practice to both avoid the heat and ensure practice will be over by the time your classes start at 8:30 a.m.

But practice doesn't go too well. After three hours of grueling physical and mental strain for the players, the coaching staff isn't happy. They saw a few fumbles, some dropped passes, a couple of missed tackles, and they aren't letting the team off the hook. The strength and conditioning coach turns to the head coach and mutters, *Should we send 'em to the concrete?*[1] After a few seconds the head coach responds, *Well, someone's gotta teach 'em what it takes.*

"There was this driveway next to the field going down into some garage with, like, some storage and stuff. Whenever the coaches didn't like something, like every week, we'd have to go to the concrete," former Power Five player Charlie Rogers told us. "[The coaches] pretty much framed it as . . . making you more into a man or whatever shit they say. We'd be told to go to the concrete, and it was like nicer concrete, but there were ridges in the concrete," he said. "In those ridges there were jagged rocks in the cement. So the coach has us doing knuckle push-ups on concrete with jagged rock pieces. . . . I think twenty-five [push-ups], but it was on [the coach's] cadence."

DOWN!! the strength and conditioning coach yells. The players lock their elbows at ninety degrees in the down position of a push-up. *I'm not sure y'all want to be here today. What do you think, boys?* the coach asks the players struggling to hold their push-up. *Do you deserve to play football?*

Time ticks by—twenty seconds, then thirty, a minute, sometimes two or three. And just as sweat starts to drip from the athletes' faces and blood begins to trickle from their knuckles, *UP!!* hollers the coach as they force their bodies up. *Why do you even come out here? Y'all want to play football?*

Rogers distinctly remembers hitting the concrete on a weekly basis. "We'd be out there probably for like thirty to forty minutes with our knuckles in the ground, and mind you, I was like 350 pounds. So 350 pounds into your knuckles on the concrete with jagged rocks . . . my knuckles would be bleeding like crazy. It took about six or eight months for my knuckles to turn back to my regular skin color . . . like they're completely scarred. . . . Ask any player that one. Everybody's knuckles will be just completely black. No matter what skin color they were." Sadly, this form of what amounts to institutionalized torture is a basic reality for many football players toiling at universities across the United States. It has also, to a significant degree, been obscured by public debates about amateurism, higher education, freedom, and, perhaps above all, compensation.

The question of whether college athletes should receive more compensation than scholarships and other minor benefits has never been more pressing. Public figures from LeBron James and California governor Gavin Newsom to Connecticut senator Chris Murphy have clearly stated, by word and by bill, that these so-called student-athletes—as the National Collegiate Athletic Association (NCAA) characterizes them—deserve to be paid. In April 2020, the NCAA announced it would allow players to receive compensation for use of their name, image, and likeness (NIL) for the first time—ushering in what many have called a "new era" of college sport. This new era was consolidated in February 2023, when a Tennessee federal judge granted an injunction sought by the attorneys general of Tennessee and Virginia against the NCAA's NIL enforcement rules. In response, NCAA president Charlie Baker issued a memo to member schools announcing that those rules would indeed no longer be enforced. On another front, in June 2021, US senators Chris Murphy and Bernie Sanders introduced the College Athlete Right to Organize Act, and in September of that year, general counsel for the National Labor Relations Board (NLRB) Jennifer Abruzzo issued a memo to the NCAA arguing that college athletes should be viewed as employees subject to relevant employment rights and protections. In 2022, the National Collegiate Players Association (NCPA) filed a complaint with the NLRB Los Angeles region arguing that University of Southern California (USC) football and basketball players have been misclassified as amateurs rather than employees, a case that positions the Pac-12 conference and the NCAA as their joint employers alongside USC. Across the country at Dartmouth College, the men's basketball team voted in March 2024 by a count of 13-2 to unionize with the Service Employees International Union (SEIU). These developments, in conjunction with recent athlete mobilizations around racial and social injustice, police lethality, and return-to-play protocols during the pandemic, suggest that we're on the verge of a revolution in the fight for campus athletic workers' rights. Note that we use the term 'campus athletic workers' and its variants (i.e., athletic workers, athletic laborers) throughout this book instead of 'student-athlete,' which masks the exploitation at the core of college football. Former Power Five player Wallace Bell explains the reasoning perfectly: "I don't identify myself as a student-athlete. I'm a collegiate athlete. A lot of us collegiate athletes do not know these things. And it needs to be brought to our attention. . . . Because if you don't understand who you are and what your identity is, that's how systems can continue to exploit you."

In the coming chapters, we argue that the reformist movement to grant college athletes their NIL rights masks the profound harm at the core of elite NCAA sport, particularly in its highest revenue-generating and most dangerous iteration: football. The NIL campaign is little more than cover for an exploitative and dehumanizing system hiding in plain sight within institutions mandated to facilitate education and well-being. Rather than retread the familiar ground of reformist policy and economics, our work challenges the premise of Power Five college football through in-depth interviews with former players who endured and sustained it.[2] Our project is not about reform; rather it illuminates the ways college football is so foundationally harmful that it *cannot* be reformed.

This book is a sociology of big-time NCAA football and a polemical call to action against a system of violent, racialized labor exploitation that flourishes within our esteemed institutions of higher education. You will read harrowing, and at times heartbreaking, testimony from twenty-five former college football players who endured the realities of giving up their labor to a system that rarely, if ever, benefits them directly (see the Methodological Appendix for details on methods). We highlight the contradictions in both the sport's logic and that of the reformist movements seeking to mitigate its harms, exposing instead the very impossibility of big-time college football as an ethical form of commodity spectacle. Unlike other work that reduces these questions to a purely economic calculus, our project brings us face to face with campus athletic workers—forcing a confrontation with the lived experience of the system's harm among those victimized by it.

This book asks us to reimagine a world without the violent exploitation of a predominantly racialized class of young athletic laborers coerced into selling their bodies to fuel the commodity spectacle of college athletics. Many scholars from a range of disciplines have considered the intersections of sport, exploitation, and athletic labor.[3] Taylor Branch, for example, has relentlessly documented how the supposedly "noble" principles on which the NCAA justifies its own existence—the concepts of "amateurism" and "student-athlete"—are pseudolegal constructions propagated by universities to justify the exploitation of athletic laborers. In fact, as Branch finds, Walter Byers, the NCAA's first executive director, created the notion of the "student-athlete" in 1964 to protect universities from having to provide long-term disability payments to players injured while playing their sport.[4] But Byers didn't anticipate the way that the concept would ultimately facilitate an enduring mass-commercialized system that continues to harm athletic workers almost sixty years later—what he later called a "nationwide money-laundering scheme" and an "air-tight racket of supplying cheap athletic labor."[5]

Alarmingly little has changed over the past decades in how the NCAA and member institutions perceive their obligations (or lack thereof) to athletic laborers—consciously labeled "student-athletes" to evade workers' compensation protections, a practice even the US Supreme Court and the NLRB have come to problematize—who generate an increasingly enormous amount of money for these institutions. Many scholars have revealed the persistence of the concept of "amateurism" in both public and NCAA discourse as a tool to subjugate athletic workers to economic exploitation at the hands of universities.[6] As it is framed by the NCAA and member institutions, putatively nonworker college athletes receive a priceless asset in return for their labor: an increasingly inaccessible college education. Yet a body of literature has emerged widely critiquing this form of remuneration on the basis that education does not negate ongoing economic exploitation, that the current structure presents a heavily racialized form of exploitation, and that education neither is a core feature of the remunerative exchange between universities and athletes nor is effectively occurring *at all*.[7] This work interrogates the deleterious foundation on which the entire NCAA model of college athletics rests—the mystification that players are "students" first and "athletes" second. Rather than operationalizing "exploitation" in a manner that rehearses the compensation debate, we follow Derek Van Rheenen by defining the concept from a moral perspective: "When one party receives unfair and undeserved benefits from its transactions or relationships with others."[8] We thus question whether education is even possible in the context of college football while emphasizing how this form of athletic labor serves a social reproductive function for the political economy of late capitalism.[9]

Framing high-performance spectator sport as social reproduction means acknowledging it as a form of commodity spectacle produced for a market—fans. There are multiple significant implications to this, both for the athlete and the spectator. For the latter, spectator sport reproduces the fan as a subject of capitalism by providing a sense of meaning and community predicated on the necessarily dangerous and sacrificial labor of athletes—necessarily dangerous because the athlete's willingness to sacrifice their body in sport is a foundational condition on which the spectacle is based. Injury and harm are therefore not incidental features of high-performance spectator sport, but inherent correlates central to the political economy itself. For the athletes, it means their work is exploitative not only from a fairly conventional Marxist approach, but also in terms of the additional harm that comes from the social reproductive dimension of their work—the demand that they reproduce the subjectivity of another through sacrifice.[10] To provide the fans with the meaning and community they seek, the athlete must play through and risk injury, even to the point of potential death. This comes at a profound physical and emotional cost, much of it borne long after careers end and the crowd's roar fades. But there is a crucial implication for the fans here too: the sacrifices of athletes like college football players are performed *for us.* By participating in fandom, we are participating in market forces that tell universities and the sports/media complex that these sacrifices *should* be made, that they are necessary. Understanding high-performance spectator sport as social reproduction, then, means confronting our own complicity as fans in the harm that athletic workers endure.

Our work builds on the theoretical intervention of Erin Hatton, who characterizes labor in college sport as "status coercion."[11] Because the work of college sport is unpaid, opportunity and status operate as compensation—the opportunity to showcase oneself to the professional leagues that may provide future actual compensation and the status of 'big man on campus' and even 'student' that carry forms of cultural and social capital. Because coaches and athletic department officials have a monopoly on opportunity and status, they exercise absolute authority over the not-quite-occupational experiences of college athletes. To challenge coaches' authority is to potentially jeopardize one's position on the team and in the university when that position is the source of all benefit accrued for one's labor. To be a college football player, then, is to be fundamentally unfree.

In addition to status coercion, we argue that players' participation in college football is premised on another form of coercion that funnels them into coaches' authoritative arms: structural coercion.[12] We draw on Jill A. Fisher's analysis of how the possibility of informed consent in medicine is often compromised by the structural factors that essentially compel patients to consent to medical research and treatment. In contexts of material privation, particularly when caused at the structural level by a system of racial capitalism, an "opportunity" can appear opportune because of its relative merit compared to the aspirant's current circumstances. Something is better than nothing, and subjection to life-altering brain injury in return for access to higher education and the possibility of professional rewards may be better than the conditions otherwise available to a young football player. This is not consent proper. Consent requires an entirely *free* choice, and a choice made under coercive conditions or constraint is not free. Thus, despite assumptions that players enthusiastically consent to participate in college football, the sport is saturated with forms of coercion that radically constrain the freedoms of the predominantly racialized athletes, indeed, that fundamentally condition the question of participation itself. While scholars have focused on consent from the perspective of the NCAA and member institutions, few have focused on the question from the viewpoint of athletic laborers.[13] The entire apparatus of the college football–industrial complex is predicated on the unfree choice of players to participate under the pressures of racial capitalism. Structural coercion and US racial capitalism are the necessary conditions for the exploitation and harm that is college football. They furnish a steady and significantly racialized labor supply for college football, which participants may (rightly) see as the best of a series of bad options.

Athletic labor performed under such coercive conditions heightens the possibility of physical and emotional harm, as players must often endure abusive coaching and overtraining to satisfy the whims of their overseers. Players ultimately bear the long-term consequences of this harm, not just bodily, but also financially, given the punitive nature of privatized health care, which universities that employ them refuse to cover.[14] One Power Five player explained how he reconciled his fear of harm: "I know that there is a chance that I could receive a concussion, I feel as though it is a part of the game and it's a possibility, but it won't deter me from the game. . . . Yes, there are risks, but the opportunity to take care of myself and the people around me is nothing compared to taking a couple of shots. The risks are huge now with the introduction of studies that link CTE [chronic traumatic encephalopathy] and concussions, but for myself and others I wouldn't be where I am in life right now [without] sports."[15]

But this isn't just a story about economic exploitation. It's about the systematic exploitation of predominantly racialized young people at the hands of disproportionately white authority figures in predominantly white institutions (PWIs). Scholars have documented how college football epitomizes what Cedric Robinson famously calls racial capitalism—a process whereby white authorities extract economic value from Black and Brown folks by structuring the labor market in which they participate.[16] Building on the intellectual traditions of Robinson and others like W. E. B. Du Bois and Stuart Hall, Billy Hawkins was among the first to illuminate how the NCAA structure embodies a new plantation model through which PWIs subject Black and Brown athletes to experiences akin to the "broader historical and social context of exploitation endured by internally colonized people in the system of slavery."[17] Building on this framework, we document some of the ways college football's exploitative dynamics are inherently and inextricably linked to racial capitalism as a function of structural racism in the United States more broadly.

This book is thus grounded in a theoretical framework that recognizes college sport as part of a system of US racial capitalism. Charisse Burden-Stelly conceptualizes US racial capitalism as:

> [A] racially hierarchical political economy constituting war and militarism, imperialist accumulation, expropriation by domination, and labor superexploitation. The racial here specifically refers to Blackness, defined as African descendants' relationship to the capitalist mode of production—their structural location—and the condition, status, and material realities emanating therefrom. It is out of this structural location that the irresolvable contradiction of value minus worth arises. Stated differently, Blackness is a capacious category of surplus value extraction essential to an array of political-economic functions, including accumulation, disaccumulation, debt, planned obsolescence, and absorption of the burdens of economic crises. At the same time, Blackness is the quintessential condition of disposability, expendability, and devalorization.[18]

While there are multiple and contested definitions of racial capitalism, for us Burden-Stelly provides the most incisive approach, inclusive of the surplus value extraction in the US context, that helps unpack the political economy of contemporary cultural systems, including sport.[19] As noted by Du Bois and Hall, a key function of race in capitalism is its role in systemic reproduction—race fragments the solidarity of the working class, allowing for the reproduction of the relations of exploitation that sustain capitalism writ large.[20] Much as others have documented across sporting environments, we hold that the premise of Power Five college football is the systematic extraction of surplus value from racialized communities to benefit primarily white institutions and authorities.[21] Contextualizing racial capitalism as such allows us to at once see the NCAA system as part and parcel of a racial capitalist political economy and a modality through which individual actors—in this case, campus athletic workers—are faced with the realities of racialized wealth extraction to benefit a small group of primarily white authorities.[22]

Both historically (i.e., slavery, Jim Crow) and contemporarily (i.e., the prison-industrial complex, NCAA college football), the cultural devaluation of Black life justifies the systematic exploitation of Black labor for the value it produces. This means that the United States (and elsewhere) is built on an ongoing racial transfer of wealth, one that began during the period colonization and plantation slavery and continues to shape access to resources and opportunities today via an organization of social relations that has also been called structural racism and white supremacy.[23] Aside from the prison-industrial complex, nowhere is this more evident in US society today than the world of college athletics, and college football specifically. Hawkins calls the system the "new plantation" because in the PWIs that comprise big-time college sports, Black athletes are subjected to substandard and fundamentally exploitative working conditions even as they generate considerable value for the universities that don't quite employ them.[24] In that this system is predicated on a refusal to compensate disproportionately racialized athletes while subjecting them to brutal labor, he—*accurately*—identifies a continuity with the system of slavery that fueled global capitalism. Following Hawkins, we characterize college football as a labor relation defined by "plantation dynamics" and contend that it is a core feature of the racial capitalist wage transfer from Black and racialized communities to primarily white authorities.[25]

Perhaps even more palpable than the economic and social exploitation is the compounding reality that tackle football is and always has been an inherently violent producer of long-term corporeal harm.[26] Deeply embedded in football culture and practice is a foundational acceptance and rewarding of heteromasculine physical violence and its consequences even from the youth level. Kathleen Bachynski has documented the deleterious consequences of a football culture premised on the "necessity" of violent labor.[27] Our project builds on, but departs from, much of this literature by highlighting the ways that harm has been lived by the college football players who endure it through their own voices. Given that between 91 and 99 percent of US college football players posthumously examined display neuropathology consistent with the degenerative brain disorder CTE, we hold that sacrifice is a nearly universal feature of Power Five college football, not merely an incidental and unfortunate consequence.[28] We thus explicitly aim to make intelligible the concerns of athletic laborers who have long experienced these damaging structural characteristics while proposing ways forward that go beyond the reformist logic that plagues contemporary discourse surrounding "compensation" in the NCAA.

Policy solutions addressing inequity in the larger racialized political economy of the United States would have profound material benefits for college athletes. Tuition-free college and a stipend for all who attend would transform the question of coercion/consent. Medicare for all would ease the lifelong consequences of the harm dealt by participation in college sport. This is not to say that the problems besetting big-time college sports are simply the problems of the United States writ large. The NCAA and universities have much to be held accountable for—namely economic exploitation, health and safety conditions, abuse, educational disparities, gender inequity, and plantation dynamics. We return to these later.

This book attempts to systematically work through the many axes of exploitation and harm that make and mar big-time college football. Rather than parsing the budgets of NCAA institutions or speculating on how we might more equitably distribute the revenue produced by college football players, we focus instead on the human cost of this exploitation. For the players we interviewed, there is little equivocation about the injustice of the system. We aim to interrogate, explore, and amplify these injustices as experienced by the campus athletic workers who have to endure them.

In chapter 1, we address key questions: What does it mean to call college football exploitation? Is college football a form of extracurricular play, or is it a form of labor? The answer for those we interviewed is self-evident, no matter their investment in the system. This is work, albeit uncompensated. Despite the exorbitant revenue produced in the Power Five conferences, players do not receive a basic wage, nor, historically, were they permitted to perform the additional labor of promoting themselves to procure some remuneration. Thus, even as athletic department administrators, coaches, university presidents, and constituents of the entire sports/media complex make a bountiful living in the world of college football, players do not. For most of the athletes we spoke to, although the precise form of compensation was up for debate, nearly all agreed pay was deserved.

In chapter 2, we focus on the putative compensation college athletic workers do receive: their education. We argue that the failure of NCAA member institutions to deliver on this most basic requirement of the 'student-athlete' experience is not a function of widespread academic impropriety—as we saw in the scandal at the University of North Carolina—but rather a structural failure to produce conditions conducive to learning. The fundamental barrier to an enriching academic experience for college football players is the burden of simultaneously having to endure a full-time and exceptionally strenuous form of unpaid labor. Interviews reveal the bitter irony that it is the relentless toll of their athletic work that prevents players from recouping an education resulting in a degree.

Chapter 3 calls for an entire paradigm shift in the debate over exploitation in college sport. We argue that exploitation in college football is not simply a function of how value is distributed, but also, and more profoundly, a question of the distribution of harm. It is impossible to adequately account for the costs borne by football players without reckoning with the physical toll the sport takes on them. The damage to bodies and minds is an inherent part of the sport, but it is compounded by a lack of occupational health and safety provisions and long-term health insurance, and by abusive overtraining practices imposed by coaches.

Chapter 4 focuses on the intersection of exploitation in college football with race. A significantly disproportionate number of college football players are racialized, particularly Black, which brings up critical questions about the racialized tenor of exploitation in college sport at PWIs. In addition to suffering the inherent harm and exploitation framing the experience of all college football players, Black athletes also experience particular hostility because of the perception that they do not properly belong on campus. We examine how the plantation dynamics of college football inform the experiences of and are understood by both Black and white players.

In Chapter 5 we turn to the question of coercion and abuse, documenting the ways in which college athletes' experiences are defined by forms of unfreedom even as the entire enterprise is justified by a fiction of consent ("they signed up for it"). Through an exploration of status and structural coercion of players, we reveal that college football requires forms of compulsion to ensure the systematic extraction of value from unpaid workers. Unsurprisingly, given the ubiquity of coercion in the sport, coaches empowered as figures of absolute authority often employ forms of abuse as the methodologies of extraction.

Chapter 6 offers the 2020 COVID season as a case study of harm and exploitation in the sport. By focusing on the complex struggles between those who wanted to play and those who opted not to, we underline the exploitative dynamics shaping player agency and also the forms of resistance that emerged, and offer a map for profound reforms of the sport.

Above all, this book is about the experiences of the athletes subjected to harm and exploitation in college football. We are not interested in paraphrasing or synthesizing those experiences, for to do so would be to both mini-mize and distort them. As Dorothy Smith puts it, "There are and must be different experiences of the world and different bases of experience. We must not do away with them by taking advantage of our privileged speaking to construct a sociological version that we then impose upon them as their reality. We may not rewrite the other's world or impose upon it a concep-tual framework that extracts from it what fits with ours. Their reality, their varieties of experience, must be an unconditional datum."[29] Reproducing the precise speech acts of the interview subjects is a form of fidelity to their "version" of the "experience" of participating in the world of college football. It is the "unconditional datum" on which the argument of this book is based and, more than that, is the single most important intervention we can make: to share experiences that did not previously exist in the public sphere.

The value of qualitative research is that it sheds light on how structure is lived. Too often, quantitative approaches fall into the trap of abstracting and thus dehumanizing the harms they attempt to chronicle. Qualitative approaches, alternatively, force us to confront or face that harm directly. Dipesh Chakrabarty writes that "the very act of listening to people orients us—opens us up—to their presence . . . this orientation is what I have called here the act of confronting suffering, of *facing*."[30] This book's primary dis-cursive strategy is to share lengthy, verbatim testimony precisely because it "positions the reader face-to-face with the victim of cruelty whose face al-ways carries the injunction: Thou shalt not [harm]. This is what makes nar-rative a political force."[31]

Yet, in this book, the face-to-face confrontation with the college football player is slightly mediated by anonymity. Players are anonymous and so too are the institutions and coaches they worked for. Although coaches' names are redacted, many are among the most famous in the sport, both at the col-lege and now National Football League (NFL) levels. These are not, in other words, outliers or anomalies. That identities have been concealed is both an ethical imperative and a pragmatic benefit: people are far more willing to dis-close the truth about their experiences when shielded from vitriol. Very few people have been willing to speak this candidly about what the sport actually looks like, certainly not in the mainstream media. Former player Steven Summers said his approach to speaking with us differed from how he tradi-tionally approached media: "If I'm doing an interview, I might hold back. I'm not really doing it with you, I'm being more myself with you, because I know this is like a confidential thing. You're just trying to get information, you're not writing like, 'Steven said, blah, blah, blah.' But if this was a more structured or public thing, then yeah, I'd be a little more reserved. But, that's just kind of the way it is. If anything, like the kind of work you're doing, you're probably getting more authenticity than other types of media."

A central premise of our argument is that the exploitation and harm that define college football are not just a function of the incentive structure of university athletic departments, but that of an entire sports/media complex.[32] The commodity spectacle produced by college football players is not only the stock in trade for university athletic departments and the NCAA; it is also the foundation on which the entire college sports/media–industrial complex is built. All of the jobs in the college football media industry, from on-air "talent" to the scribes at local newspapers, are predicated on the unpaid work of college football players. They receive a benefit (the very existence of their jobs) from the exploitation of campus athletic workers, and they also have a disincentive to critically cover the industry. Moreover, a social relationship exists between journalist and athlete that is *inherently* antagonistic to the athlete's interests, something athletes understand all too well. Former Power Five player Kurt Weiss characterized the college sports media this way:

> I think it's basically PR. College sporting events were nine out of the hundred most viewed events here on TV. So, for it to be that lucrative, networks are going to want—there's football on every day now, in the fall. And it's so lucrative, to uphold that narrative is going to be good for everyone involved. And I know the Big Ten network and ESPN are basically mouthpieces for the NCAA and conference. And down to the individuals that find themselves in those positions, I think [Kirk] Herbstreit's a total lackey. You rarely see anybody in that role express anything that looks like an opinion. It's just parroting what has been said for generation after generation from people in the industry.

By explicitly positioning ourselves outside of the sports/media complex we attempted to make this a safer space for former players to speak freely. These athletes had no incentive to participate in this project beyond the one articulated by Brock Adler: "It's done, it's finished. So, I have nothing to gain by this. I only want to tell this truth and I want people to know the truth."

This book's critique of college football will not be shared by all current or former players. Our sample is relatively small, and their experiences cannot and should not be universalized. In some respects, this testimony is exceptional, for it resists the powerful interpellatory and coercive forces that militate against speaking ill of the sport: the ideological hegemony of football as a form of culture in US society and the very material forms of censure experienced by those who push back against the system. It must be acknowledged that football is perhaps the most privileged form of popular culture in American society today. As such, most participants are interpellated into its logic and legitimacy from a young age. Jeremy Jones told us, "I have always loved it since I was a kid and never thought I would get a chance to play college ball. I remember growing up dreaming of playing at a place like [redacted school] in front of so many screaming fans." Football saturates US culture to the extent that it is difficult not to accept its legitimacy. Its very imbrication in the educational systems of the United States is testament to and tacit approval of its role as an instrument of socialization and a potential lever of social mobility. But the assumption that football is part of the fabric of American life, we argue, is a form of coercion: ideological coercion. There is a sense in which young people indoctrinated into football culture never fully and enthusiastically consent to the range of harms inherent in the sport, given that their participation begins long before they have matured to adulthood and, perhaps even more significantly, because their entry into football comes in a context wherein the sport is celebrated and embraced by figures of authority—by culture itself—rather than one of informed disclosure. Under such circumstances, the baseline expectation should be that participants in football generally endorse and embrace the sport; this is how we would expect most human beings to operate in this environment.

Likewise, there are very real material constraints acting on former college football players who might speak out against the sport. College football is often framed in familial terms as a sort of brotherhood. Anthropologist Tracie Canada has documented the many insidious corollaries of "family" rhetoric in football and how it is often internalized (even unknowingly) by participants to either justify or explicitly mask harm within those environments.[33] So, to speak out against that world is to betray those who may have come to feel like family. More than this, to do so can mean jeopardizing opportunities and access to resources. Because players are not compensated for their labor, they must seek value in alternative forms, one being the possibility of future employment opportunities from team donors. Access to these opportunities requires toeing the party line.

These factors are compounded by the fact that enduring harm and exploitation is potentially difficult and painful, requiring psychological compartmentalization and other forms of coping, including some fundamental principle of the worthwhileness of the activity causing that discomfort, a rationale of sorts. The rationale is an important psychological construct that cannot be easily traded in, no matter how much evidence accumulates against it—a kind of emotional armor that provides the strength to persevere. This rationale is necessary because tackle football is a form of systematic abuse—relentless physical and emotional harm—harbored within the very institutions entrusted with nurturing young people. To understand it as such, however, is to betray both an entire social and cultural system of meaning and one's own identity formation within it and to confront personal trauma. These are big asks. Thus, we argue that it is a damning indictment of this world that so *many* former players were willing to speak candidly about the harms they experienced. They are but the tip of an iceberg.

It must also be said that tackle football is a site of pleasure and meaning. For fans, yes, although that is incidental to our concerns here beyond the political economic implications of how those investments produce a market that directly impacts players' working conditions. More importantly, many football players love playing football and derive multiple gratifications from the game. They may not identify with the narratives and arguments in this book. This is partly because one attraction for some participants *is* the violence of the sport. As Daniel Barber explains, "I mean, I say anyone, especially if you do a lot of contact, if you're in a position with a lot of contact, you've gotta be a little bit crazy. Like, I like hitting people, like I'm into that. Not abusive, or anything like that. But it's fun for me. I'm a boy's boy in terms of, I want to jump, roll around, kind of deal. And that's something I miss, and that's something I crave. And football is the only legal outlet for that, except boxing and stuff." But the question here is, should such an outlet exist?

This book does not focus on one of the most significant aspects of harm related to the world of college football: sexual violence and domestic abuse committed by players. Our purpose is not to minimize or downplay the significance of this form of violence and harm, which we would argue is facilitated by a) the amount of power wielded by athletic departments that shield players from accountability in accordance with performance incentives and the perceived value of players to the production of that performance, and b) the violence built into the sport, which conditions players to act in aggressive and antisocial ways that cannot be turned off when they leave the field. Varda Burstyn has explained the latter issue through the concept of coercive entitlement: players are taught that they deserve any and all rewards they can achieve through domination/coercion such that this becomes the mode of engagement in all walks of life.[34] Although this was not the focus of our interviews, evidence did emerge from player testimony in support of this claim. Daniel Barber told us, "They want you to be almost animalistic. You've got to be instinctual. So can you do stuff like that [snaps fingers] and not second-guess yourself. So can you tap into just being strictly reactional, like just responding to a stimuli." To condition oneself to the point of instinctual reaction means developing behaviors that are triggered both on and off the field. Likewise, Matt Jensen explained that "I'd like to think that, for the most part, most guys were able to separate. But there are definitely guys where that football identity of aggression and constantly being in competition, that consumes their life." Terry Davis was even more forceful about it: "Somehow you're supposed to be a teddy bear off the field. . . . You have to have that killer instinct at all times [on the field]. Then them expecting for you to turn it off, how could I turn it off?"

Coercive entitlement and the forms of violence, including sexual violence, that can spill off the gridiron are unquestionably further arguments for why football does not belong on university campuses, but they were not the focus of our interviews. Valuable literature exists on this subject, and we particularly recommend Burstyn's *The Rites of Men* and Jessica Luther's *Unsportsmanlike Conduct*. Our argument is complementary to them, suggesting that campus football produces exploitation and harm in a range of forms. It is less productive to think about the college football–industrial complex, then, as an arena filled with "good" and "bad" actors so much as a site that systematically produces damaged people and benefits that accrue to others as a direct function of that damage.

In the book's conclusion, we outline how we think college football must move forward in both moral and pragmatic terms. However, we are unequivocal in our position that college football, like tackle football more generally, should be abolished. The sport is morally unsustainable given an accounting of both its exploitation and its harm. We call this book *The End of College Football* because all of the foundational features of the sport exist outside the possibility of reform. The system of college football is incompatible with any form of higher education authentically committed to teaching, learning, and the development of students. It is morally unsustainable precisely because it is grafted onto a world of pedagogy with which it is so very incompatible. As former walk-on Ross Nielsen put it, "I just realized all of college football's like this really big pyramid scheme built on a foundation of cheaply paid labor, which I now find myself in again as a grad student." Nevertheless, we remain acutely aware that part of the system's injustice is that it coerces students into making sacrifices that are antithetical to the putative mission of higher education and that abolishing college football does little to redress this. In fact, one might argue that the abolition of college football would serve to close doors of access, particularly to racialized young people too often excluded from the fruits of higher education at PWIs. This is precisely why we hold that the most meaningful change to this system of harm and exploitation must come at the level of the political economy of racial capitalism more broadly—through radical reforms like universal access to higher education, Medicare for all (health care), and, ultimately, the abolition of capitalism itself.

We thus encourage reading this book with this question in mind: Are the experiences of harm and exploitation articulated by players compatible with any coherent vision of a just and equitable society? The answer is clear for Charlie Rogers: "Honestly, if it were up to me, I would not bat an eye if football just ceased to exist. Just because of the stuff it does to people. Like that guy that fucking killed six people recently. And Aaron Hernandez. And all those other people who will just snap. And they're also, usually, people of color. . . . Whatever hardships that they had, they put it as, 'Oh, they're just a product of this environment' or whatever. When it's clearly just because they get in a car crash at least fifty times every day." We agree, and in the following pages, we demonstrate why.

CHAPTER ONE

"Play"-ing College Football

It's the day before a big game. One by one, members of a Power Five team pack a bus heading for a prime-time matchup in the South. Ryan Leonard, an offensive lineman, sits quietly by himself. The head coach—known around town as a particularly flashy guy—sits next to him. A quarterback nearby asks, "Hey coach, how much does that watch cost?" peering at his left wrist. As Leonard turns to look at the luxurious watch, the coach drawls, "More than your scholarship."

For Leonard, that incident sums up the economic realities of college football: "There's no doubt he knows how much my scholarship is worth, and no doubt he knows that watch is worth more. And literally, two days before that, I had just drained ten CCs [cubic centimeters] of knee fluid out my knee so I could continue to go play." Instances like these are not uncommon. Given the structural conditions of big-time college football, coaches can, and do, flaunt their wealth, making the economic inequities of exploitation at the core of college football crystal clear to campus athletic workers.

Derek Van Rheenen defines exploitation as "when one party receives unfair and undeserved benefits from its transactions or relationships with others."[1] In economic terms, exploitation occurs when that value is disproportionately distributed away from those who produce it via labor to some other party—the very premise of capitalism.[2] The prototypical example of exploitation is the value extraction from the worker by the capitalist through industrial production and wage labor. However, in the case of college football, the story doesn't end at exploitation vis-á-vis value extraction through wage labor alone. Equally significantly, college football represents one of the most tangible examples of *racialized* superexploitation in US society today as part of a broader system of wealth transfer from Black and Brown communities to predominantly white authorities in PWIs and the assemblage of beneficiaries that orbit big-time college football.[3]

But how does this understanding of exploitation apply to college football, given that the sport operates within the putatively nonprofit institutions of higher education? After all, there are no shareholders to pay out and no capitalists pulling the strings. Former player Ryan Leonard is unequivocal: "It's all about money. The NCAA is about power, but the NCAA is made up by institutions, who are about money." To unpack the financial logic of athletic departments, it is necessary to understand that the 'educational' and 'athletic' sides of the university have separate budgets. The argument that it is a travesty that athletic facilities are constantly being revolutionized on campuses, even as libraries and other academic facilities fall into a state of disrepair, is not only morally bankrupt (why should the athletic labor of college football players subsidize the academic conditions of other students?—per Van Rheenen, this would just be another form of unfairly distributed benefits: exploitation) but simply incorrect from a basic accounting perspective.[4] Of course, universities can muddy these waters for strategic purposes, for instance by soliciting donations earmarked for athletic facilities, levying fees on students to support the athletic department, or using scholarships paid out by the athletic department to transfer money back to the academic side. And the branding benefits of athletics for the institution at large are significant but notoriously difficult to quantify. Leonard told us, "At [redacted school], we had the president come and talk to us, and she goes, 'The way that [redacted school] is going to get on the map is through this athletic department right here, by being a top athletics [program], you will bring our university to prominence.' It's a lot easier for a university to be recognized for athletics than it is to compete with the Yales, with Rice, with Duke academically. So they found out it's actually a cheaper way to get notoriety." But, by and large, athletics and academics are discrete pools of cash.[5] For large Power Five athletic departments, revenue comes from ticket sales, merchandising, and, most of all, mega TV contracts shared with other institutions in their conference. Crucially, because these are nonprofit institutions, that revenue must be spent. This is why there is so much facilities construction, as schools use the revenue they must spend to invest in infrastructure that will lure the best recruits and in turn produce more revenue.

But this money also lands in the pockets of athletic department employees, including coaches and other administrators—some of the primary beneficiaries of the illegitimate and exploitative transfer of value that defines college sport.[6] This is a transfer from the football-playing campus athletic workers who largely produce value to the parasitic class of administrative officials who would literally not exist without that labor. As Oklahoma University football coach Joe Castiglione (surprisingly) acknowledged, "Let's face it, the whole world that we revolve around is the student-athlete. Period. That is why we exist. Without them, [we] don't need any of us."[7] Overall, the NCAA member schools reaped $18.9 billion in annual revenue in 2022.[8] In

2021–22, largely driven by football, some forty-two athletic departments each earned more than $100 million.[9] Of those, nineteen earned more than $150 million, and five earned more than $199 million, with Ohio State, Texas, Michigan, Georgia, and Louisiana State University topping the list. But the real question is: who directly benefits from all that revenue? The answer has to begin with head coaches, the overseers amply rewarded for the task of extracting value from players. In 2023, the twenty highest-paid coaches earned more than $7 million each per year.[10] Eleven coaches earned more than $9 million and six earned $10 million or more (see table 1). These coaches also often receive buyout clauses (see table 2) that pay them unimaginable sums *not* to work if they are fired without cause (i.e., not winning enough games). Between 2010 and 2021, $533.6 million was paid out to fired football and basketball coaches.[11] In the 2021–22 fiscal year alone, $90.6 million was paid to fired football coaches so that they wouldn't work at the fifty-two public Power Five schools.[12] Most amazingly, in 2023 Texas A&M coach Jimbo Fisher alone received a $77 million buyout upon being relieved of his position.[13] Moreover, it is not only the head coaches who benefit. In 2023, 66 assistant football coaches earned $1 million per year or more, and 21 strength coaches made $500,000 or more.[14].

Coaches, employed or otherwise, are not the only financial beneficiaries of this "nonprofit" system.[15] In 2021, fifty-one athletic directors earned $700,000 or more in annual salaries, with twenty-five of those earning $1 million or more.[16] For example, as of 2022, the Ohio State University athletic department paid a total of 2,158 people.[17] That figure includes 8 employees earning over $1 million annually (the highest being head football coach Ryan Day at over $8 million), 20 earning over $400,000 annually, 50 earning over $195,000 annually, 148 earning more than $100,000 annually, and 351 earning more than $60,000 annually. These positions span a remarkable range of occupations, including the expected team coaching staffs but also other departments including "athletics administration," "business office," "camps and clinics," "communications," "compliance," "creative services, and branding," "development," "event management and facilities," "facilities operations and capital projects," "stadiums," "human resources," "information systems," "legal affairs," and many more. This enormous array of jobs would not exist without college football players producing commodity spectacle for the university and, crucially, if not for the fact that the players do not receive the revenue derived from that commodity spectacle. Indeed, with increased potential for revenue-sharing with players on the horizon, it is instructive that in 2024 the athletic department at Texas A&M laid off more than a dozen

TABLE 1 Top twenty-five highest-paid college football coaches, 2023–24 (as of December 22, 2023)[a]

Coach	University	Reported salary
Nick Saban	Alabama	$11.4M
Dabo Swinney	Clemson	$10.9M
Kirby Smart	Georgia	$10.7M
Ryan Day	Ohio State	$10.3M
Mel Tucker[b]	Michigan State	$10M
Lincoln Riley[c]	USC	$10M
Brian Kelly	LSU	$9.9M
Jimbo Fisher[d]	Texas A&M	$9.1M
Mark Stoops	Kentucky	$9.01M
Josh Heupel	Tennessee	$9M
Lane Kiffin	Mississippi	$9M
James Franklin	Penn State	$8.5M
Jim Harbaugh	Michigan	$8.3M
Mario Cristobal[c]	Miami	$8M
Luke Fickell	Wisconsin	$7.6M
Mike Gundy	Oklahoma State	$7.6M
Mike Norvell	Florida State	$7.3M
Billy Napier	Florida	$7.3M
Brent Venables	Oklahoma	$7.1M
Kirk Ferentz	Iowa	$7M
Dan Lanning	Oregon	$6.6M
Hugh Freeze	Auburn	$6.5M
Bret Bielema	Illinois	$6.5M
Sam Pittman	Arkansas	$6.4M
Kyle Whittingham	Utah	$6.3M

[a] Data from *USA Today* (https://sports.usatoday.com/ncaa/salaries/football/coach)
[b] Fired from Michigan State on August 30, 2023
[c] Reported
[d] Fired from Texas A&M on November 12, 2023.

employees due to being "on the cusp of unprecedented change in the world of intercollegiate athletics."[18]

This is all playing out in the context of fundamental changes to college athletics brought about by the liberalization of name, image, and likeness (NIL) policies, adopted hesitantly by the NCAA and member institutions, to grant campus athletic workers their heretofore denied right of compensation for the use of their likeness. Don't get us wrong: the decades-long

TABLE 2 Top twenty-five highest college football coach buyouts, 2023–2024 (as of December 22, 2023)[a]

Coach	University	Reported buyout
Kirby Smart	Georgia	$92.6M
Jimbo Fisher[b]	Texas A&M	$77.6M
Brian Kelly	LSU	$70M
James Franklin	Penn State	$64.7M
Dabo Swinney	Clemson	$64M
Matt Rhule	Nebraska	$62M
Mark Stoops	Kentucky	$51.2M
Josh Heupel	Tennessee	$46.5M
Ryan Day	Ohio State	$46.2M
Nick Saban	Alabama	$44.8M
Dan Lanning	Oregon	$44.3M
Mike Norvell	Florida State	$42.2M
Luke Fickell	Wisconsin	$39.7M
Kirk Ferentz	Iowa	$37M
Bret Bielema	Illinois	$35.8M
Bill Napier	Florida	$32.4M
Jeff Brohm	Louisville	$31.4M
Brent Venables	Oklahoma	$30.6M
Chris Klieman	Kansas State	$29.6M
Lance Leipold	Kansas	$27.3M
Jim Harbaugh	Michigan	$27.2M
Hugh Freeze	Auburn	$25.1M
Mike Gundy	Oklahoma State	$24.9M
P. J. Fleck	Minnesota	$23.7M
Kalen DeBoer	Washington	$23.2M

[a] Data from *USA Today* (https://ftw.usatoday.com/lists/college-football-biggest-coaching -buyouts-jimbo-fisher-matt-rhule-dabo-swinney-brian-kelly)
[b] Jimbo Fisher was fired by Texas A&M on November 12, 2023 and reportedly received a buyout of more than $76 million (https://www.espn.com/college-football/story/_/id /38880082/jimbo-fisher-expected-fired-texas-sources-confirm).

denial of NIL rights to college athletes wasn't merely unjust; it was a fundamental violation of a basic human right to one's identity. The NCAA's prohibition against marketing oneself was perhaps the most egregious face of a system defined by little else than exploitation and harm. Nevertheless, despite the changes to NIL, the same exploitative system remains in place today. In fact, it has been further enshrined in the NCAA's most recent constitution.[19] So why doesn't NIL redeem college sport? Economist David Berri estimated that men's basketball players at an elite Power Five school like Duke hold an economic value of up to $4.13 million per year.[20] And, importantly, the labor-coach remuneration structure in big-time college athletics seems to be inversely related to that of professional athletics. Coaches in the NBA, for instance, tend to earn far less than top athletes. While the forms of economic exploitation in professional sport are worthy of their own analysis, big-time college athletics is perhaps the most egregiously conspicuous form of wealth extraction in all of contemporary capitalist sport, and the revenue produced by football far outstrips that of basketball.

The primary beneficiaries of the economic exploitation of campus athletic workers—the coaches, athletic department staff, and universities—still control the revenue generated by athletic labor, regardless of NIL. In fact, they retain complete control over the whole system, including the capacity to increase players' workload at will. For instance, in late 2022, universities agreed to a new playoff model, expanding from four teams to twelve in 2024, with that number likely set to increase to fourteen in 2026.[21] Some teams will play as many as *four* additional football games if they advance through the tournament bracket. The new two-year, twelve-team deal is worth $450 million annually of additional gross revenue for universities (the six-year, fourteen-team deal rises to $1.3 billion annually), but they provide zero additional economic benefit to the players who will play (work) the games that command such exorbitant broadcasting sums. Similarly, NIL places additional labor on the players if they want to receive compensation rather than allowing them direct access to the value they are already producing. In this way, NIL ushers in a new era of gig work for athletes while reinforcing the racialized economic exploitation of the current structure because it keeps the revenue flowing to universities while getting private enterprise to pay workers. In other words, rather than universities paying workers for their labor, private corporations are subsidizing NCAA member institutions.

Thus, even as athletic department administrators, coaches, university presidents, and constituents of the entire sports/media complex make a bountiful living from their participation in college football, players do not.[22]

For most of the players we interviewed, although there may have been dis-agreement on the precise form of compensation, there was near-uniform agreement that pay was deserved. The lack of pay was consistently viewed as a source of significant alienation in their work, partly reflected by the sense that a transition to the National Football League (NFL), although brutal in terms of working conditions, was a tremendous relief from the standpoint of finally receiving the bare fruits of their labor. In this chapter, we grapple with the ubiquitous question of compensation in college football by focus-ing on the human cost of this exploitation through engagement with the experiences of the athletes who lived it. For those players, there is little equivocation about the system's injustice. As Ryan Leonard puts it, "The in-stitution, the university, and all the staff and members are interested in profit. And for coaches and for administration, that means winning. Win-ning leads to the coaches getting higher salaries. It leads to administration getting bigger bonuses. It leads to the institution gaining more notoriety so that maybe they increase their student population or maybe they get better students. But it's driven by profits."

Playful Work

There is no question that football, like all forms of athletic labor, is in some ways distinct from other forms of work because it is labor borne of play. The activity that produces a commodity is, in this context, fundamentally, a game. Unsurprisingly, some players we interviewed highlighted the playful elements of their experiences working in college football. For instance, when asked if he felt like he was playing or working, Steven Summers explained:

> I would say that during practice, lifting and meetings and stuff, that's working. That's like: I'm showing up to work, this is a job. And you know, I enjoy it. It's not just like I love the games, I love the grind too. But that's the work, and then the play is Saturday. That's fun. That's when it's time to come out like, "Hey, this is what we've been working for," this is the reward. To get out here and compete. . . . I would relate it to when you show up to work every day, and you're busting your ass, you're working hard, you're showing up, doing what you're told, putting in the extra work. And then you get the reward, you get the payday at the end. You have to do the work first for it to be fun.

Although the tendency throughout this book is to suggest that football, par-ticularly college football, is a site of exploitation and harm, we would be remiss to ignore the fact that for many players, there is visceral pleasure found in the sport, and this pleasure is a significant motivating factor in participation and serves as a benefit even when other benefits may not be equitably distributed. From the standpoint of pleasure, it can be argued that the exploitative dynamics of college football actually detract from the enjoyment that might otherwise be found in the sport. This is something players explicitly articulated.

> JOSH HANSEN: I love the game . . . but you're also dealing with what you have to endure, will it actually get you where you want to go? So then, the kind of inherent exploitation of the game takes the fun out of the game. . . . Even when you have a scholarship, nothing is promised. It's like, you do all these things to make these coaches rich, you don't get paid for it. You're expected to show up whenever they say "show up." You're expected to be where they say "be." You're expected to endure what they say "endure." And you don't have a say in how you feel. Like, you can't talk about what it does to you or how it makes you feel, because in some sense then you become a distraction.

Campus Athletic *Work*

To reckon with exploitation in college football, an important consideration is the extent to which players perceive themselves to be involved in a form of labor, as the act of labor and the attendant value it produces are preconditions for any coherent economic discussion of exploitation. There is a quantitative dimension here to the question of the distribution of value that stands outside of players' experiences per se. But Karl Marx also invites us to consider the qualitative or phenomenological experience of doing work within capitalism and the ways it distorts and corrupts the very actions that define us as human.[23] While some players highlighted the pleasurable elements of their time in college football, the vast majority we interviewed characterized it as "work" rather than "play." Putting it this way, players framed their experience as alienated from the playful dimensions of the sport, an additional aspect of exploitation beyond the extraction of the value they produce.

If college football is sold to prospective players as an opportunity to subsidize the cost of college through the enjoyment of play, the reality often looks quite different. As Michael Thomas explains when confronted with the question of play or work, "When you look at it, you're playing but also it's work. You have to be dedicated to the gym, up early, going to practice, leaving practice, going to classes, leaving classes, going to study hall, going to dinner, going home, doing the same thing over again the next day. . . . A lot of kids, they don't really understand that until you get into those situations where it's like, 'Aw man, I didn't come here for it to be like a job.'" The oft-rehearsed justification for the college football system is that it is something that players 'sign up for.' But for athletes like Thomas, the reality of college football was far different from what was promised, and the experience was principally defined by work. For Ronnie Exeter, there was little equivocation when asked whether he was playing or working: "Oh, working. Most definitely working. Everything is mandatory, and that could start as early as 4:00 a.m. when I was at [redacted school]. If you were on the weight gain plan, you start at 4:45, and your day could end at 10:45 to 11."

Jalen Rice saw it similarly: "At some point it was like, am I being compensated enough just because I'm getting a degree, like, is that degree as beneficial to me being up so early, practice, like, sometimes you gotta get there at six in the morning, then you've gotta go treatment, meetings, meetings, meetings? Like, okay, that's why I was asking, should players get paid? Yes, at some point this is becoming more so a job than just playing."

Terry Davis had a similarly full schedule:

If you are reporting to a facility in the morning for meetings and workout in the morning and then going to class and then reporting to that same facility for your afternoon meetings and then practice and then going to your study hall for your classes in particular, and you are reporting home as late as 10, and then 11 o'clock at night after you got everything done. You fulfill your obligations for the day, only to wake back up at 5:30 in the morning for your six o'clock workout, right? So no, it was not fair. And yes, it was more akin to a full workload schedule.

The sheer quantity of the demands placed on college athletes is enough to distort even the most pleasurable enterprise into something quotidian, instrumental, and, in effect, alienated. Brock Adler puts it starkly:

I was working more than I was playing. I played maybe twelve snaps total [in] my college career. And that was in trash time, when it didn't matter, in the last two minutes of the game or so. Every day felt like it was a slog . . . like, "Why am I coming into the building?" It felt more like a job than it felt like a career. I felt though that I was getting, essentially, paid to go to school. I wasn't able to enjoy all the benefits because I was a slave to football's demands. I mean, our academic staff would always have to tell us what classes we could and couldn't take, on the basis of football practice. Some guys couldn't take classes. . . . "I can't take this class because of football." It just felt like I was working. Every day. Not like working hard, but, as in, I was part of a labor force. And I was seeing no benefits, there was no upward mobility.

In addition to the comments around academic experience, which we examine in chapter 2, Adler's combination of drudgery ("a slog") and unfreedom ("a slave") in his account does not align with the discursive construct of college football as a site of pleasure and play.

In answering the question of "play" or "work," Kevin Brown replied:

It's a job, man. A few weeks ago, I actually had the opportunity to go speak back to my high school football team and in the comments I made to those guys is, "Hey, cherish these moments, because you're playing football." You know, that joy of the game, this similar sensation of when younger kids are playing out in backyards and having imagination, "Oh, I'm in the Super Bowl," that's that same sensation of the play. And once I stepped foot at [redacted college], it's all business. It's all somebody coming to take your job every day. The environment I'm in now is very cutthroat. Very cutthroat there at playing [Division I] college athletics. So, definitely a job. The fun was sucked out of it the first day you're there.

For Brock Adler, understanding college football as work rather than play means acknowledging not only that football itself was evacuated of pleasure, but also that participation in the work of football precluded the possibility of experiencing other pleasurable aspects of college life:

A couple of us guys, we were playing Super Smash Brothers on Nintendo Switch in the locker room one day. It was after morning practice. [Redacted head coach] appears behind us and says, like, "Oh, you guys should be watching film. Why are you playing video games?" Like, not even letting us have lives. He says, "Oh yeah, you can have lives outside of football" and that stuff, but it was like it was almost football all the time with him . . . and he doesn't work very well with kids. That's who college football players are when they first get there: kids. We're kids. And we don't know better, and yeah, we're learning. But where's the true *guidance*, you know what I mean, versus being used.

Chris Andrews also felt like he missed out on the campus experience:

> I think about the opportunity cost of being a football player where, you know, I would walk through the middle of campus on my way to the stadium for practice and see all this vibrant social life and just everything going on campus, and I felt like I was forgoing all of that because I needed to go up to the football facility and get ready for practice. So I felt like there was a tremendous trade-off in terms of the college experience of giving up what most other kids experience in college versus what I was experiencing as being a football player.

That football required "forgoing" "this vibrant social life and just everything going on campus" is materially significant, given that the compensation received in return for the work of college football is the scholarship or, framed differently, access to the campus experience, widely acknowledged as the primary justification for skyrocketing tuition costs at US institutions of higher education today.[24] For campus athletic workers like Andrews to be denied that experience by the very athletic work that is supposed to provide it gets to the heart of the exploitative dynamics of college sport. Likewise, Andrew's observation that it "doesn't make any sense playing in a Thursday night game" so that it can be shown on ESPN speaks to the way in which the business of college football defines the experience of participation. This reality was acknowledged explicitly by the Duke University Department of Athletics in its strategic plan: "One of the most visible manifestations of increased commercialization is the impact of television on scheduling, particularly in football and men's and, increasingly, women's basketball. We no longer determine at what time we will play our games, because they are scheduled by TV executives."[25]

In the end, the frame of "work" rather than "play" for college sport was nearly universally agreed on by the athletes we interviewed. As Kurt Weiss put it, "I think if the student who's working at the dining hall is an employee, the student who's working on the football field is an employee." Or, in Jeremy Jones's words, "The more I've come to learn about it as a player . . . the more I've come to think that it's way more like work. I'm way more of an employee than a football player and the coaches are my fucking boss."

"Team Over Me": Exploitation Is Unfairness

Fundamental to the concept of exploitation is the issue of justice or fairness. Marx indicts capitalism because it systematically takes the value generated by working people and distributes it to others who are not responsible for its production.[26] While it is evident that players experienced college sport as alienating, transforming something once fun into what they defined as onerous work, this does not necessarily mean they experienced college football as *unjust*, unfair, or exploitative. But when asked directly, this is exactly how most players experienced it. This is not surprising, considering that the work of college football involves a median of forty hours per week of football-related activities (in addition to academic responsibilities).[27] As Brock Adler explained, "They get their hooks in you, psychologically, to where you're constantly thinking about the program, and you're constantly thinking about what to do for the team. . . . They made these T-shirts called 'team over me' and our joke was on the team is that 'yeah, fuck me. The team over me.' . . . Yeah, it says like, 'Oh, you got to put out for the team, even though the team, you know, screws you.'" For Jalen Rice,

> Nah, it's definitely not fair. You're just out there putting your body on the line each and every day and they're making so much money, they're televising you but the schools are getting all the benefits because . . . they can't have the name on the back of the jersey apparently, but if that player's number, like, Johnny Manziel, he's number two, we know who that is, they're buying a million dollars' worth of jerseys, and he's not even benefiting from it. He's just sitting there making the school millions of dollars and they're just like, "Get your degree, and that's about it. We're gonna get the next batch of kids in here and do the same thing to them."

Players like Rice clearly see football is a business involving not only the sale of commodity spectacle, but also commodities proper like merchandise. It is equally self-evident to him that this value is produced entirely by the players' labor—that it could not exist without them—and they are the deserving beneficiaries of its fruits. He is also under no illusion that a degree, an educational experience, or however one frames it, is commensurate to the value being produced. Nor is Jeremy Jones:

> If the college is like a middleman for the NFL, there's gotta be some of us who are more valuable than a college degree. You can't tell me there is no value in eighteen-to-twenty-two-year-old football players when all over the country stadiums are fucking packed and ESPN shows every game. The money is there and yet we gotta hide getting like free drinks or a plate of tacos or some shit. The biggest shit that gets me

pissed is when people say we get paid enough. That, like, we get paid with our education and that's like "priceless" or whatever shit they say. That's a fucking joke, bruh. Like, first off, the value I am bringing as a football player is worth way fucking more than college tuition and cutting me a check for rent. Do history majors fucking sell out [redacted stadium]? Do fucking computer scientists get 80,000 people out to watch them fucking code? [Laughs] The worst is when guys like [Tim] Tebow or whoever else used to play get up on TV and tell us we should be grateful for the opportunity of playing college football. Did his degree get him a job as a TV guy? Naw man, his national titles did . . . it's fucked that coaches drive around in Range Rovers and shit and make millions of dollars and I can't even get a plate of tacos without hiding it or getting in trouble.

Playing college football thus entails knowingly being exploited. Or, as C. J. White puts it, "The guys aren't really getting anything out of it, not necessarily not getting anything out of it, but from a financial standpoint, from a money standpoint, you're not really getting anything." The seductive ideological work of 'amateurism' is evident not only here but throughout the testimony of the players, who often hedge their answers as if they don't want to seem ungrateful for what they've received. Despite the conscious and very costly work of the college sport system to ideologically interpellate campus athletic workers into 'student-athletes,' the sheer blatancy of the system's inequity makes this ideological process much less seamless than it might appear. White continues:

With all the revenue and everything that they generate, I feel like college athletes should receive some type of payment . . . with all the things that you go through as a student-athlete . . . it's a high demand. I think that there should be some things that kind of grant student athletes benefits other than just saying that "yeah, we just granting them a free education." It's more during that time, because you don't get that diploma till four, five, six years later, and in all that time, there's something those student-athletes need to show that they're being appreciated for what they're doing.

What shines through here is the clear contrast between the "high demand" of the labor of college football players and their feeling of not being materially "appreciated for what they're doing"—the work they perform for the university.

Although he played in a slightly earlier era and a very different part of the country, Chris Andrews has a similar sense:

There's a whole lot of money in this and I'm [laughs] I'm not really getting any of the money that's involved with this big business. I went to [specific faculty] as an undergrad and my [faculty] is literally across the street from the stadium and so we talked about the importance of a free-market economy and then I would walk across the street right after those classes and you would start to realize that there's something that's not quite right here. And, now obviously my feeling is much different where everyone talks about what amateurism means, you know . . . and the world's gonna end if heaven forbid if somebody is paid to play college football, but I think it's silly. . . . I don't think that college sports would fall apart, there would be a big shift in the wealth of where money went within college sports, right now it's the administrators and coaches, but it would actually be a shift to the labor force, I don't think that's a bad thing . . . if you're gonna generate revenue, I think part of that revenue should go to the labor force.

Galen North agrees:

From a compensation standpoint, I think it's heavily unfair. . . . You sign away your right to your likeness, you sign away all of these things that people should be able to receive income for. I mean, your picture, your name, it's posted all over the place. And then, you're on posters, some people they sell jerseys that have your number but not your name, but it's clear who it is. It's also unfair from the aspect of you don't get health insurance, which today blows my mind. Once you're done playing, any issue you have, tough shit. They're your own problem now. You have something that flares up down the road from the football injury? They don't have to do anything. Sometimes they do, but they are not mandated to do anything. From the amount of time you spend doing it, you are not fairly compensated for what you bring in. I mean, I think there's a study done a couple years ago that the average Power Five Division I athlete is worth $185,000 a year in revenue. And, you're getting your tuition paid for, which is fantastic, great, but that only goes as far as you can take it. . . . You're not fairly compensated for the things that are done. At all.

Central to the issue of unfairness is the players' acutely feeling they were not receiving the compensation they needed and deserved as campus athletic workers. At the end of their careers they were left feeling that all the effort they expended—and the harm their bodies accrued—was for naught. Jalen Rice told us,

> All I'm getting at this point is a degree while all the coaches and the university is getting everything from me. Because, when you look back on it as a college player, especially if . . . you don't make it to the league, you wasn't capable of being an NFL player, it's like, shit, all I have now is I'm a hometown hero, I have my college jersey, I have these college trophies, all I can do is go back to college and do autograph signings and that's about it because other than that, all I have is my degree to put up on the wall, now I've gotta find a job when the whole time I've been doing so much for the school that they gave me a piece of paper.

For Brock Adler, these problems have not been resolved by the advent of NIL compensation via promotional labor:

> And even the way it is now, it's still not fair. Because the way they've opened it now, is that guys who are "players," if you will, who are on that side of the hierarchy, get those deals and those promotional deals from companies, and get money. You know, because I see guys I know now, who transfer, they get "Oh, use my code for this" now. It makes me sick. Because it's like, the guys who play, and the guys who aren't at the bottom of the barrel, they're getting hundred-thousand-dollar deals. . . . So I still think it's unfair.

Indeed, the funding players do receive often cannot even cover their expenses in college. Steven Summers noted that the funding players received barely covered the cost of rent, let alone other expenses. In Kurt Weiss's case, it didn't even stretch that far, forcing him to ask his parents for money for rent and sneak "extra nutrition bars, protein shakes, and bananas from our workout facility."

The situation is perhaps even more bleak for nonscholarship walk-on players. They are vital to the team in practices, preparing the more highly valued scholarship players. So, in effect, they work the same hours as scholarship players with none of the compensation. One wonders how they survive. The answer is, like so many students, student loans, as Ross Nielsen told us. Even some scholarship players ended up in debt. Ryan Leonard told us that despite being promised a full-year scholarship at the school he was transferring to, "I was only given a single semester of scholarship, and I had to pay for my next semester, despite having played at [elite Power Five school] in front of 80,000 people live, in front of 4.4 million viewers. . . . Ironically, I got a student loan bill coming up next month."

For some players, the financial experience of being on scholarship required them to engage in alternative methods of survival. This is nowhere better exemplified than by Charlie Rogers's experiences:

> Like that was probably the most crime I ever committed in my life. I was just stealing food. Because I was just starving the whole time. . . . Me and my friend would just go to Safeway. And that was back when they had the hot bar, where you could make your own plate with the premade food, just go in there and walk out. You know, no chase policy. And, you know, we had a meal for the day. . . . And they were saying in recruiting, that they were going to spend around a million dollars on each player throughout their whole career. If you divide it up, it's about a hundred people on the team. I paid that back by week two of my freshman year. Just by being a part of the team. And all the people that are saying like, "They don't deserve to get paid," we get free education, free this, free that. All those clothes. It's just, there's no comparison, to have to stretch $400, while having a crippling drug addiction, and needing to drink and get away from everything. That's pretty much where all the money went to.

Nick Turner had to pay out of pocket to play college football despite being on a "full" scholarship:

> It was considered a full scholarship. I was part of the class that sued the NCAA for capping member schools' living expenses. I had a surplus debt of $13,000 that I paid out of pocket with my check from the [university], and then got a check from that lawsuit for $6,000. . . . I lost money, for sure. If I had the choice, knowing what I know now, I would've forced them to give me the scholarship in cash and taken out a student loan for all of it, instead of just a portion. I think the fact that that is not standard and that it just goes to the account should be considered illegal. Anyone else who gets a scholarship from a private source, it goes to their bank account.

Ryan Leonard saw teammates resort to crime to support themselves and their families, like one teammate/roommate who had to take out loans to send money to his family who couldn't afford rent. That roommate supplemented those loans by selling acid out of the house Leonard lived in. On one occasion, that roommate and a couple of other teammates decided they could make some money by robbing a drug dealer they bought marijuana from. He explains, "They watched this drug dealer leave, go pick up the safe, wheelbarrow the safe out and bring it to our house, and they took a blowtorch to it and opened it up. Well, it wasn't full of weed at all. It was full of probably twelve guns, fifteen guns ranging from AR-15s, handguns to shotguns." A couple of months later, law enforcement officers came and arrested all three athletes. Leonard noted, "I remember these guys had no idea what was going on, and all of them lost their scholarship. This is what poverty, even as athletes, drives them to do, they drive them to go to commit crimes to try to make money elsewhere because they don't have enough to subsidize their living or do what they want to do off of a athletic scholarship."

For Josh Hansen, the solution was multilevel marketing:

[Redacted company] is like a work-from-home opportunity. It's like, financial services, like everyday services like energy and television, and you're trying to get people to sign up for [redacted company] or whatnot, and every time you get somebody to sign up, you get like, $100 or $200. And so, that was to get money in our pocket. . . . It was a couple of my dudes, on the team. They were like, "Hey bro, we've got this joint that we're doing, and y'all need to get on." So everybody tried to get on as many people as possible.

Terry Davis found his own methods to get by: "I used to buy clothes and sell clothes for teammates. . . . My closet was a shopping store basically for the basketball team and football members."

While there is often a perception that college athletes receive handsome "impermissible benefits," this really wasn't the case according to Kurt Weiss: "Only basically free drinks at bars, from bartenders or bar owners that are football fans. The occasional free meal here or there, from the same. But nothing [substantial]. One three-dollar Bud Light at a time was the extent of my benefits. . . . I think it varies by the school. I know players who were offered $100,000 to go to [SEC school]. I didn't see any of it at [his redacted school]. Even we had [three big-name NFL players] and I don't think even the premier guys, to my knowledge, got any benefits."

If the entire experience of college football amounts to the performance of unpaid labor—that requires additional work on the side to make ends meet—*overtime* football demands are particularly galling. One such demand is the bowl game, often held up as something for college football players to aspire to since it signifies a successful season and involves some minor material rewards like corporate swag. But for the athlete, it also means many additional hours of football work. For Chris Andrews,

> If we weren't in a bowl game, my finals schedule, my study schedule was much smoother than during the bowl game where we had to go up and lift or practice. . . . As a younger player, before I was in the starting lineup, I looked at those opportunities of the additional practices of the bowl game as an opportunity to move up the depth chart. But, then, after I got older, you know, I started to realize that boy these are pretty big-time commitments. There's a lot of money involved, and we get like a shiny watch and a couple of T-shirts for the time and effort that we put into this. That's not really commensurate with the level of work that we're putting in. But, at the same time too it's like, obviously my feelings now are much different, but as a kid it's like we get to be on national TV and everyone back home is gonna think this is really cool, so I really do think that it's exploitation of these college athletes that don't know their worth, and then as we get older we start to figure out our worth but we don't really have much of a way to act upon or to change the system [when] we're in the midst of being a college athlete.

The dynamic Andrews described is more rule than exception in college football: although there is no paycheck, there is also never really a vacation from the work. Kurt Weiss explains:

> We played in a bowl game every [December]. I didn't celebrate Christmas from freshman year of college through my rookie year in the NFL. . . . I would go back [home] for the first two weeks of January, after the bowl game. And then, like a week and a half between the end of spring semester, and the start of summer training. So there were no holidays or family time. I'd see my family when they came to games. So there's no, "I'm gonna miss Christmas," like you're gonna miss *every* holiday for however long you're here. No Thanksgiving. None of that.

While players viscerally and materially experienced exploitation as a feature of their time in college football, they were hardly oblivious to the fact that the coaches who exhorted them to perform were lavishly compensated. This was a key element of their sense of injustice and exploitation. As Brock Adler puts it, "You think [college football is] about playing. But really, it's about money. It's about a lot of coaches making millions of dollars off the backs of your own labor and your body, and you breaking down, and your mental health too." Players knew coaches received economic benefits and bonuses for many aspects of their work, including recruiting, as Landry West demonstrated: "If you get a four-star and you're a tight ends coach, that's more money for you rather than getting a two-star recruit, or somebody who's lower level." Or recall the story Ryan Leonard told us to open this chapter. For Wallace Bell, this power imbalance was articulated directly by coaches: "I've had coaches say, 'I can release all of you mother effers.' You know what I mean? 'They're paying me, they're not paying you.' So there's definitely a real thing that you face. They're protected by the school . . . and so many other staff members that protect them."

In other cases, it was less obvious but no less frustrating, as for Kurt Weiss: "I was naive to that stuff. I didn't know coaches had agents. I didn't know as a freshman that the program made $60 million a year. . . . But when players came to visit and I spoke with them, even if ignorant of some of the broader context, college players know viscerally, like, 'I don't have enough to eat and the coaches are driving Mercedes or Corvettes around.' So we'd talk and joke about that, but you have no recourse." Yet coaches often made it brutally clear they would not help players financially once their careers ended. Terry Davis "saw it, when other guys didn't get drafted, [famous head coach] would say shit like, 'Don't come back around with your hands out asking for help.'"

Because of the power dynamics between players and coaches, this was difficult to speak about. For Ross Nielsen, there wasn't much talk about compensation because "the locker room was kind of like a player space, but coaches were in there all the time and that's where I spent the most time with my team. So your conversational options are a little limited. Never any dialogue in earshot of coaches about compensation, *ever*, if it was ever talked about."

Given their economic challenges and feelings of exploitation, it is small wonder that players who ultimately moved on to the NFL felt a profound sense of satisfaction and relief to finally draw a paycheck for their labor. For Jalen Rice, "When you get a big check into your account, you're like, 'This is much better. I really like this way more.' I'm getting food at other times, I'm getting different deals off the field, trading card deals, they send me a check saying you're getting compensated for your jersey sales. You're getting paid for everything that you do. Even off the field, when you go back to school or something, they pay for that too. . . . It's like, yeah, I would rather do this than be in college playing football, most definitely." Rice felt no compunction about saying he appreciated his NFL time more than college, providing a sharp rebuke to the apologistic mantra of college sport that it offers a more pleasurable experience than the pros:

> I feel like playing college football is more so enslavement at that point in time, like, you had no life to yourself, you had no summer, you had no time off. . . . You're just doing it to where you gotta get a piece of paper, you're gonna get that freedom to where, hey you've got a degree, now you're free to go live your life and go find whatever job. . . . You just do whatever the coaches tell you, your academic advisors, your teachers, and that's about it. Versus the NFL, you come in, you don't have to listen to the coaches, you don't have to listen to anybody. This is truly your job, like, either you're gonna do it or not, because we can find somebody else to do it. So it's a big difference.

Name, Image, and Likeness

The liberalization of NIL rules in college sport has significantly changed the terrain in terms of compensation. While Daniel Libit and Lev Akabas have found that upward of 67 percent of Americans as of 2023 favor paying college athletes directly, NIL policies do not change the fact that universities continue to refuse to compensate the players who produce revenue; what it does mean is that players can now find new economic opportunities that will not compromise their eligibility.[28] In effect, they can now perform additional promotional labor to be compensated by third parties, allowing universities to claim that college sport is now a site of compensation—without having to do any of the pesky work of compensating. This is Jeremy Jones's point: "Guys have been doing side hustles forever, but it was always like you get caught and you're fucked. But now that shit's legal and it's about time. . . . It's long overdue. But at the same time. . . . It's fucked because it's everyone saying, "Yeah these guys can get paid now," but we aren't getting paid for football or the value we bring through football. We are getting paid for a side hustle that we have to seek out."

DS: So how do you feel about private companies paying you instead of the university?

JONES: It's kind of a slap in the face to be honest. . . . I'm out here hawking chicken for a little bit of cash and coaches be rolling up in Land Rovers. Coaches are paid by the university, right? The university always be talking about "investing" in the football team, but that investment is always buildings and paying coaches to come. But when it comes to the players, the men who actually play and bring in people to buy shit, you gotta go out and get some other job doing promo work or signing autographs and shit. That shit takes time, right? You think anyone wants to spend their time after practice showing up to a car dealership to sign autographs? Bruh, nobody wants to do that shit. So don't get me wrong, it's better than nothing. It's been way too fucking long, and guys are cool with being able to do it. But it's just another fucking thing we gotta add to our plate when we should just be able to get some of the pie. . . . Guys know they get something with the scholarship. But it's still fucked up that we get none of the money from football, you know?

Ryan Leonard sees it similarly: "It is a step in the right direction, but it is far, far less. It is a half measure upon a half measure than what should be done. And to get back to the theme, it retains to a large extent, the power of the NCAA and the profit of the institution. The interest of the NCAA remains; has been weakened but has been forced to be weakened by the court systems and the profits that is college, that is universities and the commercialization of college football is retained by the institution."

Thus, while this is a necessary and beneficial change, and despite a college sports media moral panic on the subject, the money being made via NIL is hardly transformative for most college football players. Steven Summers received an NIL deal, but the impact for him was minimal:

I had one with [a] sports drink company [shows bottle]. They do a program for college athletes. It's not a monetary deal, they basically just send [the drinks] and I do Instagram posts and stuff like that. And then this company that's a teeth whitening thing. I signed up with them, where I'm basically like a brand ambassador, so they give me a discount code that then, if people buy the products using my code, then I get like a 25 percent kickback from the profits. It's like, small stuff, you know. I think I've only made like a couple hundred. So like, nothing big. . . . And like, my mom was one of the people that bought one [laughs]. . . . I would say that's most people's experience. Some guys have reached out to some company that they like, and they'll just send them a package just for an Instagram post or whatever, that kind of stuff's cool. Little stuff like that.

For players like Ryan Leonard, in some of the most arduous but least glamorous positions, there is less to be made: "One of the things that I can say is that for people in, the players that played the position that I did that are the offensive line, that are the least marketable people potentially in sports in general, some of the least marketable people oftentimes pay the highest price when it comes to health risk."

Charlie Rogers had an even more incisive, if cynical, take:

This might sound a little harsh, but it's just as good as painting Black Lives Matter on the street or passing that Stop Asian Hate bill. Because, in reality, the government did a Stop Asian Hate bill, yet lynching is still not outlawed, and has been repeatedly rejected over decades. And people are painting all these signs and all that shit. Yet, you know, a lot of Black people still can't get the services they need, and still have to resort to committing crimes in the environment that was not created by them. So, pretty much, NIL, it only benefits star players. If you're a walk-on, or if you're on scholarship, but you're not getting playing time, you're still going to have to stretch $400 a month, while your teammate got a million-dollar deal with somebody. . . . It only benefits those who get on the field.

Wallace Bell perhaps put it most succinctly: "The NCAA is basically relying on other organizations outside of them to pay the players instead of them paying their players for themselves."

The Walk-On Con

Charlie Rogers's appraisal of NIL brings us to an often-underdiscussed issue: the Walk-On Con. Nonscholarship, walk-on players are enticed to play college football with promises of being big men on campus, sharing in a status position highly fetishized in the United States. But the reality is brutal. Coaches treat these players as the most disposable in a sport that inherently devalues all participants.

The players we interviewed painted a horrifying picture of the treatment of walk-ons. Ross Nielsen explains:

Walk-ons, especially, are kind of just treated as like . . . they're critically essential, right? You cannot run a Division I squad, much less [a Power Five] squad, without a thorough reserve of players. And bodies are valuable in and of themselves, to the point where when

I quit, I had a class with a person who was like a graduate assistant, and he was like, "Hey, we need bodies." And I was like [incredulous], "Why would you say that?" They just want to turn people through. Then, conversely, they would view you as like a parasite. I think there were more comments levied, like, "Oh, you're really enjoying that training room there," something like that, to walk-ons.

In this sense, there is a structural imperative to such treatment. Having disposable bodies on hand benefits the training of more prized scholarship players. But walk-ons are also subjected to superfluous forms of degradation, perhaps to psychologically compel them to submit to the physical demands required of them. Nielsen told us that scout-team players on his team were forced to practice in grey jerseys displaying numbers of opposing teams' players to purportedly prepare the starters. When an offensive coordinator from the NFL was hired, he was shocked and told the head coach that he was "making these scout-team players feel like fucking dog shit. Because you're basically saying you're not a part of the real team." Yet for Nielsen, "It was one of those things where I didn't realize until he brought it up. I was like, 'Wow, no. Subconsciously, that did kind of fuck a lot of us up that we couldn't even wear our own jerseys.' And that we basically had to like, pretend to be somebody else, all practice. It was a way of physically marking who the guys are that they don't really care about." In addition to psychological abuse, walk-ons also experienced material harm: the denial of access to some of the most basic forms of compensation that scholarship players received for the same work as part of their funding package, including team gear and food from the training table, which walk-ons had to pay for out of pocket.

So why do walk-ons do it? The scholarship is deployed as a dangling carrot—a promise that with enough performance, fuller compensation is possible. But the carrot is seldom given. Matt Jensen had offers to play on scholarship at Patriot League and Big Sky schools but had always dreamed of playing big-time football, so he accepted an offer as a walk-on at a Power Five school. As he approached his third year, he told his coaches multiple times he wanted to play more and be on scholarship. Eventually, the head coach gave him a list of specific points to improve on, which Jensen did.

And then I go in to the head coach, and I'm like, "Okay, I feel like I've hit all these points." And he goes, "Yeah, yeah, I feel like you have as well. But—" and that's when I knew, "Oh, great. This isn't going to go the way I want." He said, "But we noticed you had a few concussions earlier in your career, and that's where we're concerned that you can't stay healthy. So, we need you to prove that you can stay healthy before you get on scholarship." The criteria that were in my control, like get bigger, faster, stronger, get better technique on the blocks—it's completely out of my control because you can get injured doing anything. You can roll your ankle stepping off a curb. . . . That's when I knew that I needed to step away, because, not only was the criteria always changing, it seemed like he kept on moving the marker on me.

Effectively, walk-ons are told they must give everything to the team to earn a scholarship. But by the very nature of football work—work that requires bodily destruction—to give everything of oneself is to diminish, not improve, one's physical capacities. So walk-ons who satisfy coaches' demands are actually worsening their prospects with the team as they accumulate concussions and other injuries. In a world that privileges winning and performance above all, providing a scholarship to a walk-on will never be in coaches' interest, although it is certainly in their interest to perform that they will do so.

Conclusion: The Emotional Tax

An additional piece to the exploitation puzzle in the context of athletic labor is the question of social reproduction. Because the commodity produced by athletic labor is commodity spectacle, fans are the market or consumers for that commodity. This in turn creates a social relationship between athletes and fans: fans require athletes to produce emotional gratification for them through the labor of sport. When all goes well, they provide an excess of adulation. When it goes awry, they often direct their displeasure at players. So in addition to not receiving compensation for their athletic work, college players are also subjected to working conditions frequently defined by abusive or painful interactions, frequently online, with fans.

Galen North explains:

Back when we were all playing, I would see guys Google their name just to see what was coming up, which I thought was not the best idea because typically it's not gonna be stuff you want to see. And, it takes you straight to a message board or a tweet, you know, "This guy sucks," "He's an idiot," just bashing people constantly. So everybody was really, really aware of the interactions with the fans and their perceptions of performance, you know, whether they think that they're tough or weak or they actually have an injury or they just don't play or their passion for playing, that was a big speculation, "Oh that kid really doesn't care" for whatever reason. And, so people really feel that and of course you always see the great stuff and after a game you see all the admiration from the fans, but that was not typically as loud as the hate from the fans. . . . Some people didn't care, you know, they were just like, "These people don't know what the hell they're talking about. You come and live a day in the life of a high-level athlete that has basically every minute of your day scheduled from 5 a.m. to 12 a.m. and all the things that goes into every game which people don't see because you just see the end product, you don't see all the work that goes into it." So a lot of people just brush it aside because people were just ignorant to what was actually going on. And some people took it very personally.

Fantasy sports have worsened these dynamics, as Steven Summers explains: "What I can't stand is people who are like, 'Oh, my fantasy team got screwed because Christian McCaffrey got hurt again.' It's like, dude, that's a real person. That's their job and their life. [McCaffrey] doesn't give a shit about your fantasy team."

While a fundamental problem with any career in elite sport is that it comes with an early expiry date, that is magnified in college athletics when eligibility runs out early. Even when players experience tremendous emotional gratification from their college careers, they must ultimately reckon with the hangover that is the postcareer: the feeling that they will never again enjoy the high from 100,000 people in a stadium cheering for them. Ross Nielsen explains:

[Famous professional player] was a quarterback for the [redacted NFL team]. [In college] his class would clap for him when he came into the classroom after a good game. I mean, it's kind of cool. That's what they live for, right? That's the one thing that happens to them, that's actually probably what gives the experience a lot of meaning. . . . I think that when you graduate, there's a really big sense of accomplishment, but also a big sense of decompression and deflation afterwards. You go through this big adrenaline rush and then you're like, "What is the rest of life?" . . . I think that messes a lot of people up. I think that's one of the biggest problems is whenever you quit playing, it's just like a huge, huge letdown.

Galen North had a similar experience:

> You come out on a home game, road game, whatever it is. You run out of
> the tunnel and everybody's going crazy, 50, 60, 70, 80, 90, 100,000 people
> depending on where you're playing. It's just deafening and it's kind of
> like the energy and the vibe. And then you're in the game and you
> break the big play or you score a touchdown and everybody's going
> crazy. [Laughs] You know, you do great at work, there's not gonna be
> 60,000 people sitting there cheering for you, you know what I mean?
> And then once you're done playing, it's never the same in the crowd
> because you're a part of the crowd as to when you're on the field. When
> you're on the field, everything is directed to you, it's just a different
> vibe, a different energy. I to this day haven't seen anything that comes
> close to that and nobody I know that played in the NFL or is retired
> from the NFL or family members that played football have ever found
> anything that kind of matches that.

For Daniel Barber, there are very material consequences to this. Not only is
the high of athletic triumph lost, but often players are left without economic
opportunities by the teams that took so much from them during their careers:

> I get texts from guys that I was friends with . . . some of them are
> getting pushed out now. I mean, guys that weren't pushed out already.
> And they're just like, "What am I supposed to do? I have a sixth year,
> but they say they aren't gonna bring me back. The transfer portal isn't
> looking good. You know, I don't have a lot of film, they didn't put me
> on the field for real." My heart goes out to some of these guys. And for
> guys that didn't go to a top fifteen school, I don't know what you're
> supposed to do. Like you go from being a key contributor to this
> multimillion-dollar industry to being a truck driver. I mean, I know
> someone specifically, who went to my school, was a 4.0 dude, like real
> smart dude, 3.8 balling out in school. Did a fifth year. And, NFL didn't
> work out for him . . . I ran into him at Target. He was working at
> Target with a [redacted school] degree. And that's something no one
> wants to talk to you about.

In the end, from the elite player undercompensated for his production to the
walk-on, from the NFL-bound star to the player who suffers a career-ending
injury, college football is defined by exploitation and the promise of emotional loss. This system produces alienation from the pleasures of the game
through the extraction of value that benefits many others above those whose

work makes it possible. As Ryan Leonard explains, "If you look at it critically and without the propaganda that has been spewed, if you look at it from a clear value given, value received relationship, it is an employee-employer relationship. We provide a service, a phenomenally valuable service to an institution and yet they have limited the amount of value that we can return, that we can receive in return." What athletes can receive is an education in exchange for athletic performance. In chapter 2, we temporarily accept that premise and interrogate whether education-as-compensation is everything it is promised to be.

CHAPTER TWO

Failure to Educate

In late July, around the end of a summer school session and, coincidentally, spring football practice, Ryan Leonard noticed that a fellow campus athletic worker on the golf team had started missing one of their classes. He texted him to check in: "Man, where are you at?" "Dude, we've been in Hawaii for two weeks for a golf tournament," the classmate responded. Ryan thought, "I wonder how they're paying for this? I wonder who paid for the entire golf team, men and women, to go spend two weeks out in Hawaii?" He thought about all of the long, exhausting days spent in grueling spring practice sessions: "We football players are grinding, sweating . . . they're out playing golf." Ryan knew then that there was a fundamental imbalance in access to opportunities for college football players, even relative to other campus athletic workers. "Even between athletes, we don't get the same kind of treatments, same kind of opportunities in terms of access to internships, access to education, access to degrees."

When we followed up on this story, Ryan told us:

> I believe that the education that a student gets is a greater education than what a student-athlete gets, especially a football player, whether it's access to opportunities, whether it's time to actually devote to learning business, to learning your degree. It's not equal in my mind, just because there are so many other things, other responsibilities that an athlete has that he must attend to, and so many times, I've seen players who while we were traveling, be doing homework, or the craziest one is at [redacted school]. So our first four games were all night games. So they decided the best thing to do was to have night practice. So we would get out there around 6:15 and we wouldn't leave that facility till around 11:00. And so we would get our late, late dinner and while we were at dinner, I would see these athletes after going out and banging heads for an hour try to finish homework, try to turn something in before midnight, and I was like, "I have no idea how any of these players are going to graduate." And the sad fact of the matter is a lot of them won't. . . . They will not meet the GPA [grade point average], they will not get the classes. Their eligibility will expire before they get the degree.

When we asked Ryan about promises made to him during his recruitment, the differences between the college experience for athletes and nonathletes became clear:

NKL: Let me guess, they were recruiting you though as an engineer. . . . They were saying engineering, great degree.

DS: You're going to be a rocket scientist.

LEONARD: Exactly. Whatever degree you want, you can get and we'll work with you to make sure you get it. That's one of the guarantees that in reality and practicality never plays out quite as they say it does. So that is probably the biggest in terms of degree selection. Another part of it is, and this isn't even the same across all athletes, but so much of, and I'm learning this now, so much of the workforce is prior experience. So a lot of it comes down to can I go get an internship over the summer, but the reality of the situation is, well, the summer is when football players in particular are on the hardest grind. We are in summer classes just because you want to remain on a scholarship, you want to still be able to pay your rent, and you are working out, you are going through film, you are doing your optional practices. There's no time for an internship. Doesn't matter what you want to do, you have to stay in [university town], you have to be enrolled in school and you have to show up to practice. So a lot of these guys, we don't get the same opportunities in terms of career advancement that other students do or other sports.

One cannot understand the dynamics of life as a college football player without interrogating the conditions of their education. Players' education, after all, is understood to be the compensation provided for their work on the campus gridiron. While many say educational failure in big-time college football is a function of cheating or the inability of players to handle a rigorous curriculum, the problem is actually baked into the structure of college football itself: it is simply not possible to receive the education that "average" students obtain, given the physical and emotional rigors of an often-forty-hour workweek of punishing labor, restrictive practice schedules, and pervasive academic clustering practices steered by athletic departments. Nor is it simply a story about an athletic class of campus workers being treated differently than their nonathlete peers, for this story is also conditioned by the broader political economy of racial capitalism that shapes both the system of higher education and the lives of the collegiate athletes who strive within it. As Krystal Beamon has illustrated, not only are college campuses rife with racism, but racially charged occurrences and stereotypes continue to target campus athletic workers within and outside of athletic departments.[1]

In this chapter, we provisionally accept—for the sake of argument—the premise that education is the wage or compensation provided to football players in return for their work of producing commodity spectacle for the university. According to the Power Five universities, this is a significant form of remuneration. After all, tuition fees run exceptionally high at some of these schools. At Duke University, for instance, two semesters of tuition, room, and board can easily run a student more than $86,000 per year.[2] If you multiply that by five years of eligibility, that's about $430,000. No wonder universities consider players amply compensated.

The question, then, is whether college athletes receive the full educational experience they are promised. Unlike other important interventions that have focused on academic corruption—that is, cheating—we focus on how, as a function of the structure of the experience of being a campus athletic worker, it is *impossible* to receive the full educational experience promised.[3] We do not deny that cheating occurs and that it is a tremendous disservice to the athletes who do not receive the education that is rightfully theirs when they are encouraged to cut academic corners. Nevertheless, we argue that precisely because of the structural nature of the deficiencies in the education offered to college football players, they are subjected to a form of systematic wage theft. They are promised an education as wage, and they are not receiving that education. Perhaps more importantly, it follows that if those who are promised an education as compensation and do not receive it are predominantly racialized athletes, as in big-time college football, this is principally a *racialized form of wage theft*.

The educational failures are not a function of deficiencies in the players themselves. This problem is not because they do not deserve to be in the academic spaces of Power Five universities. It is not because they do not have the capacity to succeed. It is not because of some kind of cultural problem or lack of will that leads to problems with "athlete engagement," as an athletic department representative informed one of us during a faculty meeting. Rather, the problem is with the structure claiming that young people subjected to a forty-hour workweek on the football field can simultaneously receive the same educational experience offered to other full-time students. Under these conditions, players consistently spoke to the impossibility of receiving the education they were promised, no matter how much they aspired toward it. The structural constraints on the educational opportunities of college athletes inhibit their academic freedom, an alleged cornerstone of US higher education.[4] The failure of Power Five schools to offer college football players the full educational experience they are promised is an abrogation of the terms by which these institutions are accredited.[5] Thus, this issue is not merely a footnote in the debate over exploitation in college sport, but rather raises existential questions for higher education as a project.[6]

Despite the NCAA's public assertions to the contrary, big-time college sport is predicated on the sacrifice of athletes' educational aspirations. Look at any Power Five basketball team's schedule and note the number of out-of-state, or even cross-country, games scheduled in prime time. Or consider how athletes are largely precluded from the experiential learning opportunities universities promote as fundamental to the student experience, due to their off-season training and practice commitments that conflict with internships or summer study-abroad programs.

The incommensurate educational experience of big-time college sport athletes is clearly illustrated by graduation rates. While the graduation rate in 2019–20 across Power Five schools was 78 percent for all undergraduates, only 60.6 percent of Black male football players graduated.[7] Moreover, in 2022–23, the adjusted graduation gap (AGG) between Football Bowl Subdivision (FBS) football players and the general full-time male student body was –17.5 (up from -15.6 in 2021; a lower number indicates a bigger gap). In the Power Five in 2022, Black players' AGG was –25.6 compared to white players' –3.7. The differences between athlete and nonathlete graduation rates likely have numerous causes—disproportionate athletic expectations that interfere with education, athletic department clustering of athletes' academic schedules, the scheduling of games midweek.[8] Thus, on top of being denied a fair portion of the revenue they produce through their labor, they also don't receive the full compensation they are promised: an education resulting in a university degree.

Football First, School Second

In considering the educational experience offered to college athletes as a systematic form of wage theft, we should begin from the insidious premise that campus athletic workers are in fact 'student-athletes.' Rather than rehearse the history of this term (see more on this in the book's introduction), let us instead attempt to take it at face value.[9] If college football players are indeed 'student-athletes,' they are students *first*. This follows very neatly from the logic that education is compensation. Alternatively, if college football players are required to place athletic obligations above educational needs, that would suggest they are 'athlete-students' and do not receive the same experience as their nonathlete peers. If *that* is true, they are also the victims of wage theft, for they are denied the full value of the wage promised.

For the former college football players we interviewed, academics were not a priority for the institutions they worked for. Josh Hansen told us, "You feel as if class really don't matter, bro. Education is not the most important thing in college football. That's just the reality. It is only a means to an end. To keep you on campus so that you can play, that's just the facts of college football." Kevin Brown put it this way: "The majority of the people on the team were here for football and education second. . . . People were just breezing through, trying the bare minimum." Thomas Rycliff said a position coach disliked him because of his academic focus: "There was this weird psychological battle that happened with him because he only cared about, he said, 'players that are going to the three-letter league.' He only cared about players that wanted to be in the NFL. At the end of the day, that's what most of a coach's resume is, how many players they coach that play in the NFL. I wanted to excel at both football and school. There was a total disconnect with me and him."

Not only was education treated as secondary to athletic performance, but for players like Daniel Barber, coaches actively discouraged academic investment. Coaches told him, "'Why do you have your notebook out? Oh, you only take notes in school. All you care about is school.' For me, 'Oh, I need to meet with you. Why are your grades so good? You need to focus on football. . . . Why don't you have a 4.0 in football?'"

Thomas Rycliff had a similar experience:

RYCLIFF: I would literally leave practice at 5:45, twenty minutes early.
I wouldn't even shower because I'd just change my clothes and barely get . . . I mean literally seconds to spare every single day [to make it to a professor's class who punished tardiness with grade deductions]. And [my position coach] would cuss me out and call me a "motherfucking pussy" and everything, all this because I had to go to class. . . . So those experiences, I never felt like a student-athlete. I always felt like an athlete-student, that they told me that I couldn't be in the

[prestigious academic department] because it conflicted with football. So my education wasn't a priority. I did it anyways. I just didn't tell him I did it . . . so I just convinced the dean to let me do [the class].

NKL: Did they object? Did they push you?

RYCLIFF: "You're not trying hard enough." That's 100 percent. So that's what I always got that attitude from [position coach]. Because in the coach's office, when you walk into the football wing, there's the top ten GPAs on the team. . . . Now I was in the top 10 percent, my SAT, my GPA, I was in the top 10 percent of the student body. I got into the [prestigious] program on my own merit. And so yeah, I was always in the top ten on your pictures. And they put this front like, "We care about academics." And there'd be these nine photos. . . . And yeah, it puts a target on you because it's like, oh, you care more about school than football. There's this element, it's insinuated.

Ultimately, athletic departments privileged eligibility over academics and even graduation. Ryan Leonard explained:

The famous saying is "don't pass, don't play." Well, the fact of the matter is for a lot of degrees, getting a D, getting a C in a class might allow you to continue to play, but at the end of the day, by the time you're in your fourth year, your GPA doesn't meet the required GPA minimum to graduate. So by the time they're no longer on scholarship, they still need to take a semester, a year to graduate. And a lot of these guys, they didn't have money to pay for college before and they don't have money to pay for college now, so they ended up not graduating.

Given these experiences, it is no surprise that players generally felt they had very different academic experiences than their nonathlete peers. Steven Summers highlights another aspect of this:

DS: Would you say that you got the same educational experience as your nonathlete peers?

SUMMERS: No, because they have a little more time to do extra studying, extra research, if they want . . . maybe pursue something that would be harder for us to do timewise or whatever. That could be a major, that could be an internship or something . . . you can't do a semester abroad [laughs]. I mean, that's out of the question. But internships, you could do an internship in the summer. But you know there's other stuff . . . it's not as easy, I would say, to do an internship. You can't do it during the fall. During the spring, maybe. But summer . . . I had an internship one summer. Several guys would do one, [during] at least one summer. Yeah, you could do that stuff, but as far as getting really involved in on-campus involvement and stuff like that, it's definitely more of a regular student thing.

Internships were a particularly sore spot for other players we interviewed. Terry Davis "couldn't do the internships my auntie had set up for me in Atlanta in the summer because we had to practice and stuff like that. So here I am [postcareer], got a degree, and I can't get a single job." Davis also notes that career fairs were not an option for football players:

I also didn't get to participate in the career fairs that are held on Saturdays before game day or Fridays before a game day. All those events and amenities provided to regular students, they got to participate in that stuff, we didn't. We didn't get to shake those hands and build those relationships with those employers and other things like that. And I watched a lot of people struggle after college that played football, not having that network, not feeling comfortable to come back around the team to actually be introduced to these people now, at that time. They didn't feel invited back, they weren't invited back.

C. J. White makes a similar point:

Now that I'm older, and had some time to reflect on things, I feel like as a student-athlete, we're kind of limited to the education or to the academic experience that the general student body gets. Because, you know, once I got to the NFL and I was thinking back on my college career just from an academic standpoint, I knew like a lot of people that I knew that wasn't on athletic teams and they were just at the university, they would do things like study abroad, all these different academic things in the summer giving them more exposure to job experience. . . . So when I was here, I felt like I was trying to take advantage of as much of the academic side as I possibly could, but once I got older, or once I graduated in these last few years, I just think back, reflecting on it, I felt like we don't really get a chance to experience all the academic experiences that are out there.

Not only did White miss out on experiences that he ultimately regretted, but he also speaks to the difficulty for athletes to see this at the time. In this sense, there is a type of ideological work being done in athletic departments to convince college athletes it is in their best interest to focus on sports, that academics are more barrier than opportunity, making it difficult to see what one is missing until it is too late.

For many players, it is not even clear what they are missing academically because they are encouraged from all sides to focus on sports. Matt Jensen describes how his perspective changed over the course of his college football career:

When I was the initial gung ho athlete freshman/sophomore year . . . I was just kind of a husk, walking around doing stuff for school and then coming to football. And I was still giving my best effort, but at the end of the day, you can only do so much. I wanted to get on scholarship so bad. And I wanted to do that to help out my family and make it so that they didn't have to shell out $60,000 a year, you know? I wanted that so bad that that was my priority, was being the best I could at football. Academics took a little dip during that time. I wasn't failing, but I also wasn't acing all my classes. Versus when I realized that scholarship wasn't going to happen because of what we discussed earlier. And I already knew I was going to step off the football wagon for my last year, I was able to put a lot more into my classes. And that's when I noticed, not only did I enjoy just being at [redacted school] more, but I started doing very well in the classes and getting more out of them. I was engaging. I was going to office hours that I didn't usually go to before because I had practice and stuff. I was developing relationships with the teachers. You know, I didn't see them as somebody who was just there to give me these huge tests, and assignments and stuff. And I was like, "Oh no, these are cool people that love talking. They'll talk my ear off about this stuff." I was actually doing the readings well, not just skimming them. And I was like going through being like, "Oh, this is fucking interesting!" . . . I was engaged with my classes and doing well in my classes but I couldn't do that before when I was gung ho in football. And yeah, so I definitely do think that there's a lot of people that don't get as much out of their classes because they want to do so well in football, that they're just not putting enough emphasis on their education, which at the end of the day is going to take them further. Because football will only last us so long. It lasted me three years of college, like I knew I wasn't going to go to the NFL, so I had to get my education, but a lot of guys don't figure that out. There are guys that never figured it out, and they didn't even graduate from [redacted school] and now I know a guy that's serving pizza. I know another guy who just moved back home, he still doesn't have a job in Missouri and that's not to say that there's anything wrong with them or anything, but it's [that] they put in so much work to go to [redacted school] and do all that, and then to not really get the most out of it, is really hard to see.

Perhaps the most insurmountable barrier to receiving a full academic experience for players is the football workload. As Kevin Brown put it when asked whether he felt he got as much out of his classes as his nonathlete peers, "No. Because I had to rush through it. I didn't have the time. There's only twenty-four hours in a day. And so, I had to cut the corners or let things go that I knew weren't perfect. There's papers that the content on that paper was an A, I mean, the thought and the design or whatever was A-material. But it was written at a C-level or even a D-level. And I knew that I had to play the game if you will. Okay, well, something's gotta drop." Since team demands are always prioritized, untenable academic situations become the norm.

Players also can't take classes or engage in schoolwork if it conflicts with football obligations. Chris Andrews explains:

I never even thought of going to a coach and saying, "Coach, it's really important to have this review session and it's during these hours and we're supposed to be on the football field, what should I do?" because I knew the answer. The answer was hammered home for five years that your academics would not interfere with your commitment to the football team. . . . I think back to sitting in a classroom and wondering what it was like to just be done for the day and go home and study once you got out of class as opposed to going and lifting weights, sitting through meetings, going out on the practice field, then watching tape after practice and then going to training table, and then, after all that was done, because you weren't going to cut into that time, then I would go home and study. . . . I think I have a kind of unique perspective now because I actually went back to [redacted college] as a grad student for [an advanced degree] program. And so, going back and kind of being on a level playing field with the rest of the students going to the program, it made me realize even more the sacrifice I made to play football and go to school at the same time.

Likewise, for Terry Davis: "I did want a degree, I was [a STEM major]. I did want to be a [STEM profession]. And it is one of the highest-paying four-year degrees in the country as well as one of the top programs for [Power Five school]. After getting started in school, yeah, I started and played as a true freshman, and . . . me and two other offensive linemen were told that our classes interfere with football. Because our classes are in the afternoon and we are [at academic obligations in the morning]. So had to change that major after my freshman year."

The issue of fatigue is important here. Although athletic department officials like to say the academic problem for college athletes is their "lack of engagement"—a nifty neoliberal strategy of downloading responsibility for the problem on the players who are actually victims of a structural barrier—the reality is sometimes they cannot engage in the classroom because their bodies (and minds) are worn down from arduous athletic responsibilities. Dallas Adams explains, "You just have your days, especially if it's a hard practice day, and you have forty-five minutes to try to grab some food, run to class, shower, and all that beforehand. Sometimes you just sit in class and, it's not like, 'Okay, I just don't want to pay attention to whoever's speaking to me,' it's more like, 'I'm hungry, I want to go to sleep.'" Players, quite simply, were tired all the time. As Kevin Brown articulates, "It was always struggling. It was always, you're not getting, six, seven hours sleep max daily. And, then having a crash day, usually Sunday, that you just sleep all day. So, yeah, it was a perpetual state of short-term naps during the week and trying to stay focused. I was definitely always tired but it just kind of was the norm." Ronnie Exeter, Chris Andrews, and Galen North each remembered being exhausted during class. C. J. White says players could not afford to be tired at practice, so catching rest (required for any human body) sometimes came at the expense of class:

I can remember, for much of my college career, on Tuesdays, that was my hardest day. I would always have three classes, and Tuesdays was the hardest practice. So, once it came, like that third class, like 6:30–9 o'clock, a once-a-week class, I was just done for the day. I would get through that second-to-last class, but that last class . . . it would always be in my mind, like, "Do I want to go today, or do I just want to lay down?" . . . And, you know, most of the time I would just fight through it and go to class or whatever. But there were times where I just had to make that choice, like, "Look, I'm gonna sacrifice, I'm gonna get this rest, I really need this rest for my body." So I might take a day. But I would say that fatigue played a factor because of practice and obviously I always wanted to be my best performance at practice, because it was such a high demand in practice. Practice wasn't anything where coaches took lightly where you could just go out there and mope around or anything. Sometimes it was tough to stay awake in class.

For Jalen Rice, class was not where he wanted to be:

Ah, shit, like I didn't want to be there. I was probably already tired. Like, you get to the facility, I might have got there at like 6:45 or 7 [a.m.] depending on the day or depending when meetings started, maybe like thirty minutes to an hour before meetings started, then you go to practice. Practice could be done at like, let's say 10:10, it probably started at like 8:45. You practice for about two hours almost, then you've got class. . . . Then you get to class, you really don't want to be there. You're just waiting for that hour to pass by and some teachers know that. Once you get in there, they're like, "You're an athlete, you don't really want to be here, you just here to get yourself gone." Some days, practice can be hard, you get to class and you're like, "Damn, I just really don't want to be here right now." Or, some situations, you might not even go to class.

Rice raises another key consideration regarding the alienation many college athletes experience in the classroom: the perceptions of professors and their nonathlete peers that they may not belong or deserve to be in these spaces. If the compensation college athletes receive for their athletic work is an education, the basic precondition of that education is to be treated justly by the pedagogues shaping their learning. But the theme of professors (and to a lesser extent other students) acting in prejudicial ways toward college football players emerged repeatedly in player testimony. Sometimes this meant feeling singled out for being an athlete, making it difficult to thrive academically. C. J. White explains:

I always say that my first few years was a little intimidating. You know, you're sitting in class and the professor would have discussions about whatever class, whatever topic, and I really wouldn't say much. I would try to say something early so I would go ahead and get my [laughs] participation out of the way before it really got going. Because sometimes I felt like they were talking about things that I just didn't really understand or like they had different perspectives from what I had. . . . I just kind of felt like, sometimes I wouldn't say it because I felt like they would look at me different, like, "He's just here for football, anyway."

Galen North felt similarly:

You also feel, and this is not across the board, but it's very clear that you're some sort of athlete. Usually for people in my situation that are so large, they know you're a football player, so some teachers don't like you just because you're an athlete and I had that experience. I was basically told, "No, I am not giving you any leniency because I don't like athletes." I was like, "Okay, thanks." I appreciate that, I have an A in your class but you're not going to give me a little leniency here because I have an away game and I have to travel. And then you also kind of get other students are like, "Oh, there's a football player, they're probably stupid." When you get lumped into a group assignment, they're like, "We don't want you in our group because we don't think you're going to do anything or you're not going to contribute," meanwhile I'm doing better in the class than you are. [laughs] So, it's definitely a different experience. You are, I don't want to say singled out, but your presence is clearly known, whether good or bad.

This was also Steven Summers's experience:

At [redacted previous school], I feel like in my experience anyways, the athletes there, especially the football and basketball players . . . like the swimmers like they don't really get the same kind of energy or like, women's lacrosse players, like they're not getting the same kind of looks. But you know when you're at [redacted previous school], you have a bunch of, I hate to say it, but a bunch of nerds sitting in the classroom just hunched over their laptops and stuff and then some big 300-pound dude walks in, and you're like "Okay." [laughs] [We're] wearing a [university-branded] football hoodie, or we would all have the same backpack, so it was pretty easy to tell us apart. You'd get mixed reactions. I feel like you'd get some people that are like, "Oh, you're on the football team, that's cool." And you'd get some people that would look at you sideways kind of like, "You don't deserve to be at [redacted previous school]. Like you're not as smart as us, you didn't work as hard in high school, academically." Professors were the same way.

Charlie Rogers paints an even grimmer picture:

> The teachers don't really like us, because they think we're just a bunch of freeloaders, not coming to class, falling asleep in class, not doing well on assignments, and they really don't know we're pretty much fighting for our lives. Just trying to be here, being sold a fake dream of possibly going into the NFL or whatever. And a lot of students don't like us because they think like, "I worked my ass off in high school and I'm paying more money than they are." When, in reality, we generate enough money to fund every single sports program besides men's basketball. And you know, I could point to buildings with renovations, like I know I was a part of that. I helped build this.

These preconceived ideas sometimes lead to increased surveillance, regulation, and discipline of athletes in educational environments. Chris Andrews remembers when he and two teammates were called into a dean's office and accused of cheating on a homework assignment despite the fact that the syllabus said "group work is encouraged for homework assignments." Later, in grad school, he received a grade on a paper only a half hour after the deadline:

> I saw that professor walking on campus and he said, "Hey, I really liked that paper," and I said, "Yeah I was surprised that you graded all of the papers within just a couple of hours of the time that we were supposed to turn them in," and he's like, "No, just yours," and I said, "Just mine?" and he said, "Yeah, I heard you were a football player, I wanted to see if you were fucking stupid." He said it in a very playful way and he was probably my biggest supporter during my time in grad school, but I just thought it was interesting.

Sometimes the opposite dynamic occurs, with professors giving athletes preferential treatment. Brock Adler explains: "There were professors that were in cahoots with the coaching staff, on getting guys out of classes for football, or getting guys into certain classes, or even just making accommodations. Not like cheating or anything, but you know, if a guy came late that's fine. You know, not holding everybody to the same standard. Now that's not every professor, obviously. There were a lot of guys who complained about professors who were hard, but I actually appreciated that, because they were treating us like normal." This treatment veers toward cheating and effectively denies the athlete the full educational experience.

After all, the point of higher education is ultimately *learning* rather than merely procuring a degree.

The mental load that football demands from players also interferes with the classroom experience. They cannot always switch off the stress and anxiety associated with football performance to focus on academic matters. Adler told us,

> I can tell you, number one, that a lot of it was stress because I would always be thinking about practice at two o'clock versus the class I'm in now. It was always dreading the next day of the workout, "Oh, are we going to get smoked?" . . . "Smoked" is the term used for punishment, like during PT, and we would basically get that during conditioning workouts because we weren't doing something to the exact detail that the strength coach wanted. That was something that was always prevalent in my mind, and haunting my mind, and dreading in my mind because I was like, "Man, I just want to do it right." Some days were harder practices, and you would just dread it, throughout the day. You couldn't focus during class, you were just thinking about that, you were thinking about showing out, thinking about "I gotta do good this week so I can play."

Chris Andrews had similar experiences:

> I took my academics really seriously, I wanted to get good grades, but also the idea of sitting in class, like, if I had a bad practice the day before, I'd probably get yelled at by my coach, and I either got yelled at in front of my whole team, the whole offense, or my whole position group, so there were times where I would sit in class and think "How do I fix the error I made in yesterday's practice so I don't go through this humiliation of getting yelled at again," and so that would take away from the attention I could give in the classroom. Where if I got a bad grade in a class, a teacher just handed you back a folded-up exam or posted online that you didn't perform well on a test and nobody else really knew.

Between the physical and mental demands that interfere with classroom activities, the constant signaling that school is less important than football, and the differential treatment from faculty and peers, it is difficult to argue that college football players receive the full educational value they are promised in exchange for their athletic labor. They receive, at best, a poor facsimile.

Football Majors

Academic clustering is the practice of steering athletes toward degrees and majors perceived to be the least time consuming and onerous, thus freeing up athletes' time for sports. It is likely a pervasive issue across big-time college sport.[10] Ross Nielsen explains how it worked at his school:

> I had a lot of freedom to choose academically what I wanted to do—but [for scholarship players] they had this whole complex setup where you'd show up, and the academic advisors would funnel you into a major that was very low time investment, and where the department had a lot of influence, like sports management, exercise science, communications . . . they would drive them to these degree programs. Particularly at [redacted school], nothing wrong with those degrees, not to like disenfranchise them. But at [redacted school], those were low workload degrees and so they would put them in there, and the coaches would monitor their behavior. But there was definitely some thought that players were not expected to work very hard in those degree programs and still get their Cs that get degrees. And so that really hurts players in the long run, right? Most of them are the first people in their family just to be in college. I was the second person in my family tree to get a college degree on my dad's side. And so, that motivates people like crazy to come. But then the thing is, they're fighting against this pressure to put their entire hours into football for four or five years. So it's pretty extractive on the player, I don't think most people are aware of it, when they're playing. It only really arises after you stop, because you take a step back and you're like, "Where am I at now?" It's just a little bit disheartening.

Nielsen gets to the heart of why practices like academic clustering are exploitative. Players are promised an educational experience in return for their labor. For many, this is a potentially transformative opportunity, as higher education, particularly at the large research-intensive institutions in the Power Five, is, due to economic barriers and other social and cultural constraints, inaccessible to large swathes of the American population.[11] College football provides a potential pathway to opportunities often otherwise denied. But when that educational experience is circumscribed by athletic departments that inhibit what can be learned, those possibilities diminish. This is precisely why the stakes of the academic experience of college athletes are so high.

Maybe the most underhanded aspect of academic clustering is the practice at some institutions of recruiting players based on the school's particular academic specialties. This would be perfectly defensible and even laudable except for two small problems: in many cases, either the football programs make promises they can't keep in terms of admission or, even worse, they renege on the pitch they made during the recruiting process, ultimately telling players those academic specialties are too demanding and time consuming. Matt Jensen explains as follows:

> This is big. So at [redacted school], obviously we have the [redacted] Business School. Great school. A lot of guys they recruit come to [redacted school], on that [premise], saying, "You come here, we'll help you out. We'll give you the resources. We'll help you get into [redacted] Business School." One dude gets in every year. One dude. The rest of us—I was one of those dudes! I was like, "Maybe I'll do business." Then, you get there and realize how fucking hard and competitive it is, it's like getting into a Harvard within a Harvard. It's hard. And so, most guys have to, like me, just do political science or do legal studies. So, the big majors that they funnel you into after you inevitably don't become a business major are legal studies, American studies . . . those are the two big ones they like to funnel guys into. And then there might be, like, environmental econ, or stuff like that. But those are the big ones. And so they're like, "Oh, sorry, you didn't get into the business school. American and legal studies are really good degrees." It is kind of like, after you don't get into the school you came to [redacted university] to do, then you just kinda have to fall back on that. And I mean I get it, like [redacted business school] is a great business school and they shouldn't be able to get football players in there. Like 100 percent. But also, if that's the case, and it's really that hard to get in, they really do need to tell people that "look, this is seriously hard to get in. We'll give you the resources for tutors and stuff to help you, but, just know you're probably not going to get in, unless you're like, the cream of the crop."

With respect to football programs promising degrees that players wouldn't be allowed to pursue, Daniel Barber explains, "I said, 'Don't come in doing engineering.' They [recruiters] tell you, 'Oh, yeah, [redacted school] has a great engineering program.' Because your mom is saying she wants you to do engineering. Your dad's telling them you want to do premed. That isn't what you're going to be able to do, bro." Academic clustering is a nearly universal practice across Power Five college football because it is almost impossible to succeed in STEM disciplines while also excelling at football. The basic time demands of both are just too great, as this conversation with Josh Hansen reveals:

NKL: Okay. So, were you able to take the classes you wanted? Were you able to be present in class—

HANSEN: [Interjects] Hell no!

NKL: Okay, talk a little bit about that.

HANSEN: Bro, if you're in sociology, psychology, or parks and recreation, you show it. Like, my teammates who were engineers struggled. And I don't think one scholarship athlete ever graduated with an engineering degree.

NKL: Were you counseled not to take those classes, or you just make those choices yourselves?

HANSEN: No, no. I think it's a part of the counseling. Because your class schedule is already set, it's already kind of preset. Like, you choose your degree and what you want to go into, but the track is a well-oiled machine. Yeah, because you have your advisor meeting, and they tell you, "Hey you need this class, this is what you can choose," and you kind of choose it based on offerings and things like that. I mean, if you want to do like engineering and things like that, you would definitely struggle.

Likewise, Charlie Rogers explained that clustering was regular practice at his institution, based on a logic of providing players with the least demanding majors possible so they had more time for athletic work (importantly, we do not agree that some humanities and social science majors like American studies have less inherent value):

You pretty much have to fight against the entire athletic/academic wing to get a degree with any kind of weight. Like if you look at most, especially Power Five programs . . . you might have like out of a hundred people, maybe ten business majors. There was one, like my friend that I mentioned, he was a math major and he had to fight with all of his will to keep that. And the rest are just American studies . . . history. Like, not even sociology, and people give sociology some shit. But it's just these majors, like what the fuck is American studies? You know, just a bunch of these degrees that mean absolutely nothing, but it's the easiest class you can take and it fits most with the schedule, which demands that you take all of your classes before 2:00 p.m. Even if you need it for your major. They're not gonna let you take it if it cuts into football time. And anything with any sort of rigor. They try their best to get you to not do it.

For Jeremy Jones, these realities made him question his role as a supposed student:

I came here wanting to be a computer science major and was told to switch to sociology because it fit my schedule better, right? . . . Everyone always be saying we're "students first" and "athletes second," which is just lying. If we were students first then we wouldn't be missing class to travel for games. We wouldn't be waking up at 5:30 a.m. for a three-hour practice before class and then lifting for three hours after class. We wouldn't be told what classes were better for our football schedule, what majors we should take. All that shit. If we were really students first we would be able to take whatever class we want and would have to face the consequences. If I wanted to take advanced algebra as a sociology major, I should be able to take it even if I know fucking right I'm going to fail that shit. But naw, we got people looking over our shoulders at the classes we should take and directing us into the 'easier' shit. Like, they don't come out and say, "You can't take that class," but we all know what it means when they say, "Are you sure you want to take that major . . . what about this one?"

Ronnie Exeter also experienced clustering:

I wanted to be a dentist and my mom wanted me to be a dentist. Man, that was such a goal of mine. When I got to [redacted school], I was a major in bio and a minor in chemistry, and I thought I was going to handle my business, maybe go to a dental school somewhere else. It was pretty apparent that it was football first and then class second. This wasn't only me. I had a couple friends who were petroleum engineers, or just doing different harder academics. Then the coach would come, just be like, "Huh, I don't know. Maybe you need to think about going another route." That was more of usually sports management, kinesiology kind of thing, psychology.

Kevin Brown told his institution he was passionate about majoring in political science. "And so I came in and proposed that to the folks and was quickly said, 'No you're not gonna do that. You can't do that.'" In other cases, it was a lack of guidance, and the general imperative to find the easiest classes in terms of scheduling and difficulty of coursework, that produced a clustering effect:

> BROCK ADLER: I didn't really get information or counseling on what I want to do, from any of the academic staff or, you know, not like coaches made an attempt [at] that. I just had to take a major. I mean, a lot of the guys they encouraged to take sociology or American studies. And you could look at [redacted school]'s roster between the years of 2016 to now, and a lot of it is American studies and sociology. . . . It was labeled as easier, or the classes complied with football times. That's just the bottom line.

Complying with football times was a key issue. Since football comes first, classes must be scheduled around it, thus foreclosing myriad academic possibilities:

> RYAN LEONARD: I know plenty of guys that came in and we had a thing for this, that if you came in an engineer major, you were really a general studies guy, you just didn't know it yet because so many of the engineering classes happened in the fall and happened in the afternoon. That's where we practiced, and so many of these required classes were going to be conflicting with your football schedule. So if you came in an engineer, you're really a general studies guy.

Academic clustering illustrates the tokenistic way coaches and athletic departments treat the educations of players. While lip service is paid to the significance of academic success and progress toward degrees, the real goal is maximizing the productivity of the football team. Ronnie Exeter's experience clearly demonstrates this:

> I was obviously going to [Power Five school in the South], and I had an opportunity to do an internship in Ohio. I got up there, and the coach that I was doing the strength conditioning and internship with, he goes, "We saw that you have another year of eligibility." I actually had two. He was just like, "Hey, man, why don't you strength train and play football? You can get your grad degree and all that." I was like, "That's a no-brainer. Easy." Signed all my paperwork, did a compliance and all that. [The coach from his first school in the South] calls me, I'm in Ohio, and he's just like, "What are you doing?" Kind of thing. "You need to be graduating from here." He actually mentioned the word [Academic Progress Rating, APR]. He was pretty

much saying that I need you to get back, because this is going to hurt us academically.

In the end, the coach successfully pressured him into forgoing opportunities to bolster an APR score ostensibly designed to ensure academic rigor.

Our interviews made very clear that academics were, in the view of college football players, largely subordinate to athletic endeavors. The players' experiences in this chapter corroborate the findings of scholars that the authoritarian, coercive relationships between coaches, athletic departments, and athletes are at least part of the myriad barriers to the successful educational experience for athletic workers.[12] Athletic department staff have the desire and, more profoundly, the *ability* to control the pedagogical experience of college football players in almost every way. Coaches wield an incredible amount of power over not only the athletes' current playing conditions vis-á-vis football, but also their future in the sport and, despite their claims to the contrary, their scholastic careers. The NCAA system is fundamentally built in such a way that athletic programs can control the structural conditions that make status attainment possible or, often, impossible. At its core, big-time college sport is premised on these forms of coercion that target both structure and status in a US capitalist political economy: in order to receive access to an institution of higher education that may otherwise be inaccessible due to racial and economic inequalities, athletes must submit to the extraction of the value produced by their labor without seeing a commensurate return, and they must do so under threat of losing that access at any moment if they consider withdrawing their "consent."[13] Moreover, as chapter 3 illustrates, athletic labor performed under such coercive conditions heightens the possibility of physical and emotional harm, as players must often endure abusive coaching and overtraining to satisfy their overseers' whims, harm they must ultimately bear the long-term consequences of, not just bodily, but also financially, given the punitive nature of privatized health care, costs that the universities that employ them refuse to mitigate.

Conclusion: About that Accreditation

While we have not focused on academic corruption, it does occur. Cheating harms the athletes themselves most of all. It denies them the learning experience they were promised, and it ensures they will receive nothing in return for the revenue they generate. In that sense, cheating is the most tragic dimension of academic exploitation in the world of big-time college football.

One of the least dramatic but nevertheless most problematic forms of cheating is when athletes are not required to attend classes. Daniel Barber had an interesting experience with this:

> There were also professors who like went to [redacted ACC school, not his school] and stuff, who knew that, "Oh, these [Barber's school] students come to class. These [Barber's school] football players come to class! Not all of 'em, not everybody, but holy shit!" [Laughs] Like, what? [At redacted ACC school], they pay someone to go to the class with your clicker to take the daily quizzes and stuff. . . . We had a transfer from [redacted ACC school], who did not know his schedule. Like, I was with him while he was picking out his schedule, and our academic advisor was like, "Oh, you got an A in geology, do you want to go further in the scientific field?" And he was like, "What? I took that?" He was only in online classes. . . . He went through his whole freshman year, or at least, his first semester at [redacted ACC school] not going to any classes. [At redacted SEC school, not his school], they don't know what their major is. Just whatever works for their schedule, whatever works for practice, that's what they're majoring in, that semester. So they could just get these garbage credits.

At some schools the opposite is true: rather than being given a free pass to skip class, players are severely punished for missing it. They are subjected to harsh forms of punishment by the athletic department for their own attempts to exercise agency in their academic lives. This is, in that sense, an abrogation of their academic freedom. Brock Adler explained that after skipping class a couple of times as a freshman, "We basically came in the [weight room] and wiped everything up for a week." At Landry West's school, punishment involved "something after a lift. There was this thing, it's like the ladder thing that is an infinity ladder where you just climb, climb, climb. Could be something after practice, maybe running suicides, or shuttles, up downs, things like that . . . and they would be doing punishment after that practice."

At other institutions, conventional cheating on tests was so pervasive that Matt Jensen saw his decision never to cheat as a particular point of pride:

> I can actually say that I didn't cheat on any test. And that's something that I really wanted to be able to say when I graduated college. . . . The other guys, not so much. . . . They come walking into the locker room like, "Oh, I got an A on that test." And I'm like, "Buddy, you didn't study at all." And they're like, "Dude, there's multiple ways to

skin a cat, like, I just sat behind the two smartest people." I'm like, "Bro, you know that we're putting in work here. So it would be one thing if you showed up here, and you cheated, and you felt shitty about it, and you didn't say anything. You know, because you knew it was wrong." But these guys would come in and boast about it.

Ryan Leonard also described pervasive cheating on tests, explaining that "they allowed us so much more leniency than the average student, I believe. This isn't going to look great on me, but the way that it truly manifested is they looked the other way when it came to the cheating." In fact, Leonard and his teammates would have walk-on players who excelled academically finish tests before them and then leave and text them the answers via Apple Watches. He continued, "For some reason now, whether it's willful negligence or for some reason, these professors let it happen. Now I don't blame them for it. I think they understood why we were there. They understood that these guys need to play, and we had the best players. Some of the best players were in these classes of mine. And so they knew."

Leonard also describes how a professor was happy to boost his grade since it would help him stay eligible and benefit the football team:

LEONARD: I was coming off of rehab and we were going into my third year and I was going to make a 62 in this class, and I knew there was no way I was going to pass this test. . . . I go in and talk to him and he goes, "Well, I know you've been rehabbing your knee and I know you're valuable to the season coming up, but don't worry about it. Don't worry about it." I go, "Okay." He goes, "Don't even worry about the test, you'll be good." I ended up—

DS: He said, "I know you're valuable?"

LEONARD: Yeah, "I know you'll be a starter," because I had started the year prior. "I know you're going to play. I know you're going to protect our star quarterback."

Although he couldn't prove it, Leonard suspected widespread academic malfeasance at his institution that enabled players to stay eligible:

One of the crazy, crazy meetings is at [Power Five school] there was one time we came back from Christmas break. Our coach had everybody in the meeting room and he goes, "We're going to go down a list of everybody that received below a 2.0 GPA for the semester before." That list consisted of twenty-five, thirty players that ranged from GPA of a 1.9 to a 0.06 was the lowest number that I heard. Our coach told us, "If you guys don't fix this, if we can't get your GPA up, you might not play." All thirty of those players were eligible to play the next year. Nobody was suspended for academics. Nobody had to leave the facility, leave athletics so that they could focus on academics and yet they all still played. Man, somebody worked some magic. Somebody looked the other way. . . . I don't know how they did it. There were some of the top players on our team that fell into that category, that were on what they called academic probation, that were subject to not play, and yet every single one of them were eligible to play the next year.

Terry Davis said his head coach offered him inappropriate academic benefits as a sort of reward for his performance: "'What can I get you? You still want to do that degree? I can get the whole class schedule changed for you,' is what he tells me."

Maybe the most egregiously unethical academic practice was the demand coaches placed on some players to *deliberately fail* to procure more athletic eligibility. Daniel Barber told us:

You'll see a lot of universities, to get people to their fifth year, will just tell them to flunk. So we had someone [redacted teammate], he's playing for [NFL team] now. He was a double major. He was told, "Hey, for your fifth year, like, get out of here. We don't want you." He was just told in the hallway, "Hey, leave." So he went to his academic advisor, and he's just like, "Okay, I'm getting my degree." And so they fixed everything, he dropped classes, he was going to be done. And then he played really well against the [redacted]. And they came to him and it was like, "We're gonna want you for a fifth year." He's like, "What? Okay." And then they're like, "So switch out of classes. Drop credits." But it was too late. It was past the add/drop. And this was director of player personnel, I believe this was [redacted name]. He was like, "Yeah, I'm not telling you to flunk a class, but. . . . But . . ." and then the academic advisor was like, "What the hell? He is a good student, he can get into grad school." He's like, "Oh, okay, great." So [they] try to manipulate student-athletes to do stuff for their [own] benefit. That only they can do without knowing any background. They don't give a damn.

Barber also highlighted another deeply disturbing convention: exploiting disability accommodations to allow more time for football and less for school:

I think [redacted school] is the only school in the [redacted conference] that doesn't do literacy tests. I mean, they really try to get you labeled for a disability at a lot of schools so that they can get you "help" and just get someone else to do your work. And they could use those provisions to actually help educate them. Instead of actually helping them with education, because a lot of people need help, they just use it to *do* the education part, so they can do the football. So, "Hey, you've got this tutor and stuff." Like [redacted name], get called up, "Hey, why aren't you working out right now?" He's like, "Oh I'm in a tutoring session." And he was like, "You shouldn't be." So that work's going to get handled for him.

The academic side of college football is no less emblematic of the exploitation saturating this institution than the economic. The exchange between athlete and university is (problematically) premised on the (structurally coerced) agreement that an education will be offered as wage in return for labor. But the education furnished as wage is not the education promised. Instead, it is diluted and devalued: by the physical and mental impossibilities of being fully present for learning, by academic clustering that forecloses educational opportunities, by a schedule that limits what courses can be selected, by the surveillance and regulation of the student's freedom of movement, and by cheating that denies the possibility of intellectual growth. College football, according to the system's own terms and logic, is nothing less than a form of systematic wage theft from college football players.

The problem for college athletes is, at least in part, the structural conditions of the education supposedly worth more than money—conditions that make learning almost impossible. Athletes are commonly up well before their peers for gym and practice sessions and are often discouraged from taking classes that clash with training.[14] Since college football players typically do not receive the same educational experience as their peers, one reasonable prescription for this inequity is a lifetime scholarship.[15] Given that education is the only form of payment for athletic labor, all of the structural conditions described in this chapter militate against athletes receiving the full wage (education) they have earned. The only way to redress this exploitation is to create conditions whereby athletic laborers can obtain an unimpeded educational experience—and because athletic endeavors are the primary barrier to education in college athletics, that means players must be given the opportunity to complete their studies at any time they want, entirely free of the encumbrance of their athletic burden.

CHAPTER THREE

Beyond Compensation

It is a hot, humid Midwestern summer day of preseason training. The particularly grueling practice session is, thankfully, almost done. One of the last drills — the infamous Oklahoma drill where two players line up opposite one another, advancing forward at full force on a coach's whistle until one falls — is getting heated. A cornerback and wide receiver, who have been trash-talking one another all practice, are put in the drill by the strength and conditioning coach to settle the grudge. The athletes kneel down in their three-point stance. When the coach blows his whistle, they leap forward violently, hitting each other midstride. Upon collision, the wide receiver falls backward; his left hip hits the ground just before his head whips back into the turf. The coach blows his whistle and yells, *Again!* The receiver returns to his feet and resets. The whistle screams again and the players barrel at one another. This time the receiver won't fall. Instead, he pushes his teammate backward and suplexes him into the ground. The coach's whistle shrieks. *Again*, he mutters. They get back up, noticeably drained. They reset and stare into each other's eyes. The coach waits, allowing the tension to build. *Rubber match*, he yells. The players advance at one another, colliding just as their hips rise and their backs straighten. They lock arms and tussle back and forth for a few seconds before it becomes clear they are no longer performing the drill. As punches land, one after another, the coach demands, *Go meet on the T, you wanna fight on my field? Do it on the T.*

"At [midwestern state university] . . . we had a big T logo in our locker room," former Power Five player Kurt Weiss told us. "If you have a problem with someone, you just fight on the T, and solve your problem and put it to rest. There were probably only a handful of fights that I remember on the T, but this came from the strength coach. Which is crazy. I mean, he's making hundreds of thousands of dollars [as a] public employee, with young people who are students, and instructing them to get into fights." Weiss continued:

> The fights weren't fistfights. It was like wrestling, it was like a sumo match, wrestling to the ground. . . . The players would circle around and watch it. And would intervene if it got too violent. . . . [It could get] pretty violent . . . certainly it would cross the threshold of the

degree of violence that could do serious damage. So our locker room was cement with carpet over it, and there was guys picking guys up and slamming them on the ground. Throwing guys into a wall. And just wrestling, you could tear a ligament in your shoulder, knee, hip, or anything. So it wouldn't be uncommon for there to be a little bit of blood, if a guy's face rubbed against the carpet. I don't know of any injuries from the handful of meetings on the T during my time at [midwestern state university]. But . . . if what was happening on the T was happening on the street corner, the cops would be called and it would be a violent altercation, it would be a fight.

While not all athletes interviewed shared this experience, *many* did. If it wasn't "meeting on the T," it was "go hash it out on the tiger," "sort it out on the hammer," or other variations referencing a school logo or place on practice facility grounds. The normalization of such coaching tactics should shock anyone, but perhaps more profoundly, their presence on college practice fields should act as a reminder that the exploitation of campus athletic workers is about much more than compensation.

Mainstream exploitation debates are right to highlight the injustice that players are not compensated for their work. Yet this frame does not adequately account for the fact that exploitation is not just about how benefits are distributed in an exchange, but also how *harm* is distributed. College football is a site of some of the most brutal working conditions in US society, yet one unregulated by occupational health and safety standards and unprotected by labor organizing. Consequently, players are systematically subjected to brutal physical (and emotional) harm and discipline in the course of their work, compelled to play through injury, and often forced to endure abusive coaching. At the end of this process, they are not even afforded health insurance to cope with the long-term toll they must endure. Above all, tackle football is inextricable from the unconscionable level of harm caused by head injury. This chapter is the largely underwritten story of the physical and emotional harm saturating college football that compromises any claim the sport may make to prosocial development.

Deeply embedded in football culture and practice is a foundational acceptance and rewarding of heteromasculine physical violence and its consequences, beginning at the youth level.[1] While scholars have documented in various ways the deleterious consequences of a football culture premised on bodily harm, here we take a slightly different approach by focusing on the experiences of former college football players to narrate how the structural violence of college football is lived.[2] Given that every 2.6 years of participation in football doubles the chances of contracting the degenerative brain disorder chronic traumatic encephalopathy (CTE) and that 91 percent of American college football players' brains examined in a pivotal Boston University study displayed neuropathology consistent with CTE, not to mention that participation in football likely increases the chances of developing Parkinson's disease by 61 percent compared to athletes in other organized sports (and that risk is 2.93 times greater for those who play football at the college/pro level versus youth/high school), we hold that sacrifice is a nearly universal feature of NCAA football, not an accidental and unfortunate consequence.[3] We thus aim to make intelligible the concerns of athletic laborers who have had to live with the reality behind these statistics.

Compensation alone is a limited vantage point from which to view the accumulated harms proliferating throughout NCAA sport. While athletes should be compensated for their work, it is even more imperative that they are protected from harm in the course of their labor. Yet evidence suggests that the NCAA has long explicitly understood that the value produced through football is predicated on devastating physical harm. In a 1973 letter, NCAA lawyer Donald Wilson wrote to the head of the NCAA's Football Rules Committee that it should ignore warnings from medical experts of the dangers of head-first tackling because, "In my opinion, any heed paid to their suggestions will destroy present-day football as we know it. . . . Kindly bear in mind that if any of their letter, speeches and/or reports are published in any periodicals, this will form the basis of devastating cross-examination of football coaches at all levels in the future."[4]

We argue that physical and emotional harm are structural features of professionalized athletics rather than unfortunate consequences.[5] The physical pain and sacrifice athletic workers experience is *built into* the foundation of elite sport. Fans come to sport seeking meaning and community to offset the deprivations of capitalism—its systemic immiseration and atomization.[6] Investment in players' performances provides the scaffolding for a community of "we" and the possibility of ephemeral and illusory triumph that can temporarily alleviate the affective strains of capitalist life. But this meaning is predicated on the stakes of the spectacle being high enough to support the emotional weight they must bear for fans. Players must perform as if sport has inherent meaning—as if it is more than just a game, and is actually worth, even demands, their sacrifice. Injury is not incidental but in fact central to the political economy of meaning in high-performance spectator sport. This is as true in college football as it is anywhere else. The implication of this is that participants ultimately experience corporeal harm that can transform their embodied lives and thus identities — physical damage that necessarily entails subjective consequences, in the form of either maimed bodies that can no longer support the identity of an invulnerable athletic self or brains subjected to repetitive trauma that quite literally cannot sustain the subjectivities that previously existed. This is the cost of social reproductive athletic labor, a cost that must be understood as an additional form of exploitation via harm. The university takes not only the surplus-value of revenue via commodity spectacle that is drastically under- (that is, *un-*) compensated, but also the additional value that is the athlete's selfhood sacrificed to reproduce the fan, which ultimately makes college football morally indefensible as a *cultural* practice — not just an economic one.

Getting Hurt, Playing Hurt

To grapple with the centrality of pain, injury, and harm to the experiences of former college football players, we must begin with the question of how ubiquitous these injuries are. Getting hurt in football is not a question of if, or when, but how many times and how seriously.

As prevalent as injury is in college football today, its impact pales in comparison to previous decades. Ross Nielsen points to his father's experience in an earlier era: "The people who played in the '90s and '80s . . . they were way more disenfranchised by the process than I think I was. . . . My dad would tell me stories, and I'd be like, 'Wow, you were abused for somebody who was a coach to make millions of dollars.' Back then, they would give them injections of Toradol to numb pain, so they could play immediately. They would do procedures on the sidelines to fix them up. They would return to play, like they didn't have any concussion protocols or anything." While Nielsen implies that conditions have improved, the experiences of many players we interviewed suggest those improvements are largely incremental than revolutionary.

Players who competed recently described a wide array of grievous injuries. Michael Thomas played through a torn acromioclavicular (AC) joint as a freshman but lost his sophomore season to a torn ligament in his foot. Dallas Adams broke his hand and endured a second and third metacarpal spiral fracture. Kevin Brown had "a whole gamut of injuries": "Chipped vertebrae, two slipped discs . . . a clean break on my fifth metatarsal in my right foot. . . . Definitely my ankle, completely blew it out, three ligaments, three tendons. Pretty much all the metatarsals in my foot were screwed up some way, somehow. A few of them, I think the third and fourth were fully fractured. And then the first, which is the bone that's connected to your big toe, was a stress fracture. . . . Achilles tendon was torn. . . . I've broken my fingers a number of times and played through that. That's just the beast of playing offensive line."

Galen North managed through a full knee reconstruction and Achilles tendon surgery only to have his career end due to neck surgery. Likewise, Thomas Rycliff noted the frequency of damaging injuries:

> In practice that week, we had a guy who was a little bit deaf, and he didn't hear the whistle on defense, and he just hit me right to where you get what's called a stinger. I didn't get hit hard. I just got blind-sided to where the synapses in your neck where the nerves come out, when you get a stinger, your arm kind of goes numb, and you shake it off, and you just keep playing. If you keep getting numb, it gets worse and worse, and you become more susceptible. I had about eight stingers that week leading up to the game, so they strapped this thing on my neck to keep my neck somewhat in place. I had another fourteen during the game, and I played one of the best games ever.

Ryan Leonard's experience was particularly troubling given the quantity of injuries he suffered: "Before I got to college, never had an injury. By the time I left college, I had a medical record book of over six hundred pages. From rehab notes, surgery notes, to MRIs. I had over twelve MRIs total, five knee surgeries. This was while I was playing. . . . Later I found out that I had four torn labrum[s]. So I have a torn labrum on both shoulders, torn labrum on both hips. And I got one hip fixed, so this was post playing, and I also tore my bicep after I was done playing."

While damaged bodies were par for the course for nearly all the players we interviewed, so too was the expectation that they would continue playing if physically possible. Nick Turner played through two torn meniscuses and two torn shoulder labrums *at the same time*. Kurt Weiss explains how the demand to play through injury in college—a clear form of exploitation in that it is a conscious choice by coaches to extract the maximum amount of value/performance from the body with no offsetting benefit to athletes—was a stark contrast with his high school experience:

> I had three shoulder surgeries, and those would be the highlights. . . . In high school, I went to a small Catholic school. . . . They would let me, if my hamstring was tight, I didn't practice that day. At [school] that first training camp where I was basically always on the field. . . .

I was doing it all and doing too much. I pulled my groin, and it was an injury you could play with. It was subtle, a strain more than a pull. I told the trainers, and I was limping around on the field and couldn't open my hips and make turns. Coach pulled me out, said, "Are you all right? Go see the trainers." In that meeting with the trainers, I was accustomed to the high school arrangement, where if you're feeling off or can't perform, take time, get healthy. And immediately it was like, how could they get you back on the field for practice. And so, they wrapped up my [groin], I didn't miss a practice, I played the rest of training camp and started the season with that groin strain. So I learned then the difference is significant. As that season progressed, I had a torn labrum over my left shoulder. So my shoulder would dislocate pretty much every game.

We repeatedly heard players were taught the difference between playing "hurt" and playing "injured." Injuries required time off, but playing "hurt" meant coping with pain. The distinction supposedly meant that, in the latter case, significant bodily harm was not worsening through further play. But this rather subjective and nuanced distinction could easily be deployed against players to exhort or even coerce them into further performance. Nevertheless, players absorbed and internalized it and generally strove to prove they could cope with pain. Steven Summers explains:

Coaches will say, "Are you hurt or are you injured?" Because playing hurt is one thing, like I basically played hurt the whole second half of this past season with my ankle, and yeah, it sucked. It was painful. I definitely wasn't at full speed, but I could still put forth good work, so it was kind of expected like, "Hey, you just got to push through it." The coaches that I've been with at least, are pretty good about understanding like, "You have a busted knee, a shoulder that's not operable, you can't play." Versus being hurt is like, "Hey, you got a dislocated finger, like dude, it's football. Tape it up."

Summers's example of a "dislocated finger" makes clear that the level of pain falling into the playing "hurt" category is considerable. In football, being "injured" means literally not being able to perform. Evidently, that is less a medical distinction than a performance imperative. Thomas Rycliff saw it the same way:

I remember one time one of our offensive linemen . . . stepped on my foot so hard that, I think it's a metatarsal, it got knocked under the other bone. . . . I couldn't put any pressure on my foot. And somehow the trainer knew that he could snap it. He'd seen this injury before and he did the shaping and the bone would go into place, and I'm fine. And that would happen every practice during the spring until spring was over. At some point I was like, "Oh geez, got to snap my foot back into place." And boom, snapped and went back. . . . That's just kind of being a tough football player. There is an element of "Rub some dirt on it" and there is that line between, "Are you hurt or are you injured?" . . . You kind of get mentally primed for that where you're not supposed to take yourself out of these scenarios unless . . . you're severely injured, when I couldn't literally move my arm for three hours, I don't have a choice. I'm not going to play tackle football with a limp arm. . . . But you'll see guys all the time when they get hurt, and this is how you can tell they've been primed for it, they'll get a leg injury and instead of waiting for people to come out and get them, they'll just hop off the field themselves on one foot. And that's because that's this, "I'm being tough." It's that instead of, "Wait, no, this might be serious, let's take a look at it."

The coaches' ideological conditioning that working through injury is an inherent virtue rather than an instrument of extraction is quite effective, as Michael Thomas told us: "I wouldn't say it was great that [my injury] happened, but I think it was something that needed to happen because I didn't know how to handle adversity. . . . When this happened to me . . . it gave me the opportunity to learn how to handle adversity throughout my life. . . . That was one of my weak points that my coaches alluded to me about life. Going through situations, you're going to face adversity. . . . But it's all about how you handle that adversity."

During their careers, it can be difficult for elite athletes to appraise relative concern over injury. Athletic excellence requires a form of socialization that involves compartmentalizing risk. The ubiquitous cliché "no pain, no gain" exemplifies the widespread logic that some form of physical harm is necessary to build bodies capable of sporting success. Yet with the benefit of time and distance, athletes often come to see the harm that they experienced differently, particularly when forced to confront the long-term implications of the strain their bodies were subjected to. Similarly, the culture of college football produces a neoliberal personalization of responsibility for injury, or what has been called "healthism."[7] Instead of health and harm being understood as structural or environmental questions, they are treated as the individual's personal responsibility. For college football, this means holding the players accountable for their relative health and well-being rather than ascribing responsibility to a sport, culture, and political economy that require their body to be subjected to harm as a condition of participation. As counterintuitive as healthism might seem in the context of football, this is precisely how some players were taught to view their health (to the benefit of the coaches who then evade responsibility). Matt Jensen provides one example:

> It's unfortunate because we gotta have these brains—we only get one, and we have it for the rest of our lives. And so, I was like, "Okay, like I need to take care of myself here." It's not going to be the coaches that are going to say, "Hey, you don't look so good, let's bring you aside and get you to the trainer." It's going to be, no, no, no, I have to [look out for myself]. Which, you know, is part of growing up. And like it's my responsibility to make sure people know when I'm okay and when I'm not. Which, you know, I would hope it would be a little different. I would hope some people would take a little more interest, but you know, the end of day, it is my responsibility.

Jensen recognizes a moral incongruity between the harm he experienced and the lack of regard for his well-being from those in positions of authority. Yet instead of fully indicting the system, he rationalizes it through healthism, likely because this is the framework offered by the team's culture. Nick Turner explains, through the misogynistic frame of football culture, how players suffer a kind of cognitive dissonance through the internalization of responsibility for injury: "Anytime you get hurt, you're like, 'Why am I feeling this way?' But also, 'Why am I being a pussy about it?'" In Landry West's case, his institution literally downloaded personal responsibility and liability on players for the physical harm they experienced in football:

> There's a lot of guys who have lingering injuries and stuff that when you do your checkout training room form, you check all the boxes basically saying if you have any lingering injuries, you need to take care of them or have them brought to our attention now or else we're no longer responsible. So I ended up having a shoulder surgery after just because I was like, "Hey, I have this shoulder pain. I'm not going to be oblivious to it." And I ended up going to get the MRI and I had a torn labrum that I played the whole season with, and if I checked the other box would've still been living with this.

In many cases it is coaches' pure coercion pushing players back on the field. Coaches are incentivized by a system that rewards them for winning games with lucrative contracts to demand as much performance as possible from their players. If this means compelling a player to play through injury, coaches are often willing to do it. Whether it is stern command or subtle coaxing, the result is the same: players are subjected to physical harm that nobody should be expected to endure. Kurt Weiss shared that "it's a pressure cooker. So it isn't as though there's instances where you are pressured to play through pain—it's a constant, it's an expectation. And the coaching line is, 'The best ability is availability.'" Similarly, Matt Jensen describes watching a running back return to the field after obvious head trauma:

> We see him running onto the field with his helmet on, accompanied by the trainers. And we're like, "Okay, what's this about?" He's wearing a special yellow jersey that's only reserved for the quarterbacks, which means, "Hey, don't touch him. He's off limits." And he was taking handoffs, but going slower than usual, and I'm like, "Oh my god, they're really trying to get him back for this game." Knowing the head trainer and knowing the assistants, that was definitely not their decision to have their star running back out after just suffering a massive head hit. I do feel like it was more of a coaching, political decision.

Brock Adler describes an even more coercive environment:

> This guy . . . tore his groin, during a scout session . . . and kept going, just so he could try to prove to the coaches that he could play and be tough. . . . I knew a guy who, his knee was starting to give out. . . . [Coach] basically made him feel bad for not playing, saying, "You're letting down the team." He basically lost his love of football. Another example for me, would be my sophomore year. . . . I had a huge contusion in my quad . . . where I couldn't even bend it or walk. . . . The next day I came in, [head coach is] like, "Are you going to play today?" and I'm like, "Well, coach, you know, I can't." And he was just like, "Well, you've just got a bruise." Because the trainers told him I had a contusion but they saw it as a bruise. Another player I know, had a contusion like that, and just couldn't move. And they said, "Oh it's a bruise," so they weren't empathizing with the pain that we felt. . . . There were other guys too, guys who had dislocated their shoulders. Injuries are probably the biggest killer for college football

athletes, not because of the injury itself, but just because coaches hold that against them and say, "Oh, you can push through it." Because a lot of them come from a bygone era, of a lack of knowledge in medical science, in sports science, and the longer repercussions. . . . They think, "Oh, it's being tough, pushing through it for a child's game." A lot of us, we thought, "Oh man, it's my fault, I should've gone." I thought that for a long time too.

Adler's testimony reveals both that coaches expected players to play through injury and punished them for not doing so, and that this punishment caused them to feel it was their own failing, which in turn led them to play through injury more in the future. As a result, players stopped reporting even head injuries altogether. As Adler put it, "There was still the bullying [from] the coaches to where nobody would try to say their injuries anymore."

In our interviews, coercive overtraining was common—demanded from players with very little consideration given to the harm likely to follow. For Thomas Rycliff, the coercive overtraining of two- and three-a-day practices made him feel like he was on the brink of cardiac arrest:

It's already 100 degrees at nine in the morning. . . . Those three and a half weeks felt like nine months. Time would go so slow because it was so painful. Then you're hitting, and I mean, it's twenty degrees hotter when you're wearing pads. The third year, about a week before camp started, I started vomiting in my sleep. . . . When football camp started. . . . I was vomiting all day and all practice. . . . The response was to, they literally assigned a water boy to me to keep me hydrated while I was continuing to vomit through practice.

They weigh you before and after practice each day, to make sure that you're not losing a lot of weight. I don't think anyone's looking at this because I lost thirty pounds in five days. . . . On the sixth day after two morning practices, and the lifting, I just felt like my body was going cold. . . . I felt like I was seeing spots a little bit. I went to the back shower and I had lost consciousness. . . . I don't remember losing consciousness or hitting the floor or anything. I just remember this eighty-something-year-old guy trying to pick me up off the shower. . . . I went to the training room and once again, I'm reluctant to do it because I don't want to move myself from the situation. I haven't missed a practice in the third year. One of the trainers who was like premed or something, or in medical school, I didn't have to say anything. Luckily, she saw my face, saw that I was pale, and she said that my lips were purple.

Now, I later on learned that I basically had all the signs that I was potentially going to go into cardiac arrest. . . . I didn't have a pulse, so they went to put bags of saline in me. . . . If you go through one and a half bags, that means you were dehydrated. I went through seven bags really quickly, and I was still dehydrated. . . . I'd been vomiting so much that my esophagus was scarred and was starting to close a little bit. . . . I did miss that afternoon practice, and I felt super guilty about it. You know, Stockholm syndrome, whatever you want to call it. The next morning, I went and had an endoscopy. . . . They just found a bunch of scar tissue. So the next day, I was practicing again . . . and would still kind of vomit here and there, but it then eventually subsided. It was crazy. It was nuts. There wasn't really anybody looking out for my mental or my physical well-being. . . . I almost died. I pushed myself so hard that I literally almost died.

Nick Turner also noted the prevalence of punitive overtraining to extract performance: "They punish everyone — not every team is like that — but our team was. [Head coach] had that mentality that if one player is 'bad,' or not making the time, we all have to do it again. And we'll do that until the player makes it, or until everyone's passing out. You see it so extreme that in places like [rival school], they put twenty guys in the hospital at one time. We've gotten to that place, where it's starting to get scary like that."

For Kurt Weiss, too, the distinction between "pain" and "injury" served as an instrument for shaming players into playing, even against their best interests:

Learning the difference between pain and injury . . . it's a perverted lesson, but there are some beneficial aspects to actually pushing yourself and knowing you can get through something, but it's used against players. The higher you get, the more money that's at stake. So knowing the difference between pain and injury is a moot point when you're injured and have to play anyway. My sophomore year, I played for a guy, [linebackers' coach] is just a belligerent southern asshole. "You can't help the club if you're in the tub. I don't want to see you in the training room." He had an image that he put on a slideshow before we watched film, and it was a cupcake on a guy's shoulder, who was on a knee during training camp, tired and defeated. And the cupcake had a face with a smile, and he named the cupcake Freddie Soft. And so anytime he felt like a guy was milking an injury, he would just say, "Don't be Freddie Soft." It's terrible. It's good advice for a blood sport. And we had a great year there . . . and I had my best years as a linebacker. I hated [linebackers' coach]. I played hurt. But that's what football is.

Perhaps the most salient observation here is "knowing the difference between pain and injury is a moot point when you're injured and have to play anyway." This indexes the structural dimension of injury in college football. The incentive for coaches is to play injured players because they are evaluated on the success of the team, not the well-being of players. C. J. White makes these dynamics clear: "The players are how [the coaches] keep their job, so if you have a guy that's significant and he's a little banged up, they talk to the medical staff and let them know, 'Hey, we need such and such back, what can we do to get him back? Is he 80 percent? I'll take an 80 percent player if he's that good of a player, I'll take an 80 percent as opposed to not having him at all.' So there's pressure from the coaches to get back on the field."

Sometimes the coaches' messaging is subtle, but players still understand the implications. White points out:

> They'll fix it up so that when they present it to the player, "Hey, [player's name], and I know you got this AC joint injury, but we got [opponent] coming up in three weeks, but I need you back, I need you doing everything you can do in the treatment room." So it's kind of like [laughs] it's like a mind game in a way. Like I said, I haven't experienced guys coming and saying, "Hey look we've got [opponent] in three weeks and I don't care if your damn leg is gonna fall off, I need you!" I haven't heard that, but they'll fix it up in a way that's kind of like, "I'm not really telling you to get back, but I'm telling you to get back."

Sometimes coaches resort to explicit threats—the ultimate form of coercion—to push players onto the field. While Chris Andrews acknowledged part of the impetus to play hurt was a sense of accountability, there was also raw coercion: "And then the pressure from the coaches too, it's like, 'Why are we giving you a scholarship if you're milking an injury or nursing an injury and not on the field,' that somehow, your worth to the university is somehow tied to your ability to produce on the football field, on game day or even on the practice field. You know, even guys that were redshirting that were nursing injuries were pressured to get back on the field." When asked how explicit these threats were, he explains, "In so many words, 'You're milking the system,' . . . maybe not outright saying, 'Why are we giving you a scholarship,' but questioning your work ethic where you can connect the dots as a player, as a teammate that's hearing those words spoken to somebody else on the team." Coaches publicly humiliate or threaten a player not only to achieve an instrumental outcome with that individual, but also to signify to the whole team what is or is not permitted. The threat made to one player becomes a rule for the team, even if not stated explicitly. Andrews further explains, "That's how a culture is set. I think that coaches set examples, you know, and what's said to one player, it may not apply to another player, but it's part of building a culture within the team. The two things that I was praised for most was playing through injury and knocking somebody unconscious. And the unconscious part was more in the NFL than in college, but those were two things that were really praised." Discipline is imposed and ultimately internalized not only through the prohibition on some behaviors through threat and punishment, but also through the exaltation and reward of desired behaviors. Ultimately, this is how a team culture of playing through injury is inculcated.

Ryan Leonard described one situation where this dynamic was taken to its extreme, as other athletic department officials reinforced coaching pressure to play through injury. Leonard learned that one of his position teammates was involved in contact practices every day for four weeks and was sure there had to be a rule against it. There was: only three contact days a week were allowed. He mentioned it to his position group but knew they were essentially powerless to resist the demand:

> I didn't know where to turn. I didn't know what to do. So I did what I thought was right. I turned to people that I thought were meant to help. I starred 67, called our compliance department. I go, "Hey, I'm a concerned father. My son's been saying he's had headaches. My son has been saying he's been going through more contact practices a week than what is allowed by the NCAA." She goes, "I will look into this. Thank you for giving me a heads-up." That afternoon after I called, we go into our position groups and our coach comes up to us and goes, "Which one of you fucking pussies complained to your dad? Which one of you bitches said this was too hard and said that your head hurt?" So obviously that told me that this compliance

officer, the lady that I turned to for help, had called the coaches and said, "Hey, somebody may have brought this to our attention." Had forewarned the coaches.

On the afternoon of his complaint, at their regular Tuesday contact practice, Leonard realized something was strange. Typically, before walkthrough at the end of practice, players haphazardly discard their equipment on the sideline. That day, the coach instructed them to neatly line up the equipment. Then a parade of equipment managers, trainers, and graduate assistants picked up the equipment and concealed it behind a forklift used for filming. Soon after, he saw a recruiting coach, the director of staff, and the compliance officer he had just called walk onto the field. The other officials walked the compliance officer down the field at an angle that hid the equipment. She stayed for fifteen minutes and then left. Leonard explained, "In that moment, I knew that the people that were meant to protect the athlete . . . were either complicit in the rule-breaking or willfully ignorant of what was going on. In that moment, I knew I needed to be out because I knew there was nobody that was going to look out for my safety but me. So the player, my best friend, he would finish out that year going five contact practices a week and no help. Nobody came, nothing changed."

Sadly, a consequence of players playing through injury is shortened careers. Players sacrifice their bodies in college for coaches' benefit, and then they ultimately lose out on remuneration from a less exploitative professional career. Galen North saw this happen to a teammate who was pushed to play through injury: "One of the guys I played with . . . had knee surgery and was basically kind of pushed to play very quickly and played, got drafted, and then never played a snap in the NFL because of reoccurring issues from his knee surgery."

Conflict of Interest

While cases like these testify to the direct coercive authority coaches wield over players' decisions to play through injury, sometimes these decisions become filtered through athletic trainers in a process that seems to attenuate the coach's responsibility, but is in fact a structural feature of the system in that it offers a veneer of medicalization for the capitalist imperatives at root. Daniel Barber speaks to this: "[Coaches and staff] have meetings about you every single day . . . the trainers are going down the list, so,

'Hey training staff, how's [Daniel] doing?' 'Oh, he was kind of slacking in rehab.' 'Oh yeah, strength staff, what do you think?' The sphere of influence is very connected between all these different staffs. [School] prides itself on its training staff being completely different, like medically, their bosses are in the hospital. That doesn't matter. It's still football. . . . There's a lot of quackery over there. A lot of them are wannabe coaches. . . . There's a big variance in care."

Given that coaches don't have medical expertise to determine whether players are healthy enough to play, this decision supposedly falls to medical trainers. But trainers are paid employees of the team, responsible to the coach, and they are well aware that the incentives for coaches come back to player production in the interest of team success. This is an inherent medical conflict of interest. And this complicates the question of playing through injury, nearly always to the player's detriment because trainers know if they do not get a player back on the field quickly, they risk losing their positions to persons more willing to do the coach's bidding. C. J. White points out, "A lot of time the medical staff I would say is on the coach's side. Because . . . something goes wrong and the university is gonna start cleaning house. It will start with the coach, it may start with the medical staff if you have a high number of guys injured." Kurt Weiss elaborates a similar dynamic:

> Part of the bind of an unfair institution or context is that it's unfair
> to the athletic trainer. Because he's got a wife and two kids and he
> knows the reality. And it's his job to get you out there. And he asked,
> once . . . my [teammate], "Did you feel like you got good medical care
> here?" And my [teammate] said, "No." And [athletic trainer] teared
> up. So it's not like these people are evil. They're caught in the bind
> themselves. . . . That's a long-winded way of saying that of course
> their chief priority is to the program not the athlete.

Later, Weiss provided more insight: "My freshman year, we had a new head athletic trainer and the coach felt he wasn't getting players back on the field fast enough. And there'd be arguments or tension, like, 'God dammit, [trainer's name]. What's taking so long?' And [trainer] would to a certain degree, stand up for players and say, 'He's hurt. He can't play.' And so [trainer] was demoted to women's softball and helped out with track. And the next guy did what the coaches wanted him to do. So yeah, I mean, the coaches ultimately make health decisions." Matt Jensen, a walk-on less instrumental to the team's success, reported not receiving as much pressure to play through injury but also said one of his friends with a more prominent role was continually rushed back to play at the coaches' behest despite four anterior cruciate ligament (ACL) repairs, notwithstanding the trainers' reservations.

Playing through injury looks different at the professional level than it does in college. Although structural factors constrain NFL players' choices—economic incentive looks different depending on one's access to material resources outside of the employment setting—ultimately, they can choose whether it is worth playing through injury. In college, it is coaches and trainers who make that choice; for players to challenge that authority is to risk their scholarships and positions on the team. Jalen Rice describes the decision-making calculus around injury in the NFL:

It's definitely worth it [to play through injury in the NFL] because there are so many more benefits with your injury. Because you can be hurt and then your injury just nags and nags and they put you on injury reserve and you still have the opportunity to get paid. There's other ways once you get done playing that you can still get paid some different injury settlements and things. It's more worth it then, because if I have a messed-up ankle or something, they might not just cut me, they might cut you with an injury settlement, at least I'm getting paid versus college, if you get injured you're just injured. You're going back to class and chilling, like, you're not even getting paid anything, you're just getting your degree at the end of the day, that's it.

Given the sheer amount of physical harm suffered by college football players in their work for universities, the question arises of what kind of care players receive. Our discussion of dynamics with trainers and coaches suggests that treatment is uneven at best, although many trainers certainly feel an obligation to provide the best possible care. Nevertheless, conflict of interest is omnipresent. Kurt Weiss explains how economic and performance imperatives significantly dictated the quality of care players received:

They would cut costs by not imaging things. There were times when, if you weren't a good player and they did a test, let's say you sprained your MCL [medial collateral ligament] and they did the appropriate medical tests and they figured, "Oh, this is probably a sprained MCL. We don't need to image it. Here's the protocol for a sprained MCL, do that and you'll be fine." I shouldn't have had my right shoulder done. I'm sure [the doctor] made however many thousands or tens of thousands of dollars by doing that surgery that I didn't need. [Teammate], both had surgeries he shouldn't have had, and then probably needed surgeries that he didn't get because they didn't image and discover what was really wrong. So he's thirty and he needs a hip replacement. And he's in pain every day.

Although prevailing medical ethics would suggest physicians are obligated to their patients first and foremost, even if they are college football players, the tragic reality is that sometimes team doctors and university-affiliated surgeons feel an obligation—conflict of interest—to the team rather than the player.[8] Given these problematic dynamics, players are unsurprisingly steered toward and even coerced to use team doctors. Kurt Weiss shows that this coercion is entirely explicit: "They can refuse care if you go outside of the department. . . . It happened to [teammate] with his hip, he went and saw a doctor that he knew in [nearby major city], and yeah, you're in a bind. And there's something [from team doctors] about 'You're welcome to do that, but then we can't perform surgery or help you with your treatment plan, or anything like that.' So they want everybody to have surgery with their team orthos." In fact, players had very little trust in team physicians because they understood the conflict of interest:

> You learn quickly that they're team doctors. And we used to joke, [about] the medical file for [each player]. I had four surgeries, and my [position-mates] each had like a dozen plus. So our medical files were like this big [gestures to a large stack of paper]. And we used to give, not directly, but sometimes within earshot, give the doctors shit. Because before games, they're putting on their team-issued gear and their team hat, and giving each other like, the rock pound [like a fist bump], like, "You ready to go? This is the big game!" [All laugh] And we're just like, "You know we're not getting genuine medical treatment." And we would give them shit around like, "What do you mean 'we'? You've not ever made a tackle, ever in your life. What do you mean 'we'?" But yeah, it's a conflict of interest is a polite way to put it.

All too often, the requirement to work with team medical staff leads to a lack of proper care and situations that worsen and compound the harm suffered on the field. Daniel Barber described a misdiagnosed injury that he was compelled to play through in excruciating pain:

> I had an ankle injury [during a game]. I was like, "Fuck." Really bad. I ended up kind of coming back. And then I heard a pop. And I said, "I heard a pop." And I was told, "That was probably scar tissue, you're

fine." I'm like, "I'm not fine." Ended up playing, going through a whole season. This is when I was starting, hurt my ankle, "[Daniel] is a baby, don't worry about him. He's fucking soft, he just cares about school," is what the opinion of me ended up shifting to, "He's just milking this injury." So I was denied an MRI, I should have went and got an MRI, but they're like, "Just go, you're good." . . . My ankle was just destroyed. Like, I got told by [a trainer], "Thank you for putting up with this. We need you for depth. Thank you for dealing with this, I know you're in pain."

After being told to go home over the off-season and "rest," Barber aggravated the injury the following season during a warm-up, to which the trainer responded:

"You're like this. You're never going to be able to run full speed again. Just deal with it. Surgery's not going to help. Fine, we'll get you an MRI." So I go cry because I got told, "Yeah . . . deal with it. You're just a gimp. You're going to have a gimp leg." And so ended up getting an MRI. Doctor comes in, "So when are we having surgery? When do you want to schedule surgery?" And I'm like, "Shit." Mind you, anytime you get medical care, a trainer is with you. So I'm getting one-on-one advice like whatever, he's trying to schedule all this stuff, I don't know the specific terms, it's escaping me. Trainer's right there to listen to everything, to advise on stuff. . . . Doctor leaves and [trainer] was like, "Okay . . . I'm so sorry about this, but we're going to get you fixed up. Don't tell the coaches about this. I'll handle it." And so I'm like, red flag. What the hell? And I ended up going and talking to [redacted assistant defensive coach] later on, and I was like, "What did they tell you?" And he's like, "Oh, they said, 'They're just gonna fix you up and you should be back in three months.'" I was like, "Whoa. I got diagnosed with two to three things, and they said four months, and other stuff." And he's like, "Oh, okay, well I don't know why they didn't tell me that." Went to the defensive coordinator, "What'd they tell you?" [He said] "Oh, they told me, 'Yeah, like this one thing was wrong.'" Go to the head coach. "Hey, what did they tell you?" He's like, "Oh yeah, they said some blah, blah, blah, about an ankle. And they don't know when you're going to be back." And I'm like, "What? That's all completely wrong."

Barber's account is an indictment of a system in which coaches, trainers, and doctors exercise authority over young men tasked with bludgeoning their bodies on a daily basis. Yet in this gruesome world, the players' well-being is secondary to team performance. Ryan Leonard also experienced this, as he was medically cleared by a doctor for his transfer to a new school despite the doctor knowing he had a serious ACL problem. Likewise, Chris Andrews trusted the medical staff to look after him and never considered the possibility of conflict of interest. Only in retrospect did he come to understand he had received suboptimal care. When he went for an outside opinion, he was told he had received far more cortisone injections than he should have had in a short period of time. When an outside physician performed surgery, his position coach chastened him for making "other players los[e] confidence in the medical staff of the team."

Drug Use and Abuse

Another insidious dimension of health and harm in college football is the use of drugs like Toradol to mask pain, potentially creating pharmaceutical dependencies and worsened injuries. In some cases, painkiller use is a fairly quotidian aspect of life as a college football player. Galen North described how painkillers could make it easy to play through injury—at the coaches' exhortation—but also lead to subsequent physical debilitation: "And there's things they can do even if you're in horrible pain to go out there and play. Get a Toradol shot before you go play and they shoot you up and you feel fantastic and then the next day you can barely walk." Chris Andrews observed teammates who experienced life-altering drug dependency based on medication they started taking in college: "That's probably the thing that is most disturbing to me because I see how this really changed the person that I knew in college as a teammate. . . . It's difficult to see them struggle. . . . Painkiller addiction . . . impacts relationships, it can break up marriages, I've seen it take away jobs, I've seen people in and out of rehab and detox, so that's something that is a big problem."

Kurt Weiss ultimately developed a minor dependency when given Toradol for a dislocated shoulder:

> I was naive, I was eighteen, and I thought [Toradol] was like steroids because at the time, it was an injection in your butt. All of our best players were lined up before the game with their pants down to get their Toradol shot. . . . I asked a player like, "Is the doctor giving these guys steroids?" And he said, "No, no, it's Toradol. It's this painkiller that lets you play." I took Toradol for our season final and

in the bowl game, and [it] allowed me to play really well in both those games with a torn labrum. So that was eye opening. I had surgery, right after that season. . . . I had three shoulder reconstructions in a calendar year: January, October, and December. . . . I think also, I know, [I] began to get addicted to painkillers . . . it was easy to just get more and more of them from the team doctors. Yeah, it came to a point where, I know it's not the right thing to do because it gets in the water supply, but I flushed them down the toilet because I was taking them every day to just zone out and watch a movie at night. But I had the self-awareness, and I knew. I'm from [home state], so pain pills, and fentanyl, and heroin . . . not entirely foreign concepts to Rust Belt towns. So kicked the habit, not even a habit. . . . Avoided going down that road. I had teammates that absolutely did. I know at [Big 10 school] they had a heroin problem, because guys were taking so much pain medicine that they started doing heroin.

Indeed, substances other than painkillers are a common coping method for contending with the physical and emotional rigors of college football. For Charlie Rogers drug and alcohol use became a central part of his college football experience:

A lot of players would be smoking a lot, but personally, there wasn't a day where I wasn't getting absolutely drunk or high out of my mind. It escalated to harder drugs, like just anything. And I used to kind of joke about it, but I was like, get so drunk so you don't really feel the pain of the day, physically and mentally. Because I'll be walking, morning workouts. And seeing a car drive by, it's like, man, I wouldn't have to go to practice if I just jumped in front of his car real quick. Like that was a more attractive idea than going.

Drug use here is connected not only to the physical pain experienced through college football, but also to emotional discomfort to the extent of suicidal ideation. Rogers's drug use took multiple forms: "It was just weed, Adderall, cocaine, and shrooms," as well as alcohol, "probably a few times every single day. But usually, like four to five days a week, drinking heavily. Because, I'm a pretty large man . . . probably take, like twelve [beers]." Likewise, Thomas Rycliff says, "I mean I self-medicated, I smoked marijuana every day for about thirteen years. And understanding psychologically where that comes from . . . I don't smoke. It's ironic now . . . everybody does it, it's legal, and everyone that was against weed is like, 'I took a gummy last night.' And I can't do it because it kind of reminds me of that dark place that I had to pull myself out of."

Rycliff also recalls the banal and ubiquitous nature of painkillers and other sedatives while playing college football:

> There was a doctor there and if a player had an injury, he would give you that cortisone shot before it. And I remember [teammate's name] didn't play in the last season of his college career in the [bowl game] because [the doctor] hit a nerve and [the player] couldn't play. . . . There was this old doctor that used to sit around and he used to have a pocket full of pills. . . . One time, the night before a game. . . . Everybody was taking Ambien at the time and the night before a game. And I knew I was going to play the next day. So I was like, "I'll take an Ambien. Why not?" I'm like, "What a psychoactive drug that is when you don't actually have to sleep." Never took an Ambien. I had my head on the floor of the hotel room and I was watching TV sideways and then I stood up and then everything was sideways for a while.

Nick Turner reported similar experiences, but one is particularly troubling in terms of consent: "I was given tramadol before games. I don't know if I ever had a prescription for it. It was just given to me, by a single pill, by hand. When you get that, you think it's vitamin C or something. You don't realize that's something that's addictive, and it's going to make the opioids that I take less effective, make me want to take more of them after surgery."

> DS: If you knew they were handing you opioids, would you have taken them?
>
> TURNER: Probably not, because I wouldn't have taken a Vicodin if they handed me a Vicodin. I wouldn't have taken OxyContin. I know what those names are. I didn't know tramadol.
>
> DS: So you didn't know what it was, really. And they handed it to you. . . .
>
> TURNER: [Teammate] would call them "trammies." He'd be like, "Yeah, I got the trammies!" So I was almost excited when I got it, like, "Hey, yeah, we got these pills that are better than Advil but are safe."

Both Landry West and Ryan Leonard described the ease with which players could access painkillers, and how coaches encouraged their use. For West:

> There would be practices where it's like, "Hey, this guy's going to rest 'cause he's going to get a shot tomorrow and he's going to play on

Saturday." Guys who, if you saw him in practice, you're like, "How is this guy playing?" You can barely walk on an ankle and now he's running up and down the field, but then he comes in on Sunday and his ankle looks like a freaking balloon, and that's sometimes difficult for guys to understand the bigger picture because the NFL is held over a lot of guys' heads, "Hey this is your opportunity to make it there, you don't want to miss this game." They feel the pressure of the coaches, that's their livelihood and how they feed their family, so the coaches don't care about you. They want to make sure that they win enough games so they get the bowl game bonus, and all that stuff, and be able to benefit from your labor.

Likewise, Leonard explained,

We were on the goal line, and I banged shoulders with this guy, and I sprained my AC joint. . . . I came off to the sideline and I told my trainer, "Hey, I can't move my arm." It hurt extremely bad. . . . He could feel the lump of where the collarbone had been displaced and my AC sprained. And so he goes, "Well, you can still play with this. You won't hurt it anymore." So I was like, "Well, I can try." And so I go out to the next series and I literally cannot use my arm. . . . I go up to my trainer like, "Hey, I can't play like this. This is impossible." It was excruciatingly painful. And he goes, "Okay, well let's run up to the locker room and we'll get you a shot." I go, "Okay." We get into the locker room . . . [the doctor] has got a big old, probably six-inch needle full of, I believe it was lidocaine. . . . It was a miracle. It was a miracle drug. You literally felt nothing. There was no pain, free range of motion, all that. And I was able to go back down and play. Now, unfortunately, I would find out later that lidocaine only numbed things really for about . . . twenty-five minutes out of the whole thirty. The last five minutes was excruciating[ly] painful of those games.

In our interviews, it became clear that routine confrontations with various painkillers, benzodiazepines, and other sedatives might be considered a feature—not a latent by-product—of collegiate athletics. [9] While that is beyond the scope of our work here, the salient point remains: college football players we interviewed used—through coercion or voluntarily—potentially dangerous opioids to cope with the physical and mental demands of an inherently strenuous and violent form of athletic work.

Emotional Hardship

A necessary corollary of injury in the world of college football is rehabilitation. Rehab is the additional work players put in to coax their bodies back into the shape necessary for productive athletic work. The dynamics of rehab, then, have a profound impact on the experiences of college football players in terms of their understanding of the pressure to play, the care they receive from authority figures, and their emotional health and well-being in relative isolation from the larger 'healthy' team. In general, injuries take a significant emotional toll on players. This is part of the additional cost or exploitation of social reproductive athletic labor, although it is often difficult for players to confront in a sporting culture that demands stoicism. Wallace Bell explains that football "teaches you to be numb to the things that you're enduring. And that's really sad when you think about it in the grand scheme of things, because we're all human and we all have our breaking points. And even in football, physically, we know that we have breaking points. But when it comes to the mental side of it, we don't really look at it as it's a necessity for me to take care of that as well as my body."

Likewise, Michael Thomas recounts struggling to cope with being hurt:

That was probably one of my toughest times in my life I would say.
A lot of things don't really get to me, but being hurt and not being able to play a game that you truly love and that you're going to school to be able to play, and after having a really great freshman year, and coming off of that, you know, really apt to have a really big role going into my senior year, and that was something that played a huge role with me not moving forward, so [long pause] it was tough, I was depressed, I went into isolation. . . . It kind of affected a lot of my relationships. My college sweetheart, it had an effect on our relationship as well. Kind of isolated myself from my family because I didn't want anyone around me, even my teammates.

Galen North had a similar experience:

It becomes very alienating in that sense that you're just basically there by yourself trying to recover from an injury and you don't know anybody and any aspirations you had to try to play quickly are thrown out the window. So it's kind of a tough experience . . . you're not included in a lot of the other stuff purely because the time that they're doing training or players-only practices, you are rehabbing your injury with two other people, maybe, three other people and the athletic trainers on a separate field away from everybody else because you need the space. So you're kind of on your own on an island over there.

This testimony makes clear that one struggle associated with rehab and injury is structural. Players are physically separated from teammates because rehab requires different tasks, but this alienates injured players from the larger team and compounds fears associated with losing one's position.

In considering the emotional consequences of general injury, we must also grapple with the ways head injuries may cause psychological/emotional harm as a symptom of bodily damage. This was Kevin Brown's experience:

I had no other life objective after I got injured in my senior year and then had my surgery, so I definitely went into a dark place that I really at the time didn't know I was in, you know? And, I definitely have problems with depression now . . . it came to a point, three years ago . . . I went and sought out advice and said, "Look, a change in my attitude, my willingness, my desire to do things, just kind of diminished." And so, yeah, I've kind of always been curious to know, has that also been something because of repetition of hits that I did take? And, I'm definitely convinced there is. I mean, it's just simple statistics. I've always probably had a little bit of anxiety, but again, nothing that was medically, you know, needed, and then, around '16 and really '17, there were some times where, all of a sudden, my heart's racing, I'm like freaking out over just a minor meeting. . . . Not really knowing where this is all coming from, and again, I never really experienced it before. . . . I'm definitely curious, is this a part of the CTE?

Attempts to tally the harm caused by college football must consider the emotional load borne by players who live with the weight of knowing they may be experiencing life-altering head injury.[10] Players realize this even as they are playing, so they question every small change in their subjective well-being. These experiences cannot be quantified through an economic logic of value exploitation; this is an additional, incalculable form of harm built into college football.

Given the emotional hardship produced by injury and rehabilitation, it is particularly disturbing that rehab is sometimes engineered to be especially onerous to coerce players back into play. Galen North explains:

You go with the strength coach, and basically their whole goal with that move is to make your life as miserable as possible . . . just trying to make you go back to practice even if you're not medically ready. . . . Basically, you're over there with, either by yourself or with one or two other people, and you are just doing nonstop high-intensity conditioning and things that didn't really have any relevance to football training. . . . The reason they do that a lot of the times is so the people don't try and fake an injury to get out of practice. . . . But on the flip side, if you have a legitimate injury and you are medically told not to do something and you're getting crushed. I, if I'm being perfectly honest, thought that if I tear my calf, then I tear my calf. I'm gonna go practice. So I went and practiced all spring. And so in their mind, I'm sure, "Oh yeah, see, it worked," meanwhile I was in a tremendous amount of pain every day, having to spend hours and hours in physical therapy and rehab just to be able to go to the next practice. My life was very messed up.

Coaches sometimes go out of their way to ostracize injured players to discipline the team in general. This creates a culture where the entire team starts to view injured players as a 'problem' instead of casualties of a system that systematically produces bodily harm. Daniel Barber explains how his whole status on the team changed due to injury: "I felt like a burden—treated as such by the staff and even my players, to a certain extent. I think what a lot of people miss is that, how the coaches go and how they treat you—a lot of the players, especially when they're 'good' (like, I'm doing air quotes), 'good' players follow suit. They follow what the coaches say to do, and how to treat people."

Galen North described a similar experience:

Unfortunately for me, I had a ton of injuries, so that kind of hindered a lot of things and when you get injured a lot, through no fault of your own, you kind of get a little bit ostracized from the standpoint of the coaching, the strength and conditioning people, and then that kind of trickles down because other people see that they're treating you pretty shitty and so then kind of naturally, not across the board, but other people are gonna kind of mirror the coaches because that's who people are typically, they're the adults in the room . . . if you have a lot of injuries . . . there's this perception that you're soft. . . . "Oh, the coaches think that this guy's a pussy, so . . . we think he is too." Aside from the information asymmetry that goes on between what's going on with your medical situation and everyone else, because it's not like they tell everybody, "Oh, well the doctor screwed this up so they had to have this surgery, so this is a result of that, so it all resulted from one thing of no fault of their own." It's, "We know this guy is injured and he can't practice, so this guy is soft." People start to interact with you differently because they're being told, whether directly or indirectly, that the reason you're not playing is that you don't care or you don't want to or you're just here for a free ride, basically, and that wasn't so much my situation, but I saw it happen with a lot of other people.

Similarly, Daniel Barber describes situations where coaches subject players to actual punishments for their injuries:

Like specifically, [ACC team] what they do is, and they've got ways, like, underhanded ways, if you're hurt, to make you not hurt. So [ACC team], I don't know if you saw the videos of them like rolling and stuff, that's punishment for people who they think are 'hurt' [Daniel does air quotes]. So like, "Oh, you've got a sprained ankle? You don't want to practice today? Okay, go do that." For us, "You're hurt? Okay, get up at 5:00 a.m. and get here on time. Oh, and if you're late, I'm telling your coach and you're gonna get punished." And you know, there's just a lot of ways they do that underhanded bullshit.

Coaches also showed little-to-no empathy for players struggling through mental health challenges often produced or exacerbated by participation in the ruthless, high-pressure world of college football. Daniel Barber expands on this:

[We had] a player with suicidal thoughts. Went to the hospital, and they had a tough family situation. And the coach didn't try to keep it 'in house,' try to keep it as quiet as possible, and as a result, that player did not get the family support that they needed. I ended up finding out a month or two after from someone that graduated that this had happened, and they're like, "Please keep checking on him. He's not okay." And the coach has not supported him at all. . . . The support you might be able to get, like Player Support is in the same building. So if you walk down to Player Support, the coach sees you! And a lot of the times, the coach will walk to Player Support with you. Like for me, when they tried to mentally disqualify me, they walked with me to the trainers to try to get me mentally disqualified.

NKL: Player Support, you're saying, is like the training support, the health support?

BARBER: No, there's separate stuff. They're supposed to be separate resources, but it all comes back to the coach, it all comes back to the [athletic department]. So yeah, the end of the day, you can't expect people to keep stuff to themselves. There has been several times where information has mysteriously traveled. To the coach's benefit, to the program's benefit, to the players' detriment.

Notable in Barber's narrative is not only that coaches demonstrate little empathy and support, but also that they use support services as a mechanism for undermining players' status on the team, for instance, by using a diagnosis to get a player "disqualified." Coaches too often seem unwilling or unable to provide the support players need. In the following passage (which includes discussion of suicidal thoughts), Charlie Rogers explains how a coach responded to his psychological struggles:

ROGERS: In that protocol, you have to be in treatment for six months. So I had to stick around an extra six months to be able to medically retire. I was pretty much either deciding if I was going to do that, or I was going to kill myself. . . . If I were to do it, I would probably, I don't know, like, either tweet it out, or write it somewhere. So they wouldn't be able to change the narrative, like, "Oh yeah, this guy, he was using drugs, blah blah blah." Whatever. Because that's what they tried to say about the guy that lost his mind. Just because he was smoking a little bit of weed, they said he was on drugs. . . . I would've explicitly said, "It's because of these people, and this program, is why I'm doing this." I know the main strength coach is at [Big 12 school] right now. And I've even heard through other people that are at [Big 12 school] that it's just as bad. Their main thing was [for the players] to be terrified of them, into obeying their every word. I guess it's a thing, in most football programs, the main question is like, "Is your father in your life?" This guy even said to my mom that he would try to be a father figure to me and I was like, "Dude, I see my father. I talk to him, like weekly." And he's just trying to manipulate you. And I think the last straw before I just told my counselor, "You gotta pull me out, even though the six months isn't up." It was getting pretty bad. Like, he started to notice. We left for break. And then we came back. And then I had a bad workout. And while we're lifting, pulled me into his office, and he wouldn't let me leave until I told him about me being suicidal and shit.

And then after that, proceeded to say, "Everybody else has problems, you know I haven't seen my dad since I was thirteen." And I was thinking, man, like, "I don't care, I don't give a shit about your dad. If he knew you was doing this shit—I'm glad he hasn't seen you either." I was probably sitting in there for like an hour and a half, two hours, just wouldn't let me leave.

DS: And you didn't feel like you wanted to disclose that information to this person?

ROGERS: No, because that's just like somebody that raped you or killed your mom, asking you, "What's wrong?"

Similar to Barber, Kane Holden recounted how teammates connected to the coaching staff contributed to the emotional toll that exclusion and bigotry takes on campus athletic workers:

HOLDEN: There was a time my freshman year, the seniors at that time, especially in my position group, were very connected to my position coach. I would say they shared very similar values. And there was an instance where one of them saw me wearing a shirt that was supporting one of my teammates who also ended up being Black, and it was his nonprofit organization and it was about promoting sports over drugs, gang violence, etc., to children in [his home city]. So that player ended up actually assaulting me because he said, "You support these you-know-what." And was being very, very hostile and aggressive about it."

DS: Was it a racial slur?

HOLDEN: Yeah.

Not only are getting hurt and playing hurt normalized in college football, our interviews suggest they are often endorsed, and even imposed, by coaching staffs across the sport. Consistent with biomedical findings illuminating the negative health and psychological risks experienced by elite athletes, our interviews force us to confront the centrality of pain, injury, and harm to the experiences of former college football players.[11] Participants articulated the pervasiveness of these injuries during their careers. We must therefore grapple with these experiences in any debate regarding injustices in college football.

The Cost of Injury

Here we explore how former college football players experience the long-term cost and consequences of injury after their careers end. Many players we interviewed connected injuries suffered in college with issues after retirement. Indeed, injury is often the cause of a premature end to a career. Steven Summers witnessed this for more than one of his teammates: "I had two teammates at [previous school] that had to medically retire because they were so injured. One guy had a back injury that he tried really hard to come back from, but he just physically couldn't. I'm sure that's impacting him. Another guy, I think he had three injuries on the same knee. And so that dude's knee is definitely fucked forever. He's probably going to have to get a knee replacement by the time he's like thirty or forty."

Chris Andrews came to view his career differently because of the long-term physical consequences:

> If you think about it from a perspective of just aging, you know, the thoughts that I had as a teenager and somebody in my early twenties in college is much different than it is now where you're sort of thinking about longevity, seeing some of your teammates and the toll that some of those injuries take on their bodies. . . . You start to realize, "All right, my shoulder aches when I wake up in the morning." And I attribute that to football, and some of the other aches and pains that I have as I get older. . . . I have had I think seventeen surgeries now. . . . I had one surgery while I was a collegiate football player and then I had obviously sixteen after I stopped playing college football, and nine of those were related to a knee injury and subsequent staph infection. . . . Then obviously you brought up concussions and thinking about that, what does that mean long term? Like I said, I played with guys in the NFL that took their own lives and then were diagnosed with CTE when they did the autopsy, so you think about that, like, "Boy, I hit my head against that guy's head, so what's going on with me if that was obviously was going on with him?"

Even Kevin Brown, just five years removed from his career at the time of the interview, had already begun to reappraise his career. When asked if injuries currently impacted his life, he said:

> Every day. . . . I've got to be cautious about . . . bending my knees more than just using my lower back. Because I know if I just tweak it or out of line it, then I've got to do several things to get back in line. Ankle, every day . . . I have neuropathy . . . and they knew this was a risk, they told me in advance, "The nerve damage you have in this ankle and the nerve blocker they had to put in," they said there was a

high risk there would be that. So, you know, these weird sensations of stabbing comes in random and then there's some times where, literally from my knee down to my left ankle, I'm walking and it's just kind of like a sensation like where you sleep on your arm. . . . My hands, definitely, I know I've got arthritis in them for sure. . . . And what comes along with that, just holding stuff . . . the past two years now I've kind of noticed really that, my hands, and the damage that has occurred there just hitting somebody every day.

Chris Andrews saw it similarly:

Knowing that you gotta go through life with a bad knee or a bad hip or a bad back and, you know, the difference from one person to the next, some person has a back that gets sore every couple weeks, and then I have other teammates that have debilitating back pain they try to manage on a daily basis, you know, and it gets too out of whack, they're knocked on the couch for a few days and they can't go to work and that's tough because some guys have good jobs and it's not that big of a deal, and there are other guys it's very detrimental where missing a few days of work means a lot in terms of their ability to take care of themselves and their families.

Likewise, Nick Turner told us he still experiences physical disabilities from the trauma he faced playing football:

For me, it all adds up to there's the somatic control starts to fade. . . . You'll start tripping, walking up stairs. I remember one time; I was in the weight room. At one point, I was benching 315 almost ten times. And I sat down one time, and I couldn't get it up twice! . . . I had no strength for some reason. [Even now,] when I work out, I don't push myself. Because I get headaches pretty quickly, and my heart gets funky. . . . My junior year, I sprained my ankle really badly. The doctors said I was going to have to be out for six to eight weeks. They had me back in eight days. . . . I went and played that next game, and then sprained the other ankle. That was kind of the start of feeling like I couldn't be as capable in the gym. It felt very eerie and hard to figure out because the injuries start to pile up at the same time as the strength starts to go. And you're not sure what's what. You're not sure because they'll tell you that you need to be in the weight room every day. If you're not getting better, you're getting worse. And so you start to think, "Oh, I must be losing strength because of these injuries.

I'm not working out as hard." Well, that's not the case. You don't lose strength that fast. Especially not the kind of strength I was losing, which was very random and sporadic. . . . Even today, I have really bad [sciatic] nerve pain in my lower back. . . . I can't raise my left eyebrow. It's like I had a stroke. And that'll get really bad sometimes, and you can see my cheek drooping, like when I'm really tired or when I'm really stressed. I can't wiggle my right pinky toe, but I can wiggle the left one. I used to have tons of control. I was the kind of kid that would pick stuff up with my feet. These things, I started to notice them in college, and they would eat at me mentally. [The medical team] put me on an antidepressant and that just threw fuel on the fire.

For Galen North, injury ended his college career, but not just injury: also bodily harm caused by a mangled surgery by a university physician.

I hurt my neck power cleaning . . . and I had a kind of a more rare type of disrupture, which caused severe nerve damage and I couldn't really walk for a while . . . so it ended up taking from the time I had surgery over two years before I was symptom free. . . . The decision was made to take a medical hardship, which is you maintain your scholarship, but you don't play anymore. . . . Myself and my family trusted the doctors to do the right thing on my initial surgery, and they did the wrong thing and that is, in my opinion, a direct [cause] of every other subsequent injury I had. . . . [The surgery] was done by a university doctor that we've come to find out later that had never done the surgery before. . . . They didn't tell us that . . . and they used a different technique that he had never done before that was kind of new at the time. And none of this was disclosed to us ahead of time. Then you kind of get to the situation, "We kind of want to sue this guy for malpractice," but at the time, the other doctor says they're going to fix this, and you're kind of stuck between, if you sue this guy for malpractice, there's gonna be a huge conflict between you and the university and the football team. So what do you do there?

North's saga shows how little agency college football players have as they navigate their injuries. Because they are beholden to the team for their scholarships and access to playing time necessary to produce future opportunities, they must follow the team and university's guidance. But the team and university often have different motivations that can conflict with the player's interests. It may be cheaper for the school to have players receive medical care from campus physicians, but this does not equate to the best-quality care. When this information is not disclosed to athletes, the university is responsible for a significant ethical failure.

Are the short- and long-term physical harm worth it for players who are now retired and able to reflect on the big picture? This is a complex question that requires weighing a number of factors. Here is how Kurt Weiss engages it:

> I think, as it stands today, it was worth it. I've got some physical ailments, but nothing debilitating. It's a question I feel like people can't really answer until they are in middle and upper ages, particularly with the brain. That's when you start to see things manifest, in your late thirties, at the early end, and through your sixties. So you hear all the time football players saying, "Well it was worth it." And I say, ask again in a certain amount of years. . . . In terms of my body and mind at this moment, yes. But I had two screws put in my left shoulder that I think I'll have to pay to have removed, and they were always intended to be removed, so playing college football cost me a lot of money. Long term, just strictly financially, without all the other benefits of the things that you encounter and the people you meet, it will have [ended up], like I paid money to play college football.

Chris Andrews also suggests that the pay-off of his time in college football does not compute as many would assume: "When I was in school, I saw people that had academic scholarships that pretty much got the same things that we did without putting their bodies on the line. So I don't really see how you can say, and there's variability from the level of injury that somebody sustained across the board on the college football team roster, but I don't think that the level of injury, particularly of some of my teammates, was commensurate with the benefits they received of the scholarship at the school."

In the most extreme cases, players are left with posttraumatic stress disorder (PTSD) as a consequence of the physical and emotional harm they experienced playing college football. Former NFL and Texas A&M star Michael Bennett highlights this phenomenon in his memoir: "Too many of my high school and college teammates have ended up with what can only be described as PTSD. . . . A friend said to me, 'Bro, I would just cry sometimes.' I know this person as a tough defensive lineman, and he was in tears."[12] PTSD is really the only way to describe what Thomas Rycliff also endured: "I started to get sick before camp would start, right about seven to ten days before. I later on learned that I was basically suffering from posttraumatic stress disorder. . . . I would wake up vomiting every August. It became cyclical for eight years after that [until I went to therapy]. My body had kind of turned into this element of where I knew I was going to suffer. I would have these nightmares and I would be in camp. You didn't have any [relief] when I'd close my eyes and I would wake up vomiting."

In fact, the emotional trauma of college football was such that Rycliff contemplated self-harm as a way of extricating himself from the sport's physical and mental obligations:

> There was a moment where I was in the stall of a bathroom and I was trying to fall in a way to create a severe injury so I'd never have to play again. And I couldn't pull it off and it's almost like you got a gun to your head and you just don't have the guts to do it. Because rather than quit, if I'm physically injured, even if it's in a buffoonery way like in the shower or something or like, "Oh, you tore your knee going to the bathroom?" I was trying to get out of it mentally. I'd have created a lifelong physical injury that I'm glad I didn't do that to myself. But because I did have a knee problem, there was a moment in practice in camp where I fell down and I grabbed my knee and I really wasn't hurt, and I was just trying to get a break. And admitting that, coming to terms with that, was difficult, because that was the only time I ever felt like I quit.

Head Trauma

Any discussion of physical and emotional harm in football must center around the question of head trauma. It is abundantly clear that participation yields considerable long-term consequences such as CTE. Concussions and brain injury are inextricably linked to the sport, not only from the structural standpoint of participation producing that consequence, but also in terms of how football is understood in popular culture.[13] Despite lingering attempts by the NFL and NCAA to obfuscate the full magnitude of harm, it is widely accepted that football is dangerous for the human brain. In addition to all the other rigors of college football work, players must also constantly labor under the specter of potential long-term brain trauma. Many players we spoke to addressed this aspect of their experience, including Charlie Rogers: "I feel like there's a good chance that I will have CTE. Especially if I kept playing, it'll probably be guaranteed. But I won't find out until I die, which isn't comforting at all. But I don't have that many headaches anymore. But my memory is still not as good as it was before I started playing." Similarly, C. J. White explains:

I try to stay as positive as I can during a game or a season or practice, when I'm at work. But I mean, when I'm outside of football, there are times when you kind of have thoughts, with so much of the concussion conversation, just knowing it's something serious now. I try to take whatever measures that I can that make sure I'm protected once I go out there and play. Or at least just making sure I have all the protection, all the gear I need so that I can at least try to prevent concussions or injuries.

Ryan Leonard says the scariest part for him is that he does not even "know [the] price that I paid in terms of cognitive ability, in terms of how many concussions did I play through, how many times did I have a concussion and didn't report it?" Likewise Thomas Rycliff says he suffers "from panic disorder related to probably all the subconcussive blows." Chris Andrews talks about his attempts to rationalize his anxiety around the fallout from head injury:

It's hard to know what is just . . . the anxieties that surround daily life versus what is specific to head injury. . . . I like to think it's just kind of what all people go through throughout life, and . . . it's kind of a sensitive thing, because what can I do about it if it is head injury related? From what I know, the bottom line is you manage the symptoms. There's nothing you do differently if it's related to head injury versus if it's the day-to-day stress or anxiety and depression of living life. So for me it's more about managing the symptoms as opposed to attribute it to it being my head or you know something else happening to my head.

No one should have to confront a concussion as a feature of their educational or occupational experiences, but it is a daily risk for college football players. They told us about what it was like to experience concussions. Charlie Rogers, for instance, says he endured ten concussions: "I could barely do school. . . . I would forget what I was talking about midsentence. I'd be forgetting everything that happened like ten minutes ago. I would just completely zone out sometimes. It was like I was halfway there. I couldn't really control it."

DS: And it affected your personal life, with family, friends?
ROGERS: Mm-hm. I fucking forgot my girlfriend's birthday.
My girlfriend for like, three, four years.

Nick Turner explains the agony of concussion and the lingering consequences:

My freshman year . . . the running back tripped and just earholed me with the top of his helmet, like speared me. And my helmet went flying, like thirty yards. And instantly, I started crying. I lost my breath. I wasn't like I got the wind knocked out of me. It was like when you're so scared that you can't breathe . . . they sent me back out on the field. And we ran a completely different play, and I ran the same play. It's a play where I pull and I block the corner. So I'm pulling way out into the open field, and it looked absolutely ridiculous the second time I did it because it was a pass play, and I was pulling out, running into nothing. . . . Later, when watching the film, and the coach is like, "What the hell are you doing?" I was like, "I don't remember this at all." They did the concussion test, [found out] that I have a concussion. I sat out for maybe six practices, like a week and a half, maybe? Was right back out there like nothing happened.

Kurt Weiss also recounts the significant role concussions played during his football career:

We still had two-a-days. We had maybe thirty-ish padded practices in twenty-eight days . . . you hit your head in those four weeks, thousands of times at a g-force of at least twenty g's. You know it experientially, but you don't know the science behind it. So like, "camp fog" or "camp brain" was something we'd discuss. And it was just so normal. I was never diagnosed with a concussion. There's a handful of times where I was concussed. And my sophomore year, I was . . . throwing up on the sidelines. And [linebackers' coach] looked at me, and said, "You good?" And he wasn't asking, he was telling me. And he tousled my hair and kind of slapped my head jokingly, and he was like, "Yeah, you'll be good." So unless you got knocked out, or the fans saw you stumbling off the field, you just played. If the medical staff was concerned or approached you, you just say you have a stinger. . . . My teammate . . . had a neck surgery in high school. And part of this issue with, I think, the neck surgery but also brain injury, sometimes, everything would go black when [he] hit. And I learned it practicing playing with him, like if he was on the ground, just to give him a beat, because everything would be black for a second. And he would say, "Wait, wait, wait" and then [he'd nod] and be like, "Okay," and then

I would help him up. So that's [a] dramatic case. But . . . the gulf between what you can study in a lab and what's actually happening on the field is so wide, and I think either willfully or genuinely, brain injury doctors are oblivious to the fact that [redacted teammate], everything was black on the field for him . . . because he's a zero in that dataset. You know, he's "never had a concussion." It's absurd.

Weiss addresses multiple salient themes in understanding harm related to head trauma. First, most concussions are unreported—players talked about a weeks-long "brain fog" from such injury, which was not reported at all. Second, he juxtaposes this pervasive traumatic experience with scientific discourse framing head injury as indeterminate in terms of the relationship between trauma on the field and long-term pathology. Taken as a whole, this paints a grim picture of what might be characterized as the collective gaslighting of college football players who endure head trauma.

Given how threatening concussions are for college football players, and how difficult it is to protect oneself from them, discussion among teammates on the subject was limited. If they were discussed, it was often in the form of dark humor, attempting to defuse anxiety, as Ross Nielsen explains: "Surprisingly, there was a lot of jokes about it. There was, you know, if you had like a spacey moment, like, 'Oh it's that CTE kicking in.' Some dark humor, kinda. Maybe not the most respectful to people who actually suffer from that condition, but yeah, not really any serious conversations about it. No one really talked about it at all."

Despite the increasing understanding that concussions are harmful, especially when repeated, players spoke of coaches encouraging them to play through these injuries as well. Matt Jensen explains:

I was on the field goal team, so basically your role is: stand there and get hit. . . . I got a concussion twice doing that, and I wasn't happy about it. But it was playing time, so you know, that's all I could ask for. But I remember sitting down when I was still going through the concussion protocol. And one of the coaches sat down next to me. And he was like, "Hey, it's really taking forever for you to come back from this, isn't it?" And I was like, "Not really, it's only been the end of my first week. Usually, concussion protocol is two weeks." And he said, "Yeah, but you know sometimes the way you get around that is what you say to the trainers." The implication was, "Hey dude, if you still have a headache, suck it up. Like, say you're okay so you can get back out there." And the sad thing is, I don't think that was unique to our football program.

Charlie Rogers was even more blunt about how little regard coaches had for the severity and danger of head injury: "They scare you into not reporting your injuries, especially concussions, because they treat you even worse as a person, because they just think you're faking it." Brock Adler had a similar experience:

> It was light bullying . . . snarky comments. Like, "Oh, it looks like you're fine. You're moving fine, you could get out there." Or, "You're not practicing today?" alluding towards, like, "You need to get your ass out there." As a player, you would know it in your mind, and then you would feel bad. . . . [The medical staff] would reassure that "you have a concussion, you need to be careful, and you need to take the necessary steps" . . . but the coaches, they never understood. They claimed they did, but that was only for "their guys," if you will. Again, where I was in the hierarchy—this was my freshman year, because I graduated high school early for [previous head coach] and then he got fired— they used whatever they could against you.

In Nick Turner's case, returning to play after a concussion ultimately caused him to suffer further injuries that ended his football career:

> I got concussed early in the game. Went up to block a linebacker and was dizzy . . . I was like, "I'm definitely going to get hurt." I hurt my shoulder and my knee. My shoulder was numb, they call it a stinger. . . . You can play on that, I've seen plenty of guys play on that. It's not healthy, it's totally not Hippocratic for a doctor to watch you do it, but you can do it. They wanted [me] to do it. They wanted to put me in a brace, and I said, "No, I'm not gonna do it." Everyone was really confused.

Our interviews made clear that coaches not only normalized head-to-head trauma, they often encouraged it. Thomas Rycliff recalled being explicitly told to target a teammate's head with his own, even referring to it as an uncontroversial request: "He pulls me aside, he says, 'See, I don't give a fuck what you do. You bring the plastic.' And so he just wanted me to go hit this guy in the head as hard as I can, which is great because that's like my best move."

> NKL: You're hitting him with your head as well? Is it like head to head?
> RYCLIFF: Yeah, yeah, yeah. I mean, but that's just standard D-lineman stuff. . . . That's not really controversial. . . . Then I took the step

out. I took one. I got a little bit wider, just so I could have one extra step. And this is our left tackle. This is our best lineman on the team. He went to meet me, and it was just this perfect leverage moment where if you ever hit a home run or you've ever done anything, there's a thing about when you have a perfect swing or anything. It feels so effortless that you almost feel, in hindsight, like you could have done it even harder. I hit him, I hit the left tackle so hard, and he came late to meet me at the leverage point, that the first thing that hit the ground was the back of his neck.

While coaches encouraged players to play through and inflict head trauma, they also actively worked to prevent them from learning more about the potential risks. Such behavior is a form of coercion, eliciting consent for participation by concealing risk. Ryan Leonard explains:

There's also pressure to play from the coaches, tremendous pressure. Probably the most profound example of this was in my third year of fall camp . . . we had, I think it was six or seven offensive linemen received concussions . . . and we were running thin on offensive line. Not the starters, these weren't starters that were hurt, but these were the backups. . . . Our coach, maybe not directly told these players, "You need to get back here." But I had heard from these players that, "Hey, they're trying to rush us back." And so, at that time the movie *Concussion* had just came out, and I knew that it's a serious issue for all players, but particularly for offensive/defensive linemen. And so I go up to these players . . . I go, "Hey, I want everybody to come over to my house, we're going to sit down and we're going to watch this movie *Concussion*. We're going to watch what happens when you rush back, we're going to watch where this might lead if you're not careful." And I knew a lot of players hadn't watched it because they're fearful, they don't want to know. This is the dark side of, especially offensive line, dark side of football. They didn't want to know. But my head coach at the time caught wind of it. And he goes, "You're not going to do that. You're not going to get everybody in there and you're not going to watch that movie." And at the time I thought, "Okay, that is very profound. That is very warning." But I understood where he was coming from. It was for the better of the team that we get these guys back sooner rather than later. But from that moment on, I knew safety isn't necessarily the greatest priority.

The banality of violence in college football resulting in repeated head contact was remarkably common for the former players we interviewed. These experiences cannot be minimized given the long-term negative consequences associated with head trauma.[14] While not all interviewees spoke about head trauma they suffered, the familiarity of many with even the medical jargon associated with it (i.e., "chronic traumatic encephalopathy," "subconcussive blows," "cerebral cortex") indicates that such experiences may be underestimated, even in this book. Perhaps the key takeaway here is that head trauma and associated brain injury are features—not merely unanticipated, unlucky consequences—of college football. We must therefore *always* include brain injury as an integral part of our calculus when considering the harm borne by these athletes.

Insurance Malfeasance

Given the relentlessness of injury in the world of college football and the nature of the private US health care system, the question of medical insurance is central to any discussion of injury in the sport. And, indeed, the insurance dynamics for college athletes are more similar to those of other students than we might assume.[15] All students are expected to come to university with insurance or otherwise purchase it through the university. This is true for college athletes as well. For most injuries, especially minor ones, suffered during college football participation, team medical staff provide care for no additional cost. However, for more severe injuries, players go to the closest facility, which may or may not be a university facility. Regardless, treatment costs are likely billed to the player's own insurance. As with other elements of the US health care system, things tend to get extremely complicated, often at the expense of the person accessing care. For many players we interviewed, because universities were not the primary bearers of health insurance costs, campus athletic workers and their families carried a significant economic burden for injuries obtained while working at college football for universities. Kurt Weiss, for instance, explained, "My surgeries all took place when I was nineteen. I don't know if [my parents'] copay went up or whatever, but I do know that it affected [them]. Yeah, it cost them money for me to have surgery at [school]." Similarly, Kevin Brown described how the university's failures to correctly manage billing affected him and a teammate: "He had a Cadillac health plan, 100 percent covered by the university, as for mine, I got a secondary plan, and then my parent's plan, I was a primary. So whatever costs weren't covered, the university would pick up.

Well, in both scenarios, both of our credits got dinged because the university system, the process wasn't there."

The issue with insurance and billing was a repeated theme for players. Galen North explained that his family got stuck with higher premiums because, per NCAA policy, he was on his parents' health insurance plan when he was injured. The university was expected to pay part of the bill, but it simply didn't, which he discovered when applying for his first credit card. His credit score was extremely low because of outstanding debt that had been sent to collections although he had never taken on a loan. When he investigated, he discovered thousands of dollars of medical bills that had never been paid. To clear his credit, he had to fight with the athletic department and hospital for nine months, largely without success since the hospital had sold the debt to a collection agency. Ultimately, his debt was cleared only because of the threat of a lawsuit. As he concluded, "It took like nine months because I got rejected from multiple things because of it and I know for a fact that I'm not the only person it's happened to that was on my team. There are at least four other guys that this happened to. And I don't know what their end result was and how diligent they were about cleaning all of it up, but I made a point of it to fix my situation."

This was a problem for Daniel Barber too, although he played at a different institution in a different conference: "I ended up getting sent to collections, because [school] didn't pay my medical bills. And that happened to a lot of other people that I've talked to, that's not irregular. This like, [school official] was supposed to be in charge of it. I'd call her and she'd just not respond, or 'I'll handle it.' And it never got handled."

Aside from the questions around billing, perhaps the most significant factor when it comes to health insurance is that players ultimately bear all long-term costs after college associated with injury and insurance. As Chris Andrews puts it, "I had a teammate [who] played the first half of the game, his knee would blow up so severely at halftime that they drained his knee at halftime. And so, for somebody like him who obviously had that problem in college and he was encouraged to play . . . who pays for the ongoing care of that injury? And, obviously, it's he who bears the expense of taking care of that stuff, it's not the school."

Kurt Weiss adds, speaking of former NFL players he knows, "These men have spent so much money on their physical and mental ailments that they need help paying rent. There's probably going to be a lot of college athletes in a similar situation." Indeed, this is the reality for *all* former college football players: they alone must bear the cost for the harm they accrued sacrificing their bodies to produce commodity spectacle for universities and the coaches those universities so amply compensate.

While direct costs via medical care compromise the financial outlook of college athletes, an indirect cost is the potential lost revenue from NFL contracts if they become injured during their (uncompensated) time in college. C. J. White explains:

It's unfair because the NFL, you get guys get hurt, you can't bounce back, they give you a settlement. . . . But in college level, if I have a significant injury here, the team and everything will pay for me getting treatment and whatnot, but depending on how significant the injury is I really don't get nothing else out of that other than that. Just the treatment for me to get back. And, for some guys it's career-ending injuries. So it's like, they never get the opportunity to go to the next level because they're already damaged goods before they even get the chance to get their foot in the door. And it's like the only thing they have to show for it if they stay in school is the degree, which is a huge thing, but at the same time, you know, just being a professional athlete, you have jobs that don't make the type of money that professional athletes make.

Perhaps one of the least discussed aspects of physical harm in the world of college football is the harm experienced by mostly walk-on players involved in scout-team work. By simulating the opponent, the scout team prepares the players who will receive most of the snaps in a game. However, because the scout team will not be relied on in the games, coaches have little incentive to be concerned about the physical toll a scout team player experiences. At the end of the day, when a scout team player is hurt, it does not affect the team's depth chart, and it has only an indirect impact on the team's probability of success. Daniel Barber describes how brutal this can be for scout team players:

[Teammate] was like "our guy." Our star. And football is a 100 percent injury sport. And so he was in a red jersey during practice. Like, he only took game hits. . . . Everyone else, [shrugs]. They didn't like you, [shrugs]. . . . Coaches can choose, like find a way to put you in bodily harm. They don't have to do it personally. They can arrange for it to happen. . . . There's always 'that person' that kind of gets bullied, or is like the fuckup and the black sheep. And they make that person, "Oh, you messed up. Do it again. You messed up, do it again. You messed up, do it again." How's your body going to hold up? . . . People get hurt in practice. That's one of the reasons why certain schools let so many walk-ons on, is because they can be bodies. And people will sign up for that. Or they'll tell lies, or they'll tell us the right things, or give just enough praise to those walk-ons where they'll keep doing it.

Ross Neilsen, who was a walk-on and scout team player, elaborates further:

Scout team was probably like where you got banged up the most. And so I actually did scout team offense and scout team defense, just because you're in a position where you don't have anything, and you really want something, so you'll do pretty much anything to get it. So you'll sign up for a lot more stuff than you probably should. And it actually is to your detriment performance-wise, but psychologically you think that it's the right thing to do. . . . It was pretty physically exhausting. I would be done and I would question how I was going to get through the next four practices for the week. And then, on top of that . . . if you are not a squad player, which most walk-ons aren't, . . . you had to do these grueling workouts that were two and a half hours long in season, on two days of the week. That was pretty much the kicker. That was one of the reasons I didn't go longer than a year, is it was just absolutely physically brutal.

Matt Jensen experienced the same thing:

The coach frames [scout team] as, "This is your chance to develop." And I kind of knew that was bullshit, because we weren't really running *our* defense, we were running *other* teams' defenses. . . . I did get better, but it was also just hard abuse on the body. . . . Didn't care if we were tired, if we were hurt, we just had to suck it up and go in, because they needed to get the reps. So it was just a long day . . . going as hard as you possibly can, because you've got to try to make an impression, so you're taking the abuse there. . . . Then at the end of all [the drills and plays], sometimes they would do Devo, which is for all the developmental players. So that's when you would go in and you would have to say, "Okay, now I *really* have to turn it on." And now you're trying to go 110 percent again after, I don't know, ninety minutes of 110 percent.

Charlie Rogers, who played in the scout team role on scholarship, felt like "a live practice dummy" whose "only purpose was to make the starters, and all the other people ahead of me on the depth chart, better." That dynamic made him "feel kind of worthless. Because that's where they base your value on. I remember the coach pulled us into a meeting, and he explicitly said, 'If you play more, we will treat you better. And if you don't, we won't.'" What Rogers called a "live practice dummy" was for Josh Hansen "a second-class person": "They ain't going to be concerned about protecting you the same way they're protecting somebody who's a starter. Like, that's just the facts of life."

Conclusion

Why is it important to shift focus from *compensation* to *harm* in the context of college football? Rather than rehashing tired debates centering distribution of value as the redress to historical and contemporary injustices suffered by players, we focus on *all the diverse forms in which harm has affected, and continues to affect, the lives and livelihoods of campus athletic workers.* By shifting the focus from compensation to harm, we clearly see both the ways in which campus athletic workers are exploited in noneconomic terms *and the consequences of that exploitation*—to the players' bodies, minds, and pocketbooks. It allows us to more tangibly confront the true lived experiences of these players and how they navigate the consequences of participation in a brutal and dehumanizing sport. It makes visible a paradox of contemporary violent sport: what may be considered fun or enjoyable can also cause immense pain and trauma. Focusing on harm instead of remuneration destabilizes the common rejoinder that participation in college football is a desirable and "priceless" experience for which athletes should be grateful. It forces us to confront that the injustice of college football lies in much more than the racialized economic exploitation that participants are subjected to. It brings us face to face with athletic workers subjected to brutal corporeal and emotional violence that can, and often does, impact every piece of their physical, mental, and social lifeworlds well after they hang up their helmets. It forces us to consider the possibility that college football cannot be imagined outside of that harm, regardless of reforms to more fairly compensate college athletes (even if these reforms are necessary). Perhaps most importantly, it acknowledges that participation in college football must be understood in terms of its structurally coercive characteristics.

Focusing on harm reveals the multiple motivations and rationales that justify participation in an unhealthy and violent sport. But it also grants us new access to the complex feelings, regret, and grief that college football players might experience long after retiring. Take Nick Turner, for example:

> DS: With all of your injury history and everything that you experienced with college football, and now you know, you have the benefit of hindsight: would you go back and play college football again?
>
> TURNER: No. . . . I definitely wouldn't have played football. I hated football from a very early age, and was afraid to stop. I felt like it was something that if I stopped, I'll be less of a man in a way that was subconscious to me. I couldn't process that until it stopped. But my first concussion was the first season I played. It wasn't even a game. It was at practice, and most of the stupid head injuries, most of the risk, is at practice. They're lining you up. They're preparing you to hit your head in a game and be okay with it and keep going. So they get you used to the feeling of having a concussion and getting another one and getting another one. It might not be enough where you're like, "Oh, I'm knocked out and I'm gonna go back another round and keep boxing." It's not like that. It's just, "I have a headache," I'm getting used to it to a point where this is becoming acceptable for me, as a child. This is athletic competition.

Turner described a concussive blow he suffered in youth football and how his visceral emotional reaction — entirely normal for a young child — caused his father to respond in such a negative way that he still experiences trauma about it over twenty years later:

> I just went flat on my back, couldn't breathe, and was dizzy. . . .
> That's the first time I ever felt that. And I was like, "I don't know which way is up . . . I don't know what's going on." I start crying. My dad grabbed me, pulled me to the side. I took my helmet off, and threw it, and was like, "I don't want to do it." And I started crying and throwing a fit. I was like six years old. He told me, "You have to walk home now, because little girls don't get in my car." I walked home. My mom didn't do anything about it. We got home, I didn't talk about it. From that day forward, I never acted like I was hurt ever again. It felt like if I cried around my dad, I would be a little girl. That was so scary to me. After that, there was absolutely no reason why I would ever cry in front of my dad. It was so painful and subconscious that I couldn't process it until I quit and was like, "Why did I do all that?" Because I had good

grades in high school. I could have focused a little more, been part of more things. Instead of spending four hours a day on football, in the weight room, and at practice. I could have spent four hours doing anything else and been great at it.

Scholars have documented how misogyny and hegemonic masculinity are fundamental to participation in, and the performance of, American football.[16] While this is not a central focus of this chapter (one could write an entire book on this alone), our findings corroborate these studies while centering the experiences of college athletes as a form of harm that should always be considered in any assessment about injustice.

There is a reason this is the longest chapter of this book. Although economic and educational exploitation are crucial issues worthy of much attention, the most egregious aspects of college football are those associated with harm. The fact that college students bear all the risk of harm in the production of the commodity spectacle of college football makes the whole system morally indefensible. It is simply not possible to justify this sport as it currently exists with what we know about the cost to brains and bodies, certainly not in the context of a private health care system that provides no care to the players whose lives are sacrificed by institutions with a formal mandate to protect and nurture them. These sacrifices are not worth it, although players may feel like they are worth it in the moment, as Ryan Leonard explains:

> This is probably one of the most profound revelations that I had even though I was on a scholarship for a majority of my college: I will pay for that education every day for the rest of my life. Every day I will pay that price. Every day I will fight pain, I will fight the urge to take painkillers. And that was one of the biggest revelations that came after I was done playing. And it really happened after my last year where I thought, "What have I done?" Because while you're playing, you don't think long term. You don't think that, "I have to live this life. I have one body and I have to live this body for the rest of my life."

Likewise, when asked if he would go through the experience again, Aaron Peters told us:

> Absolutely not. . . . Football is just unnatural to your body. Running into something, your brain is not supposed to do that. Your body is not supposed to do that. For me, personally, at twenty-four, I'm like, "That's the dumbest thing I've done." I could have utilized my athleti-

cism for something else. If it's about a sport . . . golf. You can play golf up until the day you die. You can dribble around a soccer ball for a very long time. . . . After you're done, like you're done with college or the NFL, you don't really want to go around catching a football because you just understood all the stuff that you had to do. Football's not really fun. Running into another man is not fun. It's warfare. It's barbaric. You have to psyche yourself up to run into another man. You've defied the laws of nature, because alright, if I know a guy who weighs 250 pounds, runs this fast. He's running at me. The only way that guy is going to budge, something in his body has to give out. Whether his knee, his arm, his leg, his neck, his back. Something's got to give out because from a scientific standpoint, if we run into each other, he's going to win. The only way is to hit him in the right joint, the right [spot]. It don't make sense, the whole game don't make sense, the whole thing don't make sense.

In this sense college football can only be seen as a blight on US higher education. Everyone in US higher education should consider this a personal concern, for those of us who work in these spaces must contemplate our complicities and the ways in which we might do right by the college students/campus athletic workers under our care. As Kurt Weiss puts it, "Universities can't give their students brain diseases" precisely because it is "antithetical to the whole reason universities exist."

CHAPTER FOUR

Plantation Dynamics

Racial Capitalism through College Football

Leaning back in his chair, Terry Davis recalls:

> The only reason [Black] guys like me went to [school] was because of
> Prime Time [Deion Sanders]. Prime inspired us, that we can show up
> as our authentic selves in this predominantly white environment,
> because were the baddest motherfuckers there. . . . Me and all my
> teammates love Prime to death. Some of them are just rooting for him
> to be successful, others know how the game actually works. . . . Even
> while we're rooting for his success, we know we all didn't get the same
> latitude that Prime Time got. That affected how we showed up,
> because when we did show up as our true authentic selves, players are
> told to cut their dreads . . . by coaches' wives. . . . There's a guy,
> quarterback, that was recruited from [FCS school]. . . . He was a dual
> threat guy. He got a chance to run the Wildcat at [school] my sopho-
> more year. Told him they was going to move him to cornerback unless
> he cut his hair. He cut his hair and they moved him to cornerback,
> still, and he transferred out.

This exchange did not occur in a vacuum; it was part of a pattern Davis
experienced while playing college football. We cannot adequately account
for the exploitative dynamics of college football without grappling with the
question of how they are framed by racial capitalism.[1] In part, this is a function of structural racism in the United States more broadly—the historical
theft of value or racial transfer of wealth that has built predominantly white
institutions (PWIs) and systematically impoverished huge swathes of Black
America.[2] But these dynamics manifest in very specific ways in the context
of college football. Our interviews reveal the differential treatment experienced by Black players at PWIs and the attendant desire for protest and
resistance, albeit desire constrained by the very real power dynamics of the
sport. The interviews also testify to the profound resonance among players
of understanding the conditions on campuses in terms of what Wallace Bell
called a "plantation mind-set and system." The persistent invocation of
slavery—Bell is representative in saying of college football, "I feel it's essen-

tially the same thing as slavery with the same system set up"—as an analogue for these athletic workers' experiences is a powerful statement about the degree of racial injustice required to sustain the sport as we know it.

The social reproductive dynamics of sport are compounded by the forms of stratification and inequality that define the racialized society they are institutionalized within. As Robin Kelley puts it, "Capitalism has always operated within a system and ideology that assigns differential value to human life and labor."[3] Capital has always been accumulated through the dehumanization of race, understanding that race is not an essential fact of biology, nor simply an identity, but also, in the classic formulation of Stuart Hall and colleagues, "the modality in which class is lived."[4] Charisse Burden-Stelly pushes further: "As a *structural location* at the intersection of indispensability and disposability, Blackness exceeds the category of race, is not reducible to class, and does not fit the specifications of caste."[5] Or as Victor Ray argues, riffing on Marx, "I define race not as a thing, but as a relationship between persons mediated by things."[6] To fully account for harm and exploitation in US sport entails confronting the fundamentally material and extractive nature of 'race,' which requires a grasp of how racial capitalism shapes life chances and conditions the very nature of what opportunity looks like in a US society built on slavery, segregation, and systematic racist brutality.[7]

To be clear, the primary beneficiaries are the coaches, athletic department officials, and university presidents who oversee the labor conditions of campus athletic workers. White people disproportionately oversee campus athletic work in the Power Five conferences, whether at the level of chancellors and presidents, athletic directors, or head coaches.[8] The denial of compensation to the Black athletes who drive revenue is the single most damning dimension of the plantation dynamics of college sport.[9]

Participation in big-time college football—once denied according to the segregationist logic of an earlier moment of racial capitalism—now takes on the gloss of opportunity, socioeconomic mobility, and even the veneer of consent. But is consent possible if the distribution of life chances is determined by a fundamentally racialized political economy? To what extent does the mode of hyperexploitation and physical sacrifice flourishing in US institutions of higher education under the moniker "sport" rely on race for its reproduction?

While it is something of a microcosm for the dynamics of high-performance sport in North America, US college football is defined by nothing so much as the systematic exploitation of a group of predominantly racialized subjects at the hands of homogeneously white figures of authority.

Scholars have documented how college football epitomizes what Cedric Robinson calls racial capitalism—a process whereby racialization facilitates, via hyperexploitation and violence, an extreme racial transfer of wealth.[10] Theorists like Stanley Eitzen and Billy Hawkins argue that the NCAA system operates as a "new plantation" through which PWIs subject Black campus athletic workers to a dynamic, per Hawkins, akin to the "broader historical and social context of exploitation endured by internally colonized people in the system of slavery."[11] Building on this, we suggest college football's exploitative dynamics are inextricably linked to racial capitalism in the United States more broadly, given that differential access to life chances based on classed racial dynamics, and the social and historical racial transfer of wealth, have produced the conditions for the new plantation of college football today.

The Power Five PWIs continue to function as what Victor Ray theorizes as "racialized organizations" and Billy Hawkins calls neocolonial plantation dynamics.[12] There are many elements to such dynamics, but at the core is a racial transfer of wealth—the material extraction and transfer of value from racialized workers to white coaches and administrators. A disproportionate number of college football players are racialized, particularly Black, including 55.7 percent of players at Power Five schools, although, as of 2019–20, only 5.7 percent of the student body overall at these schools was Black.[13] This matters because of how much money these players generate and who receives the benefits. Ted Tatos and Hal Singer have calculated that Black men's football and basketball players lose out annually on a $1.2-to-$1.4 billion racial transfer of wealth, testifying to, per Burden-Stelly, their indispensability to the system.[14] Moreover, according to publicly available data, in Power Five athletic departments, 75 percent of athletic directors, 83 percent of associate athletic directors, and 80.94 percent of assistant athletic directors are white. In terms of coaching, 80.6 percent of head men's basketball coaches, 81.54 percent of head women's basketball coaches, and 80 percent of head football coaches in the Power Five are white.[15] Despite the enormous pool of Black assistant coach candidates, the revenue generated in big-time college sport continues to be distributed disproportionately to white people in leadership positions. Kevin Brown explains: "Recognizing statistically the race that is predominant in football, it is racist. And that's statistics, it's not me pointing fingers, you're avoiding national labor laws through making up a definition of student-athlete and it just so happens that the majority of the student-athletes in football happen to be . . . young Black men from low-income families. I think you're doing them a disservice and you're sucking everything out of them and then putting them back into where they came from." Or as Wallace Bell puts it, "It just goes back to the slave and the slave owner . . . you built a system on capitalizing off of the hard work of people."

Yet even as Black college football players embody indispensability in the value they produce for PWIs, they also experience disposability on campus, often subjected to the hostile perception that they do not "properly" belong. Players we interviewed revealed that even as they physically sacrificed to produce the social reproductive labor that sells tickets and merchandise and literally contributes to the survival of the entire cable television industry and the sports/media complex, they were both denied any compensation for their work and treated as interlopers undeserving of access to the ivory tower. As Daniel Barber said, "Race is just in it. It's modern-day slavery. Let's just be honest."

Before moving to players' testimony, we offer a quick note here on our subject positions as conduits for their experiences. Both authors of this book are white. We are grateful to the athletes who shared their stories, but our whiteness is unquestionably a methodological consideration when engaging with the plantation dynamics of college sport. Black athletes had and have every reason to mistrust white interlocutors, given the structural conditions of white supremacy. Therefore, it is highly likely that this chapter's findings significantly *downplay* the ubiquity and magnitude of racism in college football.

The Athletic Plantation

Players we interviewed understand college football to be a white supremacist institution within a white supremacist society—in other words, an institution and society that systematically and historically confer benefits on people racialized as white at the expense of those racialized as Black. College football is a site of value extraction and transfer from Black to white people. But the history of extraction from Black people in the United States more generally—an ongoing history with roots in slavery—also means Black people more likely face restricted opportunities for class mobility, and access to institutions like those of higher education that can leverage it, *in addition* to the cultural forms of racism that also foreclose access. We refer to this as *structural coercion*, the systemic pressure placed on individuals to participate in college football because they are otherwise denied economic and educational opportunities.[16] Thus, the choice to play college football is circumscribed by structural conditions (access to resources) *not* of the individual's own choosing or making. Individuals may decide to play college football even if they view it as a form of personal sacrifice because it is the best available option for them and their families. That is a choice in name only. In reality it is a form of coercion. This coercion, in the context of racial capitalism, is particularly, although not universally, racialized. It is a foundational predicate of the plantation dynamics of college football today.

Jeremy Jones, a Black player, perhaps best articulated this:

JONES: College football as a sport is not fair at all. . . . The whole sport is built to make money, and making money is never 'fair' in any situation, right? Like you got Bezos charging people 100 bucks for [Amazon] Prime so that you can get shit you buy from them sent to your house a day faster. You got pharmaceutical companies charging hundreds of thousands of dollars for medication people need to like survive. It's fucked. So when you take college football and look at it from that point of view you see that the whole thing is built to make money—money for universities, for coaches, for ads, for ESPN and CBS and shit. Everything in college football is about making money . . . except if you're a so-called student-athlete. Then you can't make any money. You're not allowed to. You're told you're not a professional and can't take a share of the money you are part of earning, you know? But the fucked-up thing is, bro, there's nowhere else to go. They have created this system where you can't go nowhere [else] to play football because there ain't any options. So if you want to be a professional and get paid, you have to play in college or nobody going to notice you. How is that fair?

And for me, as a Black man, it's especially fucked up because I see me and my brothers grinding every day for other people. Those other people are mostly white. I gotta say it. They are white. White head coach, white university president, white athletic director, bunch of white guys on TV. I bet the CEOs of sponsors are all white. Man, it's a whole system created to make money off the backs of us brothers. There are white guys on the team, I'm not saying there aren't, but how many Black students are there and how does that match up with the football team? So what I'm thinking is that I see me and my brothers grinding every day to make these other people money. So they can drive around in their Range Rovers. Yet I keep getting told that I'm not allowed to make any money because I'm a student-athlete. That's unfair, bruh.

DS: Did you ever experience racism during your time in college football?

JONES: Overt racism? Not really, at least not football related. I'm sure I heard white people say "n***a" or heard some drunk dude call someone some slur in [a local bar], but that shit is just life. It's part of growing up and living in [town]. You got ignorant people all over. Trump's only made that shit worse. But when it comes to the football program, naw I never had any experiences like that. [Laughs] Fucking 90 percent of the football team is Black, so I'd be shocked if anyone said shit.

DS: What about more hidden, insidious, or what some call "structural" or "systemic racism"? Did you ever experience any notable examples of that?

JONES: [Pause] . . . I'm thinking back to class, man. Like I live in a society that is racist. That weight is always sitting on my shoulders, you know? I wake up every day and gotta look over my shoulders at cops or, like, make sure I don't get into a car with five other brothers. So in that way systemic racism is everywhere around me all the time, so yeah it's also in football and in university and shit. The fact that the football team is like 90 percent Black and you walk on campus and it's white people everywhere, white professors, white students, like that is systemic racism that we gotta live through. . . . I learned a lot about this in my sociology classes . . . it's much harder to pinpoint and call systemic racism for what it is, you know? So it's harder to recognize, harder to see, harder to convince people that it exists. That's all part of the problem—people out here don't want to accept that something is racist unless it's literally someone calling someone a "n***a" or some shit. That's the problem in society, man. You can't just go out and say the whole society is racist because people go buck with that shit. . . . I live in a society that I think is systematically racist and that racism is everywhere, so I guess in that sense it's in football too. Like I said before, I'm out there grinding with my brothers for free while a bunch of white people make money. If that's not systemic racism then I don't know what is.

Ronnie Exeter, another Black player, reveals that football was his ticket to higher education and opportunity for himself and his family because of the pressures of structural racism:

I'm from a place where it's number two in the world for homicide. Not very much people getting a better life coming out of there. With that being said, for my family, me getting out of the house and doing something positive was just the number one goal. Where we're from, you end up dead or in jail. It's literally a place full of statistics. When we left, my parents were just so motivated by being in a new place. It was just, the verbiage was more along the lines of, "Hey, we can't pay for you to go to school, but here's some options for you, academics or athletics." I don't think I'm not intelligent, but I just knew that I had a better chance playing sports. I just love sports, that's what we do all day in the backyard. Why not make something out of it? Make my mama proud. Yeah, definitely I had to get a scholarship. If I didn't get a scholarship, I wouldn't have been going to school. I would've had to apply to work somewhere, because my parents could not afford it, period. Even then though, I was sending money back when I got my stipend and little things just to help. Like I said, I'm the oldest and it was always tight around the house. Anything I could do to make it less tight or make my parents worry less, or just aim that direction into the other kids and not me kind of thing, that was always my goal.

Ross Nielsen, a white player, spoke of how he saw structural coercion affect his Black teammates:

I kind of felt like all the white people who played were viewed as people who had a lot of money, like their connections got them into the team or whatever, like their lives weren't as hard. And honestly, that's kind of true. A lot of the players that I played with that were African American had very, very tough financial situations. And so, I don't think there was any player-on-player hate for that, I don't think there was any coach-on-player hate for that. The system just kind of thrives on that, if that makes sense? I mean, there were people who would tell me that they grew up and they couldn't afford to eat before college football, regularly. They had the school meals. And those are the kind of people that, I mean, there's like a huge drive to be good. But you've got these people, their lives are really hard, they play college football, and something filtered out hundreds of people that were in that same situation. Most of the people on the team didn't have high socioeconomic background, and so, the team was everything to them. That experience was their entire life, like their whole life built up to this. But that is the racial dynamic, I guess, is you've got a lot of people from low socioeconomic status backgrounds that are really dialed in because it's like the biggest-bang-for-their-buck investment on their life's work. And it does affect, I think, African American players more than it affects white ones, to be totally honest with you. I do think that the stereotype was right, most of the white guys on the team had a ton more resources growing up, and that's how they got into the situation they were in.

Nielsen suggests white players often earned opportunities to participate in college football *because* of the resources required to produce an elite high-performance athlete. Conversely, because of the history of racial capitalism in the United States, Black players were often propelled by a desire to create opportunity out of situations where resources didn't exist precisely because they have been systematically denied. "Everything" was at stake for them, an ideal situation for a coach interested in extracting maximum value through performance. Wallace Bell told us, "Them not paying their players for the work that they're doing, that's essentially what enslaved Americans have to go through that look like me within the society for four hundred years. And it's the same system, capitalist system that is manifesting within the NCAA."

Even as the material dimensions of the plantation dynamics of college football must be kept in view, these dynamics also impact players' subjective experience. While the economic exploitation of college football does steal from white Americans, it takes far more from Black Americans because of the additional racism and alienation involved in the experience of attending a PWI in the Power Five. This represents a form of harm dealt to Black athletes that white athletes do not contend with. Kevin Brown was keenly aware of these dynamics when he told us about his perception of college football:

Clearly, this system's rigged. It's really systematic, it's definitely a great example of systematic racism. You have a statistically majority of the folks [who] are low-income young Black men that statistically never had a father figure in their life. And, now you have a father figure that's making, that's their head coach or their position coach that's making millions of dollars off of them, off their performance. And, it's not fair in the sense that they're subconsciously and emotionally seeking that leadership, that young man leadership they're needing and they're receiving it, but they're receiving it because of their athleticism, they're not genuinely receiving it. These coaches wouldn't give a damn about some of these kids if it weren't for their athleticism. So that's not fair.

Josh Hansen explains what makes college football an institution of white supremacy and why the experience is different for Black players than for white players:

That is white supremacy, is that, at end of the day, those who matter most, whether it be coaches, whether it be fans, whether it be what we do, is white people. Who's making the decisions for our lives? White people. Who's the desired fan? It's a white person. Whose respect do we take into account? So like, when [head coach] makes his comments about Martin Luther King, he's not taking into account how Black fans feel. When he talks about protesting and Colin Kaepernick, he's not taking into account what he's saying, how it makes his Black athletes feel. He's thinking about what white people feel in that moment. But at the end of the day, the people who benefit the most from college football, in general, are white people. From the standpoint of coaches, from standpoint of athletes, from standpoint of fans, etcetera, is white people. So yeah, I think college football is fundamentally white supremacist.

Ryan Leonard agrees: "I think it's similar to the drug laws that are in place in our society today where the law in itself is not racist, but it predominantly impacts the African American community, and that's why, justifiably so, so many athletes look at the college football system and say this is the plantation mind-set where all the labor, all the risk, all the sacrifice falls upon the workers, and in this case, a predominantly African American workforce, and all the profits are left to the administration, are left to the plantation owner."

For Jeremy Jones, the same racial undertones present in college football extended into professional football:

I went [draft pick] in [draft round] even though I was better than a lot of guys who did. I thought I might get drafted in the top rounds and was kinda like, "What the fuck?" when I slipped. So I was like scrambling around, man. I had another year of eligibility but there was no way I was going back to college, and you actually can't after a certain time. So I thought I was fucked. But my agent told me to chill out and that he was getting some interest in me as an undrafted. The [team name] were always calling us, even as the draft played out, so every time they picked, I was like, "This is it." At one point they called me the night of the draft and said I was probably going undrafted, but they would offer me a contract so I actually just stopped watching the draft. I always thought that the draft was sort of fucked up from an optics standpoint — like a bunch of n****s sitting around waiting for these rich motherfuckers to "select" them as if they should be grateful to be picked. It's fucking backwards . . . I'm like, "Bruh, I'm about to make you money."

Or take what one college football player told us for a piece published in the *Guardian*: "I would purposefully not wear any team-issued gear to class for the first few weeks in order to not be labeled as an athlete. Attending a PWI like I did brought enough negative assumptions about me without football adding to it."[17] The player added that "professors didn't treat Black athletes the same. They looked down on us . . . like we didn't deserve to be there." Given the power that coaches wield in the world of college football, and that they are the foremost beneficiaries of the racial transfer of wealth, it is unsurprising that they often reproduce racist dynamics. Josh Hansen recalls an incident where an SEC head coach told a player, "If he chose [a different SEC school], he would end up pumping gas for the rest his life, like all the other players from the state." As Hansen elaborates, "That gets at the kind of inherent whiteness of the sport as well, like, when has it ever been a white dude who's been told that? . . . The narratives about failure and success [are] oftentimes racialized, and these white coaches can get away with it. Just think about [ACC school], where the white coach said the n-word, and there was no consequences." Daniel Barber describes how coaches drew on racist stereotypes as 'motivational' techniques to extract violence from players:

> We were called in for a meeting, and we were basically called soft. . . . They put up a lion roaming free, and they're like, "That was y'all before you got here." Then they played the slideshow and showed a lion in a cage, and they're like, "That's y'all now. You go over to campus, and they tell you all this soft shit about 'you belong,' all this stuff. That's bullshit. Y'all are like, 'We're gladiators,' like on Saturday nights, you're lining up across from someone from [rival team] who doesn't give a fuck, doesn't have to go to class, all this stuff. That's what I need, I need some heavy drinkers, some weed smokers, I need some of motherfuckers that don't give a damn, that got some dog in them." Mind you, he literally said, "I need some weed smokers. I need y'all to be smoking weed. I need y'all to not give a damn. I need y'all to be from the hood." And then, will turn around, and if he doesn't like you, he's gonna drug test you off the fucking team.

The references to "lions" and "dog[s]" (the latter albeit often a term of endearment in sporting cultures) plays on traditional dehumanizing assumptions about the animalistic nature of racialized people. The deployment of race here is evident to players via references to stereotypical tropes around "weed" and "the hood." These terms dog whistle—with a bullhorn—that the coach is making a racist assumption around an ostensibly natural relationship between Blackness and a capacity for violence he wants players to tap into. Terry Davis recalled an incident where his head coach had to fire his own cousin "because he called an unassuming nice kid walk-on a n-word. That [fired] coach is now in the [state] Hall of Fame since probably like 2014 or something like that." For Josh Hansen, the racism of coaches is connected to their understanding of religion:

Especially in the South, college football is so wrapped up into white Christianity and conservative politics. Like, I think when you talk about what type of religious experiences are desired in that space, it's pretty much the white conservative Christian experience. And if your coach is a white Christian conservative, that's going to shape how they think about Black people. And I've had, literally, my friends who still work at [school] to this day, that tell me like, "Yo, I don't think certain people like Black people" or whatnot, but these people also paradoxically, would believe themselves to be the biggest Christians.

Terry Davis articulated moments where he felt he was treated differently than his peers and colleagues:

Here we are going to this bowl game against [team]. . . . In comes [referee] and his officials to the locker room. I go around the locker room and shake everybody's hand. I know I'm not going to make it [through the game], he told me he's going to kick me out.
 But my white center that played at [school], an ACC player, told me that, "Oh man. [Referee] loves me, man. We talked about [a small town they were both from] all the time, every game we have, because you were an underdog, bro. . . . You were a player who didn't have a scholarship, who earned a scholarship just from his hometown. We can be proud of that." But I'm an entitled motherfucker. I'm a big entitled guy, that's why I made it, not because I worked hard. He don't look at me the same way he looks at you, especially as a Black man.
 But I, as a Black man, don't look at [the referee] that way because he has a fucking gold tooth. No respectable Black man has a gold tooth, especially with all the stigma that goes with stuff like that. He gets to be a hip-hop, gold tooth, Jerry curl–having, this goddamn referee. But as soon as one of them players show their urban culture, they're a 'me first' player. They're this, they're that, right?

Charlie Rogers experienced less overtly racist dynamics: "It was really just, indirect. Like, coaches talking about some of the Black players, and their demeanor, how they carry themselves. Like, 'Who does he think he is.' Yeah like, 'Who does this n***a think he is?' pretty much. They never really said the n-word. I've never heard him say it, or anything like outwardly racist. But it was all like microaggressions. And you could see that the only reason that they're around this many Black people is because they make 'em millions of dollars."

For Kane Holden, teammates who were close to the coaching staff, as well as coaches themselves, all contributed to the plantation dynamics in the locker room:

DS: Were the senior players almost acting like pseudocoaches or acting on behalf of the coaching staff?

HOLDEN: Yeah. I would say that they themselves saw themselves as an extension of the coaching staff. My former coach, again, our position coach, we shared the same position coach. He wasn't outwardly racist, you could say, but he did things that you could probably say were. . . . It seemed like he was. There was an example of one time where he brought up politics in the middle of a meeting and started talking about just very, I would say, racial topics in terms of segregation or even police brutality, things like that. And we also had a couple of Black players in the room too. And to me it seemed like they were just very uncomfortable being there, talking about it or even hearing about it, especially from one person's perspective they may not necessarily agree with. And then there were times where he would do things that were very violent and very aggressive. He would show videos of a goat getting shot in the head. . . . Random things like that. And he would just talk about how that could be one of you right there as the goat. And it was just things like that where it's just you were kind of owned. It's like, "I own you" kind of thing. So I can see how maybe those seniors thought themselves as the extension where they felt like they're in a position of authority as a senior.

DS: That example with the coach talking about segregation and police brutality, do you remember what he was saying? Any specifics?

HOLDEN: There was this former Baltimore police officer that came out. I think he did an episode on . . . *60 Minutes* or something like that. He did some documentary about detailing the brutality of cops in the city of Baltimore and their profiling measures and things like that. And then it turned into a conversation about, is this stuff even real? Do cops really even do this? It's like you're always going to have a bad few apples in your batch or whatever. And it's just some of the common misperceptions or common, I would say, arguments that people tend to have with that conversation. But then again, though, no one was ever disagreeing with him because then again, there's that fear factor where it's like, if I disagree then what's going to happen to me?

Daniel Barber added that, despite the fact that many players used marijuana regardless of race, coaches often used drug testing to target Black players:

It's [marijuana use] widespread. I mean, the whole [Pac-12 school] team uses it. You can probably look at it, there's a disproportionate amount of African Americans that end up suffering from this. It's a good way to get rid of your Black players. I mean, white players smoke too but [shrugs], you know. I was talking to one of my former teammates and he was like, "Yeah, it's a zero-tolerance policy. . . . The new head coach for [SEC school] hates weed," and I'm like, "I know [another player], who was a four- or five-star recruit tested positive. Like, his third or fourth time, tested positive." [Shrugs] They don't care. They use it to, I guess, keep them from some things. And it's weird, because someone else who tested positive . . . running back. He's gone. He got kicked off the team, off of it. So it is subjective. But that is one of the underhanded ways marijuana testing [is used] to get rid of players.

Sometimes coaches reproduce a racist logic assuming natural Black athleticism—an idea tied to dehumanizing historical fabrications linking Blackness with the animal, which justify via the idea of 'natural proclivity' forms of brutal forced labor (i.e., slavery). Daniel Barber explains,

There are plenty of light-skins. I'm light-skinned. So I'm Black and white. And I've grown in a mixed household, I have mixed family members so, yeah, that's the thing that probably helped me get any insight. But I know during my recruiting [by another school], [gestures a phone call], "Hey, you hit pretty good for a light-skin. Oh yeah, I thought you were white for a minute and then you were moving too well." And I've never had a conversation with this man. And I'm sure he's still in the industry, like he was at [another school], but he was a defensive coordinator.

The racist logic that Black players are naturally predisposed to superior athleticism can also have negative implications for white players. Barber points out, "I mean, they suffer from stuff too like, 'Oh, you aren't a Black player. You aren't athletic. Fuck you. You're just here. You're just a body for me to use in practice.'" Additionally, Barber found that the racial dynamics in football were distinctly classed, so that Black people employed by the athletic department in positions of power consolidated that power at the expense of the Black athletes subordinate to them on the football team. He said of Black figures of authority on his team and in his athletic department: "They made me realize not all kinfolk is kinfolk. They screwed me over like anyone else. They don't care. They aren't here to help Black athletes like they say they are. They don't care, at all."

Coaches are not the only figures in the college football world who reproduce plantation dynamics at the level of social interaction. Sometimes the problem is with athletic trainers, a particularly significant issue since athletes are beholden to trainers for crucial medical care and that medical relationship should be predicated on a basic level of trust. Barber describes how trainers had "Fox News on, when they're treating [players]. Which, I think is a conflict of interest, like you're treating majority Black athletes, and there's the whole thing with medical people, not respecting [Black people's] pain, like them having a 'higher pain tolerance.'" Importantly, Barber underlines how racism is institutionalized in US medicine and manifests through a logic that Black people have more capacity to absorb pain, a dehumanizing assumption connected to the notion of Blackness as animal. For Barber, trust was compromised in his dealings with the mostly white trainers, thus undermining the quality of his care.

Some players noted that the plantation dynamics of college football manifested through the preferential treatment afforded to white players. Charlie Rogers explains:

[Redacted school] is kind of a different place. They really value their white boys. Because on any good team, their starting O-line [offensive line] would be consisting of maybe one white person, but the rest are all Black. They brought me, and that other friend that's at [Group of Five school] that I mentioned.[18] He's also like 6'8". His arms were even longer than mine. He was stronger than I was. And neither of us saw the field or had a chance to see the field. We were the only two Black people that he recruited, or that he got to get to the school. And the only other one, he was already there with the other coaching staff, before the one that recruited me. So it was out of twenty people, it was three Black people. And we were all ridiculed. There would just be a lot of stuff that we just simply couldn't relate to. Like, my friend, he's a Black man from [redacted region], and the coach would try to relate to him about shit like hunting, and stuff like that. You knew this guy was not on your side. And, yeah, and the other Black guy . . . he's from the South. You know, they think a little different over there. They kind of let some of that stuff slide. Like being from [city in California] and growing up on the [Black] Panthers and stuff, you can't not notice that type of shit. And I remember we had to do these speeches to let the O-line room know about yourself. And one of the guys, he was pretty much saying some racially motivated things about the defense. Because, in football, Black people weren't allowed to play offense at first. And so, it's still kind of like that. It's racially, and on a kind of intellect level, you could tell the difference between the offensive and defensive player, for the most part, generally speaking. But he was saying how every time they would get a stop, he hates how much they're screaming and dancing, and pretty much, how Black people would generally celebrate doing well in football. Instead of keeping a stick in the ass, like, 'alright, let's do it again,' you know, type shit."

Brock Adler also saw favoritism toward white players:

[Player A] is an example of a player who was a Black player, who may have had an attitude issue, yes, but then, [Player B], who is a good player, but [Player A] was a great player too, who went to [Big 12 school] and did great. [Head coach] replaced him with [Player B] and a lot of other white guys on the team who played. I was Black. . . . But in talking racial dynamics, you know, certain positions, like yes, they play a lot of Black players, but they don't understand what it's like for Black players. I mean, [coach] messaged all of us, Black D-linemen [defensive linemen] during the George Floyd incident, "Oh I can't imagine what it's like for you right now, I'm sorry," and that stuff, and we just thought in the back of our mind, "Man, we don't know George Floyd." I mean, it's a horrible situation, but you feel obligated because of guilt, right now? As for the racial dynamic, I would say that there was a favoritism towards white players.

Favoritism not only manifests in football-related affairs; it can also affect opportunities once careers end. Daniel Barber elaborates:

> The boosters will give [white players] jobs way quicker than Black dudes. They'll watch [Black players] on Saturday, but they don't want to give you a job on Sunday. So, like, it's a big problem. That's one of the reasons I didn't go to state schools is because you got to rely on the booster network, in a lot of instances. Like, your degree doesn't carry as much weight, and it turns into a subjective thing, you aren't going to get helped out. So [at school], we watched bankers, people just hire the white boys. It's just a big issue of your worth outside of football.

Networking opportunities, that is, social capital per Pierre Bourdieu, accrued via participation in the 'family' of the college football team, are *supposedly* a form of compensation players receive for their work (instead of monetary compensation).[19] If these opportunities are systematically denied to Black players, this is racist exploitation.

Chapter 5 makes clear that drug testing is a central apparatus in college football of status coercion. It allows coaches to rescind scholarships, particularly given that marijuana use is pervasive in college football. Thus, the targeted use of drug testing against Black players should be viewed as a racialized form of surveillance, discipline, and coercion serving a racialized political economy of value extraction. Josh Hansen explains the different standard for white and Black players in terms of drug use:

> When it relates to who is punished and what is punishable, I'll give you [an] example. I done been at parties where white dudes on the team done did some stuff that they will get in major trouble for. But when it comes to Black dudes and weed, from a standpoint of drugs, that is like the greatest sin almost, is with drugs and Black athletes and things of that nature. So when it came to punishment, I'll never forget one of my teammates. He did weed. But he didn't flaunt it, it was like his thing that he did, by himself, on his own time. It kept him straight, mentally. It kept him straight, emotionally. . . . He struggled mentally and emotionally. He needed something to keep him grounded and going. That would be kind of beyond the structure of the locker room, or the dynamics of the kind of equities of power that is college football, coaches, and things like that. And like, you got to perform, everything is about what you do on the field, and things like that. Well, my boy [ended] up getting dismissed from the team. And

without them being concerned about getting him the proper help that he needs.

Marijuana use in college football is a tool for managing physical and mental distress and anguish *directly produced by the sport*. This fact is widely known in team cultures, including among coaches, which is why it is so striking that coaches choose to actively regulate Black players for their use of the drug. Kurt Weiss explains this dynamic further:

> I tried marijuana. I wasn't a marijuana smoker, or edibles. I didn't take edibles really ever, for that reason of coping with the stress and pain of football. I think it's a good coping mechanism. It's certainly better than the alternative of painkillers. I also think culturally, like a lot of African American teammates smoke. It's just more culturally prevalent to smoke. And I had one teammate from Jamaica and he and his family would smoke weed together at night in high school. And so there's a few things at play. I think players do it to manage stress and pain. I think more so my Black teammates than my white teammates just were around weed all their lives. So it's a convenient leverage point for the industry and for the department if they ever want to use it to their advantage.

A primary virtue of sport, we are often told, is that it brings us together. The locker room, in that telling, is a place of integration—the authentic realization of America as a multicultural project. We are sold this narrative through films like *Remember the Titans* (even as the school depicted remains as segregated or more segregated today than it was at the time the film was set). This is also the story told about college football. Yet players revealed to us that much as the promise of the civil rights movement and full integration is illusory for America more broadly, so too is it overstated in the locker room. Kevin Brown explains:

> I was [an] anomaly in the sense that there definitely was clique-ish in a sense, and it wasn't directly open, like it was just this thing in which my roommate, I mean he's my brother from another mother, we come from two totally different life experiences, but yet we're pretty much the same person. We got dropped in our freshman year together, didn't even know each other, but boom we just hit it off great, and, so I definitely ran around, if you will, I didn't view it this way, with the majority of the Black guys on the team. Again, the majority of the whole team is Black. But there was times from other white teammates of mine that would say

something to me, like, "Stop acting like that," I'm like, "What are you talking about, acting like what?" and it was pulling from experiences that I was imitating in a joking way that they somehow thought it was me trying to, I guess, appropriate their culture. But I was definitely accepted, and now that you bring this up, there were at least a handful of white guys that still to this day, majority of the teammates just don't jive with. I don't jive with them either. I didn't view it as, "Hey I'm hanging out with all Black guys," until it was brought to my attention, and I was like, "They're your teammates too, why does it matter?"

Josh Hansen also meditates on this theme:

When people always say "the locker room is a microcosm of what America can be," I don't know if y'all have ever heard that? There's this kind of idea woven into the 'national myth,' and I'm thinking myth as like, not just something that's untrue or a false statement, but like a story that gives us meaning. So the kind of national myth about college football is that the locker room, much like what people say about the military, that the locker room is what America truly is and can become. When in actuality, so much of the racial narratives and realities are reinforced. We may shower together, we may play together, but oftentimes once we leave, we walk into very different realities and even those realities that we already live into, you know as being athletes, are already very much segregated. You go into these locker rooms and if you don't see and know it, you're going to feel the racial divide, as it relates to you. Like, who's going over to whose house, and who's hanging out with who outside of that.

Hansen indexes the superficiality of college football integration. While white and Black players may work (that is, experience exploitation) in the same spaces as an occupational requirement, this in no way sutures the cleavages between them in their lives outside football, lives they return to after leaving the field. Aaron Peters was frustrated by white players on his team performing solidarity with Black Lives Matter in 2020 despite previously behaving in racially problematic ways. He said of white players prior to 2020:

They're not speaking out on anything, they're not going to say anything, they're not going to be like, "Yeah bro, I understand how you feel." Yeah, it's funny, because after I leave, I see a lot of my same teammates saying Black Lives Matter, and I'm like, "Bro, you've witnessed countless players be disrespected. You've witnessed countless players [be talked to] like they're animals." And now it's, my life matter[s] or something like that. Come on. Miss me with that. That's the type of stuff that I would say. "Why are you even marching? Last year, you said X, Y, Z. Or just last year, you did X, Y, Z. So now, don't march just because they make you."

For Josh Hansen, an additional dynamic is at play in the relationship between Black athletes on campus and other Black students:

There is an inherent difference between Black [school] and Black student-athlete [school]. . . . My wife, who was my girlfriend at the time, we dated while we were at [school]. And my wife is Black. And the things she would tell me about like [school] is that Black [school] experience was much different than us. So, like, even though we in this kind of racist experience as a Black athlete on a white campus, the white supremacy that everyday Black students experienced and that we were shielded from, is a reality simply because we're athletes. Like Study Hall, and the help that we get, as well as the support we get simply because we're Black athletes. But, then, also how we are weaponized against Black [school]. It's almost like we're separated from them. So everything is separated. So it's this inherent division that we live in. So we're different. Like, the message, the underlying script is, "Yo, you're better than them," and things like that.

Black football players, as members of the campus community with relative status, were treated with more respect than their nonathlete Black peers. This is a window into a PWI's dynamics and a racist campus culture: Black athletes are told to avoid other Black students, whose "Blackness," it is clearly implied, would somehow tarnish the athletes.

In contrast, some white players denied the presence of racism. Matt Jenson told us, "I didn't really observe a lot of racial dynamics. Thankfully, I mean, there wasn't any institutional racism that I noticed. I think for the most part, everybody was very good about treating people equally, respectfully, at least from a racial standpoint. I think, for the most part, it wasn't troubling from that point. There was nothing that really shocked me that people were being, you know, racist or anything like that. For the most part, people were very respectful and very cordial in that respect."

Similarly, Ryan Leonard said:

I have talked to players that feel that they weren't played because the coach was white and he's Black and he feels like abused, he feels like he was lied to, he feels like he's been persecuted against, prejudiced by the coach because of race, but in terms of seeing evidence for that, I truly believe that's not the case and I might be naive, I might be ignorant to it, but I believe that was a hurt human being that fell upon that because of the emotions involved of not being played, of being guaranteed a spot, being told you are going to be the next greatest thing, and then once you get on campus, you are treated an entirely different way than when you were being recruited.

Although it's possible there wasn't as much racism at these institutions, the likelier reality is that these denials show how normalized racist dynamics are and how difficult they are to spot for those benefiting from them.

Conclusion: The Academic Plantation

We have focused on the racialized experiences of college athletes on the football side. But campus athletic workers are also students, and their primary compensation for athletic work is their education. Any compromise of their academic experience by racist dynamics is a racialized form of wage theft — part of the racial transfer of wealth. The function of race in capitalism as a tool for reproduction puts the "structure" in structural racism: race fragments the solidarity of the working class, thus allowing for the reconsolidation and reproduction of the exploitation that makes capitalism operate.[20]

The plantation dynamics of college sport operate through the production of Blackness as difference/otherness/outsiderness, undermining the potential for labor solidarity both on college football teams and among students/faculty/players on campus. These potentially natural alliances do not form because Black athletes are seen to 'not belong' in PWI spaces, which is articulated in myriad racist (ideological) ways (i.e., assumptions about cultural difference or lack of academic preparation) that fundamentally serve a political economic project to extract value and consolidate coaches' and administrators' power. A key way this manifests for Black athletes is simply feeling othered on PWI campuses, where Black students make up a disproportionately small number of students. Steven Summers explains:

I feel like it's less overt, where they're saying like, "You don't deserve to be here." But it's more like, you get a look, and you're like, "All right, I can kind of feel—" or like, I know a lot of my friends. . . . I don't know the numbers exactly, but basically the vast majority of Black students at [previous school] are either on the football or basketball team. And they would be like, "Yeah, I can tell when I'm walking around campus, I'm looking around, and I'm the only Black person. In a group of a hundred people or whatever. Yeah, I definitely get some looks. Because I stick out in this crowd. It's like, I have my [team] men's basketball backpack on, and I feel like I get stereotyped," and I'm like, "Damn, I can see that." You can walk around, and even the white guys on the team, like the dudes that are huge, walking around through a crowd. . . . I could see [them] getting some looks. Like, it's not necessarily always hateful, but it's just kind of like, you feel a little tense. Especially in social settings, like going to the bars and stuff. Walking around, it might be dark out, and [if we] see a group of chicks and we're just like, "Okay, maybe we should cross the street so they don't feel like we're being like scary or whatever." So you need to kind of feel it out sometimes.

C. J. White had a similar experience:

Once I got [to school], it was a little bit intimidating from a class standpoint, but also from a cultural standpoint, because it was a different culture than what I was used to. And there were times where you could kind of feel and sense some kind of racial barrier where I felt like some of the students just knew that the group of Black guys were part of the athletic realm at the school. But I would say for the most part, I don't think that my race had much to do with the academic experience here. But I was saying that first part to say this, when I came here, I didn't spend a lot of time on campus. . . . [School] is right down the road [laughs], that was a historically Black college and university, and that was similar to the environment that I grew up in, me as well as other guys. . . . Any free time we had, we would go over to [historically Black college and university] and hang out a little bit over there, just kind of get the culture that we were used to.

Ryan Leonard, although white, noted the pervasive assumption that Black athletes were only on PWI campuses because of their athletic aptitudes: "There are some institutions . . . if you see a Black person on campus, you automatically know it's an athlete. He's here because he plays sports, and unfortunately, the stigma comes with it that these athletes are here not because they are smart enough to be here, but because they play sports." Charlie Rogers felt jealousy fueled some of the animus toward Black players: "It's pretty much jealousy, and all the little frat boys that don't like the big Black players because you know we quote unquote take their women that they're going to try to get drunk and have sex with without their consent, you know, some shit like that. . . . They're mad that they will consent to us and not to them. It was, pretty much, you're kind of ridiculed. But I found my way around it. But yeah, for the most part, people didn't generally like us."

Terry Davis experienced this sense of being othered viscerally: "You go into this environment and you're charged up. [White members of the university community] are like, 'Oh, Godzilla. King Kong. You're the thing that doesn't belong here. You make us less safe because clearly you're not about to play by the rules of being talked down to and treated as a lesser.'" Ronnie Exeter had a similar recollection: "Anytime we were out or anything like that, people might want to get macho and stuff like that. I hate to think about it, I hate to say it was race, but of course, a lot of the times, it was a lot of us being provoked. Mainly campus life, just different colleagues or classmates treating us different. Like I said, it was really a scale. If we win, it was always good. If we lost, it was pretty nasty." For Josh Hansen, that sense of being out of place was most palpable at moments of national racial crisis:

> If you were like me, somebody who was not really trying to [push] against the system, then you won't feel the whiteness of [school], until something like Trayvon Martin happens. And you feel the response. When Trayvon happened and athletes wanted to stand in solidarity, you know, the coaches . . . it was like they were reluctant to do that. And it wasn't "a team thing." So when George Floyd happens, and now it becomes advantageous for college coaches to be seen as not racist or to be seen as inclusive, then they'll say, "Okay, let's put together a demonstration." But during Trayvon Martin, when you didn't have that same clout, it was a "distraction" and then they distanced themselves. "Y'all, this is something y'all could do. It's not something I'm going to speak out on, or do anything about."

Then there is the question of faculty. We firmly believe that faculty owe all their students who are campus athletic workers a duty of care and responsibility given the exploitation they are subjected to in their athletic role. Yet, too often, faculty are responsible for reproducing plantation dynamics by making Black athletes feel like they do not belong in the PWI classroom. Daniel Barber chose not to wear team-issued gear to class because he worried about the treatment he might receive from his teachers as a consequence: "I tried to avoid it, at least for the first couple days. I was like, 'I want to make an impression of me, and not necessarily my teammates or what they know from what's going on over there,' which a lot of the professors who didn't have experience at other universities, and are strictly academia, like, kind of slighted you. There were professors that we knew not to take [courses with] and might take some cultural things completely wrong, because they don't interact with Black people."

Although white, Chris Andrews noted that some faculty "had some preconceived notions of what it meant to be a football player and so I think that oftentimes the color of somebody's skin and the size of them would lead a professor to believe that that person was a college athlete and they were treated differently." Charlie Rogers noted how white special teams players would overhear faculty comment about Black players being overly privileged and then impose draconian conditions in syllabi meant to penalize them: "Some of the special teams players who look a little more regular would hear them just like talking about how we get all this stuff and 'they don't try that hard in class.' A lot of the syllabi would specifically say, 'If you miss a test, there's no exceptions,' especially for games and shit. You just knew that was charged towards athletes that had to travel every week." He euphemistically refers to white players as "look[ing] a little more regular" and Black players as those who "had to travel every week," terminology speaking to both the normative status of whiteness in that PWI space and the extent to which the commodity spectacle, or value of college football, was being produced by Black players.

Sometimes these dynamics play out in absurd but revealing ways, such as when faculty make the assumption that all Black students on campus *must* be athletes and act accordingly. Daniel Barber relayed one such situation: "Any Black person in a class, who is male, or even female, because there are other female sports too, essentially, you're on a team. Like, straight up. I mean, there have been Black regular students who have had issues in the classroom. Guess who gets a call? Coaches. Coaches get a call. It's like, 'We don't fucking know him!' [Laughs]"

Aaron Peters contended that academic clustering targeted Black players specifically:

Look at the Black athletes on the team. A lot of them went to the NFL and stuff like that. But for the guys that didn't, keep track of what we went to school for. Check what other guys are going to school for. We had good resources and everything. But . . . basically, a lot of us were pushed to do African American studies, sociology, psychology, right? I know when I came in, I wanted to do computer science.

I thought, yeah, it was going to be hard, but . . . it still should have been the same amount of time. . . . But all the swimmers, majority white. Baseball players, majority white. Fencing. Any sport but football and basketball, where it's not majority Black, ask them what they're going to school for. I had a 25 on the ACT, like, took it one time. So clearly I wasn't dumb. But it's like, they don't care. You're here for football, you're going to play football. We don't want you here [otherwise].

The dynamics with campus law enforcement are also notable in a society marred by racial profiling and systematic police violence against racialized people. Ross Nielsen explains how police racially profiled Black college football players, treating them as trophies, even as the team exercised power and status to extricate players from legal troubles:

Essentially, two players at one point were arrested for being super intoxicated in one season. And [coach] had his assistants text everybody for an emergency meeting. . . . One player was intoxicated and tried to evade the police, and was tackled by the police. And [coach] was like, "Our star player can't outrun a stumpy, donut-fueled cop . . . he runs probably like a six flat forty [yards]. What do you run, like four-six, and he outran your drunk ass?" And he was like, "But I don't really care because the cops are your enemies . . . you're like a trophy to them, they're out to get you." And, yeah, especially at [school], it's very bad. I think a lot of things happen with the football team and the university, and the criminal justice level that are. . . . I think a lot of players and a lot of coaches are able to get away with a lot of stuff that the average citizen would not because they played football at [school] in that town. And it's ingrained in the culture at, public-eye level, and then also where the political elites reside in that town.

While exploitation is foundational to college football, the racialized nature of that exploitation—the plantation dynamics—makes it morally intolerable. Given the history of US society being built on accumulation via the forced extraction of value from racialized people, and the ongoing reproduction of that history through a century and a half of transfigurations, the plantation dynamics in college football are symptomatic of a structure in desperate need of remediation. But the racism of college football is not an anomaly. It is a product of racial capitalism, and as such, the solutions require a transformation of racial capitalism itself and reparation for the harm done.

In the 2018–19 academic year, Power Five universities collectively generated $8.3 billion in revenue through athletics.[21] Yet, aside from scholarships, players don't see any of that money directly and most players systematically denied the revenue they are responsible for generating are Black or otherwise racialized. Based on the NCAA's own figures, at the PWIs that comprise the Power Five, as of the 2019–20 season, Black students comprised only 5.7 percent of the population, yet Black athletes made up 55.7 percent of men's football rosters. At revenue-darling schools like Texas A&M, the disparity is particularly striking. Despite Black students representing only 3.1 percent of the general student body, its football team was 75 percent Black. At the University of Georgia, the fifth-highest revenue producer at the time, although the school boasted a slightly higher Black student population at 7.5 percent than the Power Five average, 74.1 percent of men's football players were Black. At the conference level, in the SEC, for example, while the overall percentage of Black students was higher (8.4 percent), so too was the disproportionate reliance on Black campus athletic workers in revenue sports. It is hard to deny from these numbers that Black athletes are disproportionately admitted into institutions that otherwise largely foreclose access specifically to have their labor exploited for the universities' gain.

These numbers are even more galling given the number of racist incidents that occur on campuses across the country.[22] When University of Texas Longhorns football players left the field during the singing of "The Eyes of Texas" in fall 2021 because of what they called its "racial undertones," wealthy alumni threatened to pull donations and spammed the university with racist vitriol. Consequently, players were told that if they did not stay on the field during the song, they could lose access to job opportunities after graduation.[23] Earlier that year, Creighton University men's basketball head coach Greg McDermott admitted that he casually demanded players "stay on the plantation" in a postgame locker room talk. Although he claimed to have offered to resign, the university refused to accept the offer, presumably due to his success. Players spoke out against McDermott, with Shereef Mitchell powerfully saying, "For slaves, life on a plantation was filled with mental, emotional, physical, psychological and sexual abuse. You were owned as property and not human . . . they were branded like cattle," with teammate Denzel Mahoney adding, "What Coach Mac said hurt me and my teammates."[24] In 2021 in Tennessee, GOP (Republican) state lawmakers called on universities across the state to prohibit athletes from engaging in (antiracist) protest during the national anthem.[25] The Northwestern football hazing scandal in 2023 revealed an alleged culture of racism in the football program, including reports that a Latinx player was assumed to be good at cleaning and that Black players were called "monkeys" and told to change their hairstyles.[26] These incidents ultimately caused one player to be diagnosed with posttraumatic stress disorder. Each of these cases offers just a hint of the too-often veiled racist climate Black athletes endure on campuses across the country—a climate that is part and parcel of a broader system of racial capitalism structuring the political economy of the United States.

Using a lens of racial capitalism to explore the world of college football reveals how disproportionate opportunity, inequitable resource extraction and distribution, and racialized power hierarchies shaping US society also shape the day-to-day lifeworld of college football players. Observing college football through the prism of racial capitalism forces us to confront the troubling reality that the sport is an extension of the same white supremacy embedded in US society through the historical and ongoing existence of colonialism, slavery, and racialized resource extraction. And if college football is part of that history, it's long past time for change. Power Five revenue sport is saturated in plantation dynamics that essentially amount to forms of unfreedom for Black workers laboring to earn revenue for white institutions and the predominantly white officials governing them. No matter what label we use—racism, white supremacy, or a new plantation—that is what big-time college football is, and it is exactly what a lot of wealthy, powerful white people want it to be.

CHAPTER FIVE

They Signed Up for It

Coercion and Consent in College Football

"Something happened before my junior year," Aaron Peters told us, visibly upset:

> I didn't truly understand what I was getting myself into from an academic standpoint, and even a football standpoint. . . . I played a little as a freshman, then I didn't play enough. Sophomore year wasted some time. So, it was like, okay, I'm going to leave. I'm not from [city]. My family never comes to the game because everything is so far. Flying in and out of the [local airport] is very expensive for us. I just wanted to go back home. I told my coaches. And they sat me in the office for like, three days straight. Like, "This is the worst decision you're making. You have a very important role on the team. We really want you to stay. This is not a good idea." I wanted to transfer. Ultimately, after having the discussion with my parents, I decided to stay. But I feel like deciding to stay after telling everybody I wanted to leave kind of left a sour taste in everyone's mouth. . . . My junior year, I think I played less than I did during my freshman [year], which is crazy. But my production was a lot more. But they still didn't play me as much as I wanted. But at the end of the season . . . right before the bowl game . . . coach sent me a text like, "Can you meet me in my office?"

What happened next left a lasting mark on Peters:

> [The coach] just told me that, basically, "We don't want you here anymore." I'm shocked. I'm like, no, this doesn't make any sense. I could have left last year when I wanted to. I'll use the term "clean myself up," because that's when I really locked in on school, locked in on football . . . I could feel myself growing up. . . . [One coach] told me to leave. The coaches that recruited me were there. My position coach was there. And they really couldn't say much. The coach gave me a whole bunch of reasons of why, trying to use academics. But I

was like, "How could you use academics, I'm doing well in class?" . . .
I'm just trying to plead my case. They're like, "Okay, if you don't leave,
we'll call the police." And I'm just like, "What?!"

By pushing him out when they did, the coaching staff not only compromised
his athletic career at a Power Five school, they also essentially cost him the
ability to transfer as a graduate, which he could have done if he remained
enrolled for another semester. This would have allowed him immediate
eligibility and presumably the right to earn his degree at a prestigious
school. Although Peters had been on a full-year scholarship—the de facto
compensation promised in return for his football labor—he was not permitted to redeem the second half of that year, costing him tens of thousands of
dollars in tuition that he had earned. As Peters saw it, his unceremonious
firing was influenced by much more than football or even academics.

> I've never had a DUI. I was just outspoken on the team. I think it's so
> funny that the things that got you suspended out of school are things
> that are acceptable now. Like when we had the George Floyd thing,
> teams, everybody was doing the whole Black Lives Matter thing [holds
> up fist in resistance]. But when I was in school, being outspoken, it
> was like, "Nah, say what we want you to say. You can say what you
> want, but not too much." At that time, me saying, "Oh, no, we're more
> than football players. We should have a say so. We should have this,
> we should have that." The way I went about it, not cussing out coaches
> or anything, but not having a filter . . . just saying it . . . right before
> I left, I sat down with some guy . . . and he was just asking questions,
> like, "The guys on the team, they have a lot of respect for you . . .
> why is that?" [I respond,] "I don't know. They just respect me. I say
> things that should be said." [He replies,] "Okay, okay. Well, the
> coaches are kind of wary about that." [I said,] "Why? I'm not saying
> anything wrong." [He replied,] "Yeah, true, but still."

Coaches have immense power in controlling not only the current playing
and working conditions of college football players, but also their *future*
socioeconomic potential. Perhaps the single most popular and pervasive
rhetorical defense for the current college football system is that "they signed
up for it." In other words, all manner of exploitation and harm is justified in
a situation consented to by participants. While the question of authentic
consent to harm and exploitation is complex, we are not forced to confront

it today, because that is not the reality experienced by college football players. Still, apologists for the system, leaning on rickety consent-based arguments for college football, are onto something: a theoretical and empirical exploration of coercion and consent are required to fully unpack the illegitimacy of the system. Consent in big-time college football operates only in the most formal sense—players do sign documentation acknowledging their willingness to participate. Yet when considered in the context of structural constraints on players' agency, it becomes difficult to deny that the concrete reality and defining feature of this world is coercion.

Structural and status coercion work in concert to constrain players' agency and subject them to exploitation and harm. We build on Erin Hatton's argument that college football is defined by status coercion, or the power of coaches to determine access to the limited resources available—scholarships and playing time—by arguing that status coercion is in turn informed by structural coercion.[1] Coaches' monopoly over cherished forms of capital compels players to submit to exploitative conditions they might otherwise reject. The fundamental inaccessibility of higher education, and the dream that participation in football might lead to socioeconomic mobility in the context of a punishing system of racial capitalism, effectively requires players to submit to coaches' discipline and control.

Status coercion, as Hatton demonstrates, is a defining feature of college sport, accounting for why players *must* act in accordance with their coaches' demands, no matter how unpleasant or unreasonable: "For [college] athlete workers, the primary threat is not that they will lose their jobs, though that may also be of concern. Rather, it is what might happen to their bodies, families, and futures if they refuse to comply with their bosses' demands."[2] This accounts for the specific nature of the power dynamics that operate in the world of college athletics. Hatton expands on status coercion: "The type of coercion that permeates [college athlete] labor does not operate through either pecuniary or corporal mechanisms. Rather, it operates through status. Their supervisors have the power to discharge them from a particular status—as prisoner, welfare recipient, college athlete, or graduate student 'in good standing'—and thereby deprive them of the rights, privileges, and future opportunities that such status confers."[3] While "status coercion" captures the punitive ways power is wielded in Power Five college football, we argue that it should be paired with the additional formulation *structural coercion* because it captures how status coercion relies on a broader system of racial capitalism that produces the necessary conditions of privation, immiseration, and discrimination that render individual subjects vulnerable to status coercion. Why succumb to the status coercion of college sport unless one's body/family/future, to borrow Hatton's framing, is not already constrained through privation and lack of access? Thus, unlike the prison, where the institution itself imposes maximal coercion, the structural coercion of racial capitalism is a necessary precondition for the status coercion of college football. Without it, one might simply opt out.

We draw on the term "structural coercion" from Jill Fisher, who argues in the context of informed consent in medical research that we must understand the capacity of an individual to consent to participation to be influenced by power dynamics beyond the individual relationship with the researcher. For Fisher, these factors include the political economy of US health care, a system that often enacts violence on individual actors by producing impossible choices between health and economic harm. Fisher writes, "Structural coercion occurs primarily outside of the research clinic, yet shapes the ways in which potential participants perceive the researchers and institutions, as well as how they interpret information about specific studies."[4] This is why status coercion is contingent on structural coercion: it relies on a subject *already* constrained by forms of material violence that foreclose a range of agential choices. Fisher's medical context is also instructive for college football because the most egregious form of harm there is to health. For all the injustice in the economic exchange between the college football player and the university, the full measure of the exploitation can only be understood through a focus on the inherent physical sacrifice involved. Consent to this sacrifice is directly analogous to informed consent in medical research (and, as we shall see, often literally involves consent to medical research) because it is a process of signing one's body over for physical harm, knowing it will occur but hoping it will be outweighed by potential benefits. Yet these benefits are only benefits because of the structural conditions in which they are offered. Were a university education and robust economic opportunity freely available in US society, regardless of racial, economic, or gender status, the choice to participate in the physical rigors of college football would have a radically different cast. There would be *no material benefits at all* to counterweight the profound risk, beyond ephemeral pleasure or love of the game.

Coercion is a defining feature of college football. While there may be putative freedom to choose whether to participate, that freedom is constrained by coercive dynamics—something players understand better than anyone. "It's a choice, but it's a Hobson's choice," Kurt Weiss said. "Would you rather

jump off a tower or eat glass? Like, give me the glass, but I don't enjoy it."
Or as Chris Andrews characterized it,

> As I get older I start to understand the disturbing wealth and power
> between different groups of people within our country, and so you can
> say, "Yeah, we signed up for it," but there are also protections in place
> to make sure that too much power isn't accumulated in one area and so
> that's why everyone thinks that, "Oh college sports is so much differ-
> ent, it's not like a T-Mobile and Sprint merger where antitrust laws
> kick in," it's exactly the same to me. It's a business. If antitrust law is
> applied to college sports that is the way I think it should be. You can't
> have these little carveouts just because it's convenient and just because
> this disparity in power has existed for such a long period in time.

Yet this is hardly the prevalent sentiment in popular culture. It is rare to
hear players speak publicly about issues of inequity in the world of college
football. Why? The answer comes right back to coercion: speech is a form
of freedom, and if there are direct material consequences that can result from
speaking the truth, it is reasonable to assume in most cases that it will not
be spoken. Former Ohio State cornerback Marcus Williamson offers a perfect illustration of what happens when players do speak the truth. In a
Twitter thread, he explained his reading of the injustice of college football
(@WW_Marcus, January 1, 2022):

> Ask ANY college athlete if they can take their studies as serious as they
> need with our athletic schedules. Most won't understand. . . .
> Participate in your lecture/discussion in your 8 a.m. class after a mat
> drill at 6 a.m. (arrive at 5 if you're a freshman). . . . PROFESSOR My
> hands are bleeding from the rope pull but you want me to grab my
> pencil?? . . . I was repeatedly pushed past my injuries as if I was
> completely expendable. (You are). 2018 I used to wake up, put my
> shoulder in place . . . & go to practice. They bandage u up like shit
> sweet. . . . The industry is often silent because everyone is obviously
> chasing the big pay day. But the injustices these players face just isn't
> right. We literally put our bodies and lives at risk with 0 guarantee. . . .
> Why don't you leave? Quit? Most of us have only been athletes our
> entire lives. This is how we try to feed our families and children. It's
> either play their game or have 0 chance at the lottery.

Williamson received considerable backlash from his testimony, which also
included a critique of racist imagery shown in a meeting by former coach

Urban Meyer's staff, including from a handful of former players. This raises an obvious question: if the system is unjust, as Williamson and the players we interviewed point out, why would other players challenge that premise publicly? Kurt Weiss offers a clear answer:

If you don't toe the line, you're ostracized. And the team is everything. The pressure to not disrupt the focus of the team, even if you're experiencing a lot of things that are unsettling, you just keep it in-house. And there's many ways in which you pay the price if you speak out on something that the team, the coach, doesn't want said. . . . The locker room is sacred in ways. And I disagree with this, and I think it's embellished. But it's like a gang, or a unit. You keep everything in-house, "What happens here, stays here," "We're all in this together," that type of thing. So when someone like Marcus Williamson speaks out, it kind of breaks that imagined circle of trust. Even if players know it's true. And I've experienced this. . . . One on one, a player will agree with me, but publicly disagree with me. And it's a little crazy-making. . . . When they're introduced to something that they know is true but can't embrace, because it would be a chink in the armor of their football story, it's just hard to hold two conflicting ideas in your mind at once and most people don't want to do that. . . . Players won't step out of line because it risks everything they've worked for . . . from your position, to money, to the coaches telling scouts that you're a trouble-maker. So you do everything you can not to upset the status quo, because though you're being exploited at the moment, there's a chance for a payoff later. You know, figuratively and literally.

Weiss observed situations in his own college career where players were punished for speaking out:

My sophomore year, there was a campuswide walkout and protest. And so, part of the paternalism of football, you have class checkers. Literally students that are hired and paid money to stand outside your class and see if you attend. And so, I was at class early, and we walked out of class, as a class, to attend the protest, and my checker marked me as missing class. And so, I was punished with time on the Stairmaster. . . . But from the coach's perspective, when a player begins to get out of line, whether that means dogging it in practice, or not watching enough film, or being distracted, whatever, the coach kind of reins him back in and reinforces what you must do.

Structural Coercion in College Football

When the choice to participate is shaped and constrained by a systemic context beyond the individual's control that forecloses options—agency—that is structural coercion. Structural forces like racial capitalism limit subjects' ability to carve out the life paths they want by unequally distributing access to resources. For instance, your opportunity to pursue higher education might be limited because your high school is under resourced, limiting the quality of the education you receive and your preparation for university. The high school is under resourced because it's in a community with a low tax base, and the community has a low tax base because of a history of slavery, segregation, white flight, and redlining. Or the opportunity to attend college might be limited, even when performance warrants access, because the cost of higher education will put your family into a lifetime of debt. Or the ability to achieve employment offering class mobility, even with a college degree, might be limited because of systematic discrimination. Given such circumstances, if there's a chance to play football and receive a free education and potential professional opportunities, it is hardly a choice at all and certainly not one that is freely made. As Theresa Runstedtler puts it in a brilliant discussion of child labor in the US athletic industrial complex: "The business of recruitment works best when it has an ever-replenishing pool of highly motivated, even desperate, youths without access to quality education and facing diminishing job prospects."[5] Indeed, it is precisely because one's agency to make *any* choice is limited that the decision to make *this* choice becomes desirable. That limitation on agency is structural coercion, and it is the fundamental condition on which the exploitation and harm of college football are predicated.

Coaches "prey on" players' desires to improve life chances for themselves and their families. Kurt Weiss explains:

> [When I stopped playing, I got] dozens and dozens of text messages like, "Bro, I would have done the same exact thing, I just can't afford to." So players, more so in the league, but also in college, are fully prepared to be sacrificial lambs to uplift their family from generations of poverty. It's like, *The Hunger Games*. And coaches prey on that. The NFL preys on that. They say, leading into the predraft process, for half a century, it's been a cliché that "We want players with PhDs—poor, hungry, desperate" . . . because they'll do whatever you say,

be a wedge buster, and play through injury. Because you know that your guy that has an engineering degree from Stanford might sit that one out.

Thomas Rycliff noted how much "pressure" is exerted on college football players trying to succeed for their families and communities:

> You're carrying kind of everybody with you. . . . *Hoop Dreams* is an interesting documentary and there's a part of it that really sticks out to me where one of the guys is talking about how, "Man, everyone comes up to me, man. 'Hey man, when you make it, don't forget about me.'" And he says, "All I can think about is if I don't make it, don't forget about me." And there is this pressure of you're the best in your area, your whole state, you're All-Area, you're All-American, you're all this. And if you're not playing then you're failing.

Ross Nielsen saw the same thing:

> You've got people who grew up with not very much money, who think that college football's like their lottery ticket . . . college football is going to absolutely liberate them. . . . My parents always provided for us, and we always had a roof over our heads. So I was actually one of the more fortunate people that I knew who played college football. But we never had hardly any spare money or anything like that. So my thing was like, "Yeah, I'm gonna play college football because my dad did. My dad barely made it to the NFL, I'm gonna play for like five years, and our family's gonna be millionaires, that's like how my life is going to go and this is my lottery ticket on the way out. I'm going to grow X and Y inches, like gain this many pounds when I start playing college football, and whole world's going to change." Like, the classic capitalism lottery ticket, like, "I'm going to get this position and everything's going to be better." And it's just so not true.

For Neilsen, the prospect of opportunity afforded by college football is the single reason the sport can reproduce itself. Without structural coercion, it simply could not exist in its current form:

> If there was no scholarship, nobody would do it. I can tell you that right now. They would pick another sport, they would play baseball, they would play soccer, they would do something. Nobody can endure the things we endured to play college football with no light at the end of the tunnel. . . . There's a light at the end of the tunnel, there's a

carrot dangling on the stick. I mean, you want to quit, every day, at some point, for an extended period of time. Everybody goes through this, and if they don't, they're lying to you. You're just like, "This is brutal, I can't physically endure this much, I'm doing twenty hours of workouts, twenty hours of practice, and doing twenty hours of film, like all my time is at the sports complex." It's very draining on you, and if there's no grand lottery ticket at the end of it waiting for you, you're not going to do that.

Wallace Bell said that if given a choice of sports to receive a scholarship for, he "would choose basketball just because it's a lot safer on your body, for sure." Charlie Rogers echoes Neilsen and Bell; without the promise of a scholarship, he would never have chosen to play football over other sports:

Fuck no. Because I played basketball my whole life. And then my high school coach started fucking with my confidence and then convinced me to play football, because I was bigger. Instead of, you know, helping me become a better basketball player. I was actually about to go to [Patriot League school] for basketball. But I turned it down because that's when I was offered by [school] for football and that was my dream school. But then, I was considering, before I signed, just saying "fuck it" and going to junior college for basketball instead of going on a full-ride scholarship to [school]. So yeah, no, I would have never played football. I would say that's probably the worst mistake I've ever made. . . . If I knew what I knew, I would have never played.

Landry West chose football over baseball for the same reason:

My younger brother is playing college football at [another school], and my dad played, had a couple uncles play. And what they would say for this is, "Football is a vehicle to get you where you want to go. And you always have to remember that." And I kept that same mentality because I was like, "This is something that I'm good at. This is going to open doors for me that may not have been open without it, and I need to do this to get where I want to be." But personally, I wanted to play baseball in college and it came down to, "Hey, my family's going to have to come out of pocket for me to play baseball." Or [if I choose football,] "My family's not going to pay a dime and they can focus on the younger siblings after me." And that was my sole focus. I was like, "I don't want to have to make my parents pay for me to go to college and just for me to be happy. It's a bigger picture." If I had a full scholarship to play baseball, I probably would've went the baseball route just from a longevity perspective, but I definitely couldn't turn down the free opportunity.

When asked about the dangers of CTE, Wallace Bell returned to the theme of structural coercion to explain why he was willing to play through risks: "It is in the back of your mind, but at the same time, we're doing this sport for our families. [For] a lot of people that look like me and other collegiate athletes who don't, this is our only way to attain a higher education and get a degree . . . we don't come from a financially stable situation where [our parents are] able to pay. . . . It's just like, let me make these sacrifices for my family."

Similarly, Josh Hansen said people play football to improve their potential for class mobility: "Where I come from, bro, like, that's one of the main ways you make it, is you play ball. If you don't play ball, you go work at the factory. You go work at the gas station. One of my high school teammates, one of the coaches who expected him to get recruited, was like, 'Yo, if you don't come here'—I think was [head coach of an SEC school]—'then you're going to be back at [home] pumping gas at gas stations.'" This was also Galen North's observation:

You have a certain subset of people, that this is their only avenue that, one, they'll ever go to college, or, two, that they perceive they will ever have the opportunity to make, you know, a lot of money. . . . You want to play whether you're injured or not . . . because this is your one shot. . . . There is a carrot in front of you that could be hundreds of millions of dollars potentially, and you have to personally ask yourself that question, "Is the risk worth that reward?" and the vast majority of the time they are people already that are playing, the answer is "Yes."

For Kurt Weiss, that structural context produces a desperation to do anything to escape: "You're gonna have to play with pulls, tears, strains, bruises, breaks, concussions. That's the game. And if you're unwilling to do that, like the poor kid from Dade County, he will. And there's kids that are fully prepared to—'die' is strong—but they'll do *anything*. Because if you avoid catastrophic injury, you might make a million bucks in three years."

The violence of structural coercion is perhaps most evident in cases where an athlete does not fulfil the promise of economic opportunity through football. Kane Holden told us about the devastating experiences of his best friend and teammate who ultimately took his own life after coaches denied him the chance to live his dream:

HOLDEN: He was a freshman whenever I was, I think, a sophomore. He was the player that came from North Carolina. He didn't have anywhere to go to during the breaks and things like that so I let him live with me. And then we became really close there. We became very close, very good friends. And when I transferred, we were still in close contact, keeping up. And it was all love. It was mutual respect, mutual love, and we were very close and then all of a sudden his playing career ended, not by injury or anything like that, but I think just the coaching. The coaches wanted to go a different direction with that position group and they benched him his last year for underclassmen. And for a guy that started multiple years and then he get[s] benched, especially since he always talked about going to the NFL and getting a good-paying job and then helping his mom get out of the hood, so to speak.

He was broken from that. He didn't know what to do. And he eventually went down a very, very dark and just very depressed path. And he got involved with other drugs and things like that and then he passed away very shortly after that. And I mean, it's insane. I know we talk about grief and trauma, but I remember exactly what I was doing, where I was when I got the text from a former professor of mine, and it was very hard. And from then there, I was going to let him in a way kind of use me as a voice, if that makes sense. At least try to tell his story for him and let him not go silent. Because in my opinion, he is just a product of this system. And he saw it as a way out. People saw him as a tool. . . . A tool to an end.

And he got thrown out in my opinion. And people allude to the fact that you have a choice. And I know you said that too in the beginning. And that's typically the rebuttal here is like, oh, it's always your choice. . . . But the thing is, it's very easy to think that when you're a position of privilege here, when you can say that you have the choice whenever there's people like him that don't necessarily know any other way or weren't ever taught any other way or know they have any other choice.

DS: Do you think football ultimately led to your friend's premature death?

HOLDEN: Absolutely. I would say so. And I would say the truth for a lot of former players.

The tension between the opportunity offered by football in a racial capitalist system that provides so few others and the costs of participation is ultimately something every participant must reconcile. So is the sport morally sustainable? We return to this question in the book's conclusion. For now, Charlie Rogers gets the final word:

DS: In your view . . . should football in general be abolished?

ROGERS: That's kind of a hard question. Because if football ceased to exist, then, for one, a lot of poor Black people wouldn't have the chance to get any sort of education. There would also be a lot less Black wealthy people. Given that the majority of the football world is Black people. So, on that hand, I would say no. But football is absolutely the worst sport ever created. Like, I would be more okay with two people just trying to kill each other in a boxing ring, because at least that happens once every few months. This is like, every day. Including practice, sometimes it'll be like, five days a week.

Status Coercion in Big-Time College Football

If the broader structural context of racial capitalism drives college football players into participation in the sport—structural coercion—coaches' power over opportunity shapes and constrains their experience once on campus. Of course, this is connected to structural coercion, for coaches' power is a direct function of the fact that they control access to future professional opportunities or, now, NIL opportunities. The point of playing college football is to ultimately access economic resources, whether in the present (NIL) or the future (pro earnings). But accessing those resources is entirely contingent on performance. The better players perform, the more promotional value they (and their team) have and the more potential value they offer to professional teams. In that sense, playing time is the ultimate form of capital in college football for players, and coaches control playing time. This is status coercion, and coaches make their power as plain as possible to players, as Ryan Leonard explains:

One of the very first things that they did there is they got us all up in the line . . . all the freshmen, and they said, "Look to the man left of you and look to the man to the right of you. By the time you leave here, both of them will be gone." And that was actually an understatement, all of us will be gone. The amount of people in my recruiting class by the fourth year was in the single digits. Very little people stuck around for long. And that speaks to coaching staff, that speaks to the dynamics of replaceable machine parts in a cogwheel that is college football.

Coaches can control players because if they withhold opportunity as punishment, then players receive essentially nothing in return for their efforts, nor do they have the realistic possibility of a professional career to compensate them for the sunk costs. This would, of course, be different if they received a genuine wage at the college level. Thus, for instance, Steven Summers said he "would do pretty much anything" to win a starting job. Nick Turner explains that coaches threatened to sabotage players with professional teams if they didn't follow orders: "'Oh, you don't want to play? You don't want to practice today? Maybe the Ravens scout will like to hear that.'" Jeremy Jones says, "[The coaches] hold all the power and I just gotta play along unless I want to quit or get kicked off the team or some shit."

A primary mechanism of status coercion in college football is surveillance. Coaches place players under near-constant surveillance to exercise power and ensure compliance. Ross Nielsen explains:

> They literally had attendance checkers for their classes . . . they couldn't do anything without the coaches hearing about it. [The players are] also in the limelight. So it's really hard for them to do any action that escapes public knowledge, in general. So it's not hard for the coaches to run a surveillance state on players because—even if you're a walk-on, you're, like, the center of attention on campus, because everybody wants to know what's happening on the team. They see you wearing that jacket or having that backpack that you got from the team and they immediately flock to you, they want to ask you questions, want inside information, and so everything you do is very visible.

One of the most exemplary ways that coercion structures the experience of college football players is the notorious off-season 'voluntary' workout. Its very name implies that players do not *have* to participate. But, just as participation in college football is not nearly as consensual as it appears, the voluntary workout is anything but freely consented to. Its compulsory nature is a perfect synecdoche for status coercion in the sport: one can 'choose' not to participate, but there will be consequences. Ross Nielsen explained:

> I don't know if the rules have changed, I hope to God they have, but like a lot of stuff was considered 'voluntary,' but if you didn't do it, you had no chance to play ever. So coaches could levy infinite workloads at

you, and you had no choice but to comply or quit. So I think it was like twenty hours, maximum, that we were allowed by the NCAA to work, but our team workouts were considered 'voluntary' workouts, so that was an extra . . . fifteen to eighteen hours a week is not unheard of. . . . There was so much volume in that weight training, I could barely recover from it. It was just part of the reason I stopped playing.

Charlie Rogers saw it similarly: "One of the craziest things that I found out was the fact that summer workouts are completely optional. Yet they never say that. It's very deep in the contract that we signed, that nobody reads. And they make it seem like if you miss one day, that's it for you. If you come back, you're gonna wish you never came back." Ryan Leonard explained, "The famous quote that every coach says is, 'Yes, it's optional that you be here, but it's optional that you play.' It's a motto and it's a catchy one. It gets the point across." It is so self-evident to players that these workouts are not voluntary that Kurt Weiss's team coined a neologism for it: "Volun-tory, rather than voluntary. . . . Guys will get punished in direct and indirect ways for missing. . . . The coach would call you, like, 'Why'd you miss?' or 'I heard you were late today.' And there's pressure with that, like 'You're supposed to be a leader,' 'We need you here,' all of that. Sometimes punished with extra workout. . . . Our offensive line coach, if guys missed summer workouts, they would do thirty to sixty minutes on the Stairmaster with a stick on their back like Christ with the cross." Likewise, Daniel Barber found the idea of summer work as voluntary to be laughable: "I did not know that was fucking voluntary! I didn't know! [Laughs] We got told, 'It's voluntary. You have to sign up to get in though. It's your decision. I cannot promise you playing time, if you do not come though.' Verbatim. 'I cannot promise you playing time.' And it was told to us, 'I can't help you, if you don't come' kind of deal." Whether through the threat of punishment or the withdrawal of playing time, status coercion is a pervasive instrument coaches employ to extract the maximum amount of effort and performance from players.

To exercise status coercion, coaches must have power not only over playing time, but also over membership on the team and scholarships. Given the emphasis placed by the college sport system on the academic aspects of the experience, it is no surprise there has been some movement to protect scholarships and move toward a putatively guaranteed four-year scholarship model.[6] Yet coaches still find ways to rescind scholarships. Drug testing is a key tool for coaches to exercise status coercion by taking back—or perpetually threatening to take back—scholarships. Marijuana use is prevalent in college football as it provides physical and emotional relief from the rigors of the sport. Coaches tend not to mind players' ubiquitous marijuana use, partly because it means that *when* they want to cut a player, they can simply test him. Ryan Leonard was the first player to introduce this to us:

> Drug testing is one of three predominant ways that the university, the coaches, use to get a scholarship spot back. Because marijuana in particular is so prominent within football culture, it has been weaponized by drug testing to get a spot back. . . . I started noticing a trend, at least for my team in college football, is that there were two [kinds of] people that were getting drug tested. First one were what I call straight shooters. Guys that the coaches weren't worried about failing a drug test and they were meeting a quota.
>
> And then the other guy is players that weren't panning out, players that they recruited and these guys weren't going to play, but maybe we can get them on a drug test and we can get a scholarship pulled . . . that [we] can then offer to somebody else that might pan out. And it has been weaponized against college football players because frankly a college football player searches for ways to self-medicate, or ways to cope, whether it's just to have a good time. But I don't think it's ever that simple. I think a lot of these players turn to marijuana as a way of dealing with pain.

Similarly, Josh Hansen explained that "discipline and punishment and tests coincide with performance." Those who did not perform or otherwise acted against the desires of the coaching staff found themselves disproportionately tested. Daniel Barber explained more about how the testing structure served the interests of coaches:

> I got tested like three to four times my first summer/first fall. Because I was a 'good kid,' they knew I wasn't gonna test positive. Whereas a lot of star players don't get tested. So new coaching staffs always have ways of getting rid of people. Basically, they'll just get rid of walk-ons, they'll implement team rules and you break them, so then they can get rid of you. They'll lie on you, they'll have people lie on you. . . . But they used drug testing to get rid of people. [Marijuana use is] widespread. I mean, the whole [Pac-12 school] team uses it. You can probably look at it, there's a disproportionate amount of African Americans that end up suffering from this. It's a good way to

get rid of your Black players. I mean, white players smoke too but [shrugs], you know.

Charlie Rogers noticed similar dynamics: "They [would] test a certain group of people. . . . It would be Black/white, but mostly Black. But especially when they're trying to get rid of you, because, you know, that rule, you can't get rid of anybody based off performance anymore in the NCAA. One of my friends, who's now at [Group of Five school]. They were trying to get rid of him first. They tested him, weekly, and some people hadn't been tested in three years."

This is all possible because coaches are acutely aware of the marijuana use dynamics of college football. Indeed, they *participate* in those dynamics, as Ryan Leonard shows: "On every team that I played on where marijuana was not legal, there was a player that was the plug, that was the drug dealer to the coaches. . . . Because these coaches smoke marijuana, these coaches are football players. They've grown up in the same culture that we have. And so they turn to players because it's actually safer for a coach to go to a player than it is to go to a drug dealer, because we're in this together." On one occasion, Leonard knew he was about to be tested and would fail, so he told a coach, who simply pulled some strings and got him out of the test. Drug testing allows coaches to protect players perceived as crucial to the team's performance while punishing those who are not, as Landry West also told us: "I know a player who probably failed five to six drug tests and stayed on the team and somebody who may have failed two who got kicked off. I think there is at least one player kicked off every year, majority from weed."

Tragically, pervasive marijuana testing can push players to take harder drugs that are not as subject to testing. Ryan Leonard explains: "We figured out that we always got drug tested on Tuesday. So after a game, we could go to the bar, drink as much alcohol to numb the pain as we want, and to do as much cocaine as we wanted on Saturday, because we knew by Tuesday it was going to be out of our system. . . . I did many eight balls of cocaine before I ever smoked a blunt. That is what drug testing does."

Another coercive strategy coaches use to rescind scholarships is medical exemptions, sometimes colloquially referred to as medical redshirts, although the medical "redshirt" is technically different from what Daniel Barber discusses here[7]:

They'll push you to medically retire to get paid for college. They'll highly discourage you, try to manipulate you, and tell you how you really feel about the game. I was told, "You won't to be able to walk anymore." Like, "I want you to be able to play with your kids" kind of deal. And that didn't work on me, I ended up rehabbing and being fine. My doctor was surprised—that medical advice was strictly coach-driven counsel. And I had four or five other players that year who accepted that. They were approached the exact same way, they took it, they took the medical redshirt. So that freed up four or five scholarships to go recruit JUCO [junior college] people, to recruit high schoolers.

Brock Adler saw the same thing: "One of the tricks they can do is use an injury as an advantage. Basically say like, 'Oh, you're injured all the time' . . . or 'You're never going to play here, so you might as well transfer.' You know, just screwing them out of a world-class education."

Academics are yet another mechanism coaches use to rescind scholarships. While eligibility is a persistent concern for players who are performing well—teams need them to achieve minimum GPA standards to remain on the field and will bend over backward to make this happen—when it comes to players perceived to be underperforming, the same academic regulations can be employed to push players off the team. Ryan Leonard explains, "Academic negligence . . . can be as simple as not showing up to class, missing a tutoring appointment, not turning in homework, getting a zero. Something so subjective and so easy to point out that it was almost a shoo-in. I knew one guy who wasn't playing, was severely overweight, wasn't really into the athletics, and they got him on academic negligence because he didn't show up to two. That was profound. It was within a year. He was a senior."

Brock Adler describes one situation where a teammate—who had come from Europe for a top education—was pushed out of a scholarship because his performance was deemed insufficient on the grounds that his grades were not high enough (likely due to the frustration of a lack of playing time and distance from home). Teams can also undermine the academic experience of players they *don't* want to see transfer by limiting their options. Daniel Barber explains: "I know schools like [major Power Five school], I mean [different school] will do this to you too—they'll just trash your GPA. They'll just [punches hand] your GPA, and go, 'Oh, you're on academic probation, but we'll still play you. Oh, you don't like what we're doing? Okay, then leave.'"

NKL: But you can't leave because you're on academic probation, you're saying, so that's a way they prevent you from transferring.

BARBER: Let your grades fall, but still focus on football. They want to be the only hand that you can eat out of.

Likewise, Landry West saw how coaches could "have an impact on schools that would potentially take you. They'd ask [the coach] [about players] and he had the ability to say, 'Hey, I wouldn't take this kid because of X, Y, Z reason.' Whether that's true or not, I saw it hurt guys and impact them directly." Moreover, the awareness that coaches had this power is itself a tool of discipline and coercion.

Sometimes, coaches rely less on technicalities and more on raw coercion, whether in the form of deception or ill treatment. As Daniel Barber puts it, sometimes coaches "just straight-up lie, not finding any technicalities, but just try to mislead players. So say, 'Yeah. I'm taking your scholarship.' And then the players will follow. Like, they'll influence the players, they'll 'help the players out' to do stuff to take care of the player, but it's really just to get the player out. So they can coerce a player to basically lose their scholarship of their own accord. Just by misleading them." Or coaches will essentially bully players until they leave "of their own accord":

> Coaches are the alphas in a lot of sense[s]. . . . So coaches treating you poorly, teammates are going to treat you poorly. If you aren't feeling like your game is getting respected and if you're investing all this stuff, like all your energy towards it, then you're going to feel disrespected, abused. [Bad treatment can be] lack of playing time, or, in some instances, they'll overload you with playing time in practice, they'll completely just dump work on you. I mean, they have all sorts of underhanded methods. They'll tease you. It could be passing comments. Things like, "Oh, you're looking pretty small."

Charlie Rogers experienced this firsthand when his head coach told him toward the end of the season that he "just wasn't good enough" to keep playing for the team. Kurt Weiss saw this too:

> You would see this unfold in the spring and in spring ball, after scholarship players' redshirt season. So they bring in a guy—any redshirt, who's not ready to play, or he's not as good as they thought he would be, or needs development. And if he wasn't working hard and if he wasn't practicing well, really when spring rolls around, they try to run these guys out of the program . . . just treating the player like shit. Like, criticizing him in front of his teammates, being really hard on him in practice, telling him like, "You're never going to play here, you should transfer."

Again, it's one of these unofficial things that's common is if they're riding a player really hard, you can sense they want them to shape up or ship out. . . . And sometimes coaches, they get it wrong. We had a player that they were trying to get rid of that wound up becoming one of our contributing players, and then played in the NFL for eight years. So, you know, the coaches are under immense pressure. There's only so many scholarship spots available. They're also recruiting—they're recruiting your replacement.

Thomas Rycliff's coaches consistently undermined him, hoping he would transfer. He remembers "walking into the D-lineman [defensive lineman] room on the Tuesday. And my position coach stopped me, and he said, 'The head man just let me know when you're going to be starting this Saturday against the number three team in the country.' Before I walked in, he stopped me, he says, 'I just want you to know that I'm against it.'"

Sometimes, to eliminate players from their program, coaches tell them they do not fit the culture, essentially code for assuring them that they will not have the opportunity to play if they remain on the team. This is Ryan Leonard's third method of taking back a scholarship: "'You don't fit the culture so I will not play you, but I will find you a new home where you can play' . . . which, frankly, is 'We don't think you're good enough to play or we think we can go out and get a better player so we want your spot back' . . . you better hope that the next place that offers you [a spot] has the same degree plan. You better hope that all your credits transfer. Otherwise, you're starting over, and if you start over, your likelihood of graduating continues to fall."

Thomas Rycliff experienced this sort of pressure from a coach shortly after he came to campus. On his first meeting with him, a meeting twice delayed by the coach, he was told, "So I hear you're transferring." He was shocked, given that the thought had never crossed his mind—he had chosen to attend that school as much for its unique academic programs as for football—let alone been articulated. When he told the coach he had no intention of transferring, he was informed, "Well, you're not going to play while I'm a coach here." At least eight of his teammates had the same conversation and ultimately left. Ronnie Exeter endured the same thing when a new coach was brought in to run his team: "He was pretty much saying going into spring, fall, like, 'Oh, just letting you know, man, I don't know you. It's like, no way possible you can play for me. You won't be playing here. You can stay on special teams and all that if you'd like to, but yeah, you won't be playing linebacker.'"

The job security of college football players is precarious, regardless of putative scholarship protections. Coaches control access to playing time, and they can instrumentalize it to extract value and performance or drive players from the team.

Coaching Malpractice

Coaches' use of structural and status coercion is motivated by a desire to optimize team success (winning), which in turn benefits the coach in terms of a lucrative and long-term salary and the university in terms of revenue from the sale of commodity spectacle and the difficult-to-quantify value added to the institutional brand. These coercive tactics may be inhumane and unjust, but they are certainly logical. But some coaching practices cross the line even for those who might suggest that status coercion is a legitimate mechanism for maximizing team success. This includes, but is not limited to, disingenuous pitches during recruiting and outright bullying and abusive behavior. Abusive and harmful coaching behaviors have become a major story in college sport thanks to the reporting of Northwestern University student journalists, who exposed an alleged culture of hazing and abuse on the school's football team, leading to the firing of coach Pat Fitzgerald in the summer of 2023.[8] We argue that abusive coaching practices, including the alleged sexually abusive hazing in the Northwestern case, exist on a continuum with the forms of coercion discussed above. In the context of a sport premised on violence, harm, and value extraction, coaches' abusive behaviors are more a difference of degree than kind when it comes to their general methodologies. As such, we do not characterize the following testimony as describing 'exceptions' or 'bad apples,' but rather as showing the logical outcome of a political economy predicated on the destruction of students' bodies. These coaches are who we collectively ask them to be, at least implicitly.

One of the more insidious practices coaches engage in is dishonesty with players during the recruiting process. Coaches often sell a vision they know will not be reality once the players arrive on campus. Charlie Rogers explains:

> When I was recruited as an O-lineman [offensive lineman], I specifically told the coach . . . I played one season of football in high school. They asked me if I knew a lot about football. I said, "No, not at all," and they said, "Okay, we're going to teach you." And then when I got there, they handed me a book, they said, "Learn on your own." I was

talking to my mom, and she was telling me about somebody who had a family member who was getting recruited for [Division I] football. And she knew that I was playing at [Pac-12 school]. And she asked my mom for advice. And she was like, "I don't know, there's not really an easy way to say, like nine times out of ten, unless you're a number one, five-star recruit, four-star recruit, everything they're telling you is a complete lie." She was trying to figure out a way to say that to that other parent that was about to send their kid to play football.

Ryan Leonard adds, "The first profound piece of advice that my dad gave me was, college coaches are the best used car salesmen that you'll ever meet. They will sell you a load of shit wrapped up with a perfect bow. They will guarantee you things that can never be guaranteed. And once you sign on the dotted line, if things go wrong, they will act like they never knew you. They are some of the greatest recruiters in the world and they get handsomely paid to do so."

That moment of signing on the dotted line—of 'consenting' to the world of college football—is a foundational aspect of the disingenuity at the heart of the relationship between player and university. Kurt Weiss explains:

You'd sign the stack of papers, first team meeting at training camp. And first team meeting when you were back in January . . . we would be like, "What the fuck? We're signing away whatever." But again, you don't have choice, real choice, or time, and the people that are giving the presentation and handing you the papers are the doctors that work with the team, and athletic trainers that work for the team. . . . Do you not sign? Or do you say I need some time? Or I want to get this to my attorney? Or find an attorney? And you mentioned the term "coercion." There's a little bit of that. Like everybody on the team is in the team meeting room, and you're handed the documents, and it's, "Hey guys, sign these, and give them to [name], and then we'll start watching film." So everybody signs it. . . . It was more a sin of omission than it was a lie. I think they just said like, "This is something we have to do. It's protocol. Do this paperwork and then we'll get on with things." And players, to varying degrees, the kid that doesn't know better from background who's like, "Okay, I'll sign my name." There were guys, like me, that understood kind of what was going on. But I don't know of one instance where a player ever didn't sign, or said, "I need time," or anything like that. So it was coercive. In a just world, it'd be a different meeting, and then a different environment, and with a third party.

Ryan Leonard makes the same point:

When we signed our scholarship, when we signed away our name,
image, and likeness, and we signed away our consent to drug test, it
was often in the summer, and they would bring us in groups of thirty
to a computer lab and they would tell us, "Hey, you guys got lunch,
and then you guys got meetings." So it became a race for all these
athletes to sign these documents on the computer as fast as they can,
never reading it, never having anybody look over it. You don't want to
be that guy, and you're hungry, you want to go eat, you just got done
with practice, and they leverage that, kind of keep people in the dark
because they know athletes don't read. So they leverage that against
us, and it'll be interesting to see how fast people have signed their
names fifteen times on these documents that end up being some of the
biggest contracts they ever sign in their life.

While the issue of consent is certainly problematic, players were even
more aggrieved by how coaches promised they would be treated like family
and then failed to make that a reality. Aaron Peters told us:

After we leave, he ain't going to ever call us, unless we go to the NFL or
we donate some money. He isn't going to call or check on our family.
I'm expecting a daughter with my fiancée. Like, you're not going to call
me, asking how I'm doing, or asking when's the baby shower, or asking
when is your wedding, I'd like to come. You're not going to ask us none
of that. You don't care. But y'all try to tell us, "It's family this, it's
family that," like, if it's a family, I know how a family is supposed to
act. Yeah, you'll do the post for the guys coming back, but only
because they went to the NFL.

Players were frustrated that coaches withheld compassion in moments of
genuine crisis. Terry Davis explains:

What I found was that the street, the monsters, the gang leaders, the
drug dealers, they have more compassion than our coaches have. They
are more human than our coaches are. So these monsters of these
dark alleys will show you compassion and concern and care before
your coaches would. Because they're not actually committed to their
community, committed to the team, committed to the players they
coach, they literally aren't doing that extra job, the job that that local
coach does. It's more than just taking these players home. It's more

than just buying these players some food. It's really tapping in and seeing where they're going.

Yet those same coaches who would not offer players the care they deserved *did* require compassion from players toward their own families. Davis continues:

> [My teammate's] mother died, so I told two of my other O-line buddies like, "Hey bro, we got to go. His mama died." We showed up. The coaches didn't show up, but when the coach's daughter, [who] was born developmentally disabled and in a wheelchair most of her life, she passed, it was kind of mandatory that the whole team go to the wake. But the teammate's grandmother who died, that raised him, that's in the county adjacent to [the school], died and y'all didn't show up to her funeral, y'all didn't tell the whole team they had to show up to her funeral.

For Aaron Peters, if football was like family, it was a toxic and abusive one, as he laid out in a metaphor comparing coaches to a spouse: "Your wife is somebody you trust, and then they're manipulating . . . it's like, if I do this, it's an issue. If I do that, it's an issue. What's going on? It's going to drive you nuts. Because I'm trying my best, I'm trying to do everything you're asking me to do. It's just, the way you're laying it out is a way that doesn't make sense, but [you] try to understand it. Then you're still going to get yelled at."

Many players we interviewed felt coaches crossed lines in how they treated and interacted with players, producing toxic working environments antithetical to the mission of higher education. Reporting from the University of Minnesota underlines this point. In 2023, an anonymous player explained that paying obsequious deference to coach P. J. Fleck was a literal job requirement: "We had to [give Fleck ovations] multiple times—the first time, because some other people in the back were not moving as quick as he wanted." Two other players added that "Fleck would reenter a room if he didn't like the ovation he received."[9] Daniel Barber summarized these dynamics in his conversation with us: "Coaches were biased, nothing was fair, nothing was for the sake of the team's goals. At the end of the day, it was for the sake of the coaches' paycheck. In some instances, if they liked you or if they felt like doing you a solid, or doing something that made them feel good inside, they'd help you out."

But the worst we heard was about coaching that veered into the realm of abuse. We define abuse here as harm caused deliberately and gratuitously, whether in physical, verbal, or psychological form. That abuse is prevalent in the world of college football is perhaps the most damning indictment of the system as it currently exists.

Ross Nielsen experienced abusive behavior during his time at a major Power Five program:

> My first day of practice, I was hazed. . . . I was participating in a drill, and somebody came into the drill that wasn't supposed to be in it, and knocked me clean onto the ground. And [coach] basically blamed me for the whole incident, and told me that he was going to cut me on the spot since I was a slapdick, walk-on, piece of shit. Like, barking up to me. . . . Then, basically, I went to the locker room. And I was so depressed, because I was so excited for that first day. . . . Basically, everybody, when I came back in, they were like, "Dude, don't worry about it, he does that to everybody. It's like, his character test." I mean, but that was his tool to motivate people, was just constant verbal and psychological abuse. Like, he would use people against each other, he would say, "Oh, you better watch out today because so-and-so's going to take your scholarship, and you're going to be back to wherever," like some [Division II] college he would just name. Like, "You'll be playing there next time you hear it," or like, "You'll be like working on [local Main Street] flipping burgers next time we all see you because so-and-so's going to take your scholarship." That was constant.

Verbal abuse is a ubiquitous feature of the sport, to the extent of normalization. Landry West remembers suffering from the specter of public humiliation:

> Sometimes you would just dread . . . those meetings where you know you had a hiccup and it's like, "This is going to be that meeting where I'm going to get chewed out." That was what we expected in terms of how harsh it would be. . . . It'd depend on the coach, but even when guys would get in trouble, maybe outside or off the field, it was the team meeting, "Stand up X, Y, Z person, why were you doing this on the Saturday night? Why did I get a call from so-and-so? You were doing that." And I know guys who changed after that public humiliation and were never the same, which is sad to see.

Charlie Rogers explained that it was commonplace for coaches to "just like demean you. And just make you feel like less of a person. Call you a 'bitch.'"

Sometimes, coaches directed their ire at specific individuals who were ultimately subjected to bullying no doubt intended to discipline the whole team:

ROGERS: They would be cussing [my teammate] out all the time. And honestly, I don't know, I feel like if he wasn't there, that would have been me. Because I was out of shape a little bit. But they didn't even refer to him by his name for about a year, they would just call him "stupid." I remember one specific time, a little bit before he had that mental breakdown, they had him read out the workout. And, of course, he was terrified. Because if he messes up, even stutters a little bit, he was thinking they're going to do something. So he went up there. He was stuttering. And every time he stuttered, the coach slapped him on the back of the neck. It's like, "Come on, dum-dum. Come on, idiot. Spit it out."

DS: Wow. And this caused a mental breakdown, as you put it?

ROGERS: Yeah, because this would be every single day for about two and a half years.

For Aaron Peters, coaches transformed his earnest attempt to discuss playing time into an opportunity to publicly discipline him for exercising agency:

When I confronted him, I said, "You say it's a meritocracy. We're clearly playing the best. Why are we not playing more?" [The coach responds:] "Oh, Aaron, you know, this is selfish." The next day, we come in, there's a whole PowerPoint laid out. It's literally like, "What a cancer is." I'm like, I already know this is about me. [They're like,] "A cancer is malignant and destroys everything in its path." Next slide. "You don't want to be a cancer." Next slide. [Points finger outward] "If you're a cancer, you're not going to be part of this team." Next slide. I'm just like, "Alright, okay, I get it." They started yelling, stuff like that. Everybody knows, it's probably something [Aaron] said. But they're looking at me, I'm just like, "This was not what I wanted. I just wanted to talk to him, justify why we should play."

Nick Turner's experience shows the deliberate nature of this verbal abuse. After practice, Turner suffered a panic attack and couldn't breathe. The trainer knew and didn't inform the coach, who followed him upstairs into the locker room:

Then in front of everyone, I start throwing up in the trash can when I got to the top of the stairs. And he's standing over me, saying, "You fucking piece of shit. You're gonna hurt this team. I'm going to make sure you don't make a fucking penny." In front of everyone. Everyone's standing there wondering what the hell's going on. And so he's assuming I have some drug or alcohol problem. [He] didn't hear anything from the trainer. The trainer is also watching this go on. Still didn't say anything. Then magically later, like two hours later, after team meetings and everything is over, [coach] pulls me aside and is like, "Hey, I heard you're having a little something going on." Like, privately. Of course berates me in front of everyone and then privately apologizes for it. . . . That happened to a lot of players all the time. You slowly become this type of person that's like, expecting it?

One player told us about a coach who took this humiliation beyond the locker room: he walked around practice with a microphone, broadcasting his belittling comments to players for the whole university.

Ross Nielsen explained why institutions allow such conduct: "What the coaches do is hazing, there's no way around it. If a fraternity brother did this to their pledge brother, they would be kicked off of campus. But the coaches can do it because they're million-dollar employees." Daniel Barber agreed:

They're unchecked, a lot of 'em are "good ol' boy" babysitters that get paid millions of dollars to just rehash, resay shit that's been developed for the past forty years. So, I mean, everyone does the same thing. I think coaches are overpaid, plain and simple. And they're just monsters, I mean, like think about the qualifications for being a coach. . . . Are you able to stomach the industry long enough for someone to call your name? And it's political and all that. It's who you tag along with as a GA [graduate assistant], who you're willing to just let shake his stuff down your throat long enough.

Charlie Rogers indicated that the amount of abuse players received from coaches was often directly proportionate to status on the team: "If you have a higher chance of getting on the field, they will treat you better. They refer to it as equity. . . . You wouldn't get cussed out all the time. They would say 'Hi' to you. The strength coaches would probably be less likely to do those punishment workouts on you. And pretty much getting treated like more of a person, if you played more." Ronnie Exeter experienced the silent treatment from coaches who only acknowledged those perceived to be performing sufficiently: "Coaches will just literally walk past you if you don't play, like, 'Hi.' They won't say nothing back. It's just, 'What have you done for me lately?' kind of thing. If you ain't producing, you ain't getting a lot of talking to."

College football players often become acclimatized to abuse because it begins long before they get to college. Thomas Rycliff explains:

That [high school] coach was actually abusive to me. He hit me across the face a couple of times after practice with the helmet off. He had this big ring, and he had this fat hand. I actually got the flu one time, and I lost ten pounds. I was trying to gain weight. And I said, "I just lost ten pounds." And he smacked me across the face hard. And I said, "I just had the flu." And he smacked me across the face again, and I said, "I'm going to gain it all back." And he is like, "That's what I want to hear."

It should be no surprise that coaches sometimes engage in physical violence in college as well. Terry Davis explains:

My O-line coach does like he normally does. He start going in on the people who made a mistake. . . . I sit there and say, "Yes sir. No sir. Yes sir. No sir." Look you in your eyes. So he kept going. I'm like, "All right, coach, you going a little bit farther right now, so clearly something else is going on. I'm going to walk away, give you a little space." And I got up to walk away and he's like, "Don't fucking walk away from me!" And I stopped and said, "Yes sir, you're right. I apologize." I put my hand out and he knocked my hand down on the sideline, televised game. I'm like, "You ain't no fucking man. I fucking apologized to you. You going to knock my fucking hand down?" So he starts fucking rushing me. My left tackle gets in the way.

Coaches generally seemed particularly rankled by players who stood up to their attempts to verbally and physically dominate. Thomas Rycliff describes one such incident with his position coach:

When [the position coach] would yell at me, I'd look him in the eyes and I wouldn't look away because that's what I was taught. And [the position coach] grew up in a swamp with a frog in his pocket. He's like that junkyard dog where if you look at him too long, he'll bite you, he'll start growling at you. And so there were multiple times where he tried to fight me, just for that reason alone. [One time] he's lighting into me in front of everybody on the team, it's like a show. And he's calling me every name in the book, "You motherfucker," all this. And he's getting closer, and closer to my face, and closer, and I'm just staring at him, and I'm doing what my dad taught me and he starts losing his mind and he's like, "You stop fucking looking at me. You stop fucking looking at me." And he lunges at me and they have to pull him off of me. And I'm still staring at him because that's what I was taught to do. And they literally had to tear his shirt because they had to pull him off of me.

Nick Turner endured years of a coach's verbal abuse, and when he finally couldn't take it anymore, he was threatened with physical violence:

It felt like this whole weird thing where [my coach] wanted to make me feel less than just so that I worked harder? Because he even said something to my dad, my freshman year, at the banquet, like, "Nick will be a really great player one day, we just have to keep our foot up his ass every day." I didn't understand that, because I didn't feel like that. And other people felt like it was obnoxious. And you'd hear him screaming my name at practice anytime I messed up. The strength coaches, the trainers, the water girls, [even] reporters at practice when I would run by them, going into the locker room, they [would imitate the coach yelling Nick's name], as a joke. That's how bad it was, that this coach was just harping on me. I didn't understand it, and I was done with it. So after the game, in the locker room, he went to shake my hand and I said, "Get your fucking hand out of my face. I don't want to touch your hand. I'm not giving you anything. You can leave. You can just get out." And he was standing there, listening to me say that, and [said], "I oughta punch you in the fucking jaw." He starts stepping towards me. I was sitting down, he was standing up, and he stepped over me, and I stood up. Then players separated us both. And that was the end of it.

One of the most brutal aspects of the harm built into the sport—harm that can only be understood as inherently abusive—is the punishment inflicted by strength and conditioning coaches on behalf of the general staff. Recall Charlie Rogers's harrowing story in this book's introduction about his coach forcing players to do push-ups on jagged rocks as punishment. Matt Jensen had his own saga of abuse at the hands of strength coaches:

It was hell. We'd show up, and the first few weeks we didn't get to go through a single workout because, it was like boot camp, but for three years under him. And it was more about psychological conditioning and mentally tormenting you more than physically preparing you. And that is part of the reason why my body feels like shit to this day because we weren't built up the way we should have been. It was just an everyday kind of [thing]. The sense that we couldn't do anything right, the sense that we were wastes of space. If we didn't do the exercise specifically to the way he wanted to, we'd have to do it again. . . . A lot of people would be like, "Oh yeah, it kind of sounds like boot camp. He's trying to instill camaraderie, in the sense that you need to be detail oriented." It was more than that. At a certain point, it was sadistic. . . . A bunch of my friends had to quit for mental health reasons, and that was really hard to see. . . . I do believe a major factor in all those guys losing their minds is the constant and consistent and unnecessary stress that they were subjected to from the strength and conditioning department. Because the strength [and] conditioning department is supposed to build you up, and get you strong and get you prepared. But our strength and conditioning department was just not that. It was all focused on breaking you down, and making you a subservient dog, rather than a competent football player. . . . It was just like, "Fuck you, you guys aren't shit. Don't forget your place. You're the players, I'm the coach." It was just constant gaslighting, making us seem like we were the problem. . . . Looking back on it, some people asked me, "Hey, do you regret it? Like, would you go back and do it again?" Fuck no, I wouldn't do it again.

Sometimes coaches discriminate against players based on their identity. Brock Adler said he had this experience based on disability:

One day, I stood out in front of my entire team after a team run, because we were sharing stuff, and I said, "Hey, I'm high-functioning autistic. That's my mountain to climb, but I'm not gonna let it affect me." And everybody gave me props for it, it was very encouraging. And then, in an individual meeting, I talked about it with [head coach] and my position coach, and you know, after that, I started getting treated different in the regard of, "Oh, [Adler] doesn't know the plays, oh, [Adler] is just all over the place, [Adler's] going to get mad." They never said anything explicit against it, because obviously if they did, I could go and say something. But it was a way of discriminating. A subtle discrimination. Because, as a Black man, also, you know discrimination because of your race.

One of the practices most disturbing to us, as academics who have worked at Power Five universities, is how the academic side of the university is recruited into complicity with abusive athletic practices, notably corporal punishment, for supposed academic missteps. Ross Nielsen, for instance, explains that missing class resulted in "conditioning, or weight training, some kind of physical punishment–related." For this reason, Charlie Rogers wasn't comfortable speaking with academic counselors, who he understood were "in cahoots" with the strength coaches who doled out discipline: "You'll be dealt with after practice. There was another punishment they called the 'Lieutenant Dan.' You had [to] army crawl, like forty yards, without using your legs. I've only done it once. And mine wasn't as bad as everyone else's. There'll be a lot of people, their arms would be kind of raw, like if you took some sandpaper and just aggressively rubbed their skin off." Landry West described how coaches would read players' grades out loud in front of others to both applaud those succeeding and shame those struggling.

Sometimes coaches' toxic and abusive behavior manifests indirectly, by fostering a culture of violence and mistrust among players. This is one explanation for why players do not speak out about the harm they are subjected to, as Brock Adler explains:

> [Coaches] try to hammer in that play time is equal with your loyalty to the team, and with your effort for the team. . . . They made us wear on our back, and I hated wearing, was "team over me." You can't say anything because it's going to hurt your playing time, and on the team, it's going to hurt the team, your teammates. They also teach teammates to be dogs at each other, so if a guy is screwing up or is not complying with the team, then everybody's against them. Our coach encouraged guys who were against him, or against the team, or calling certain things out, to bark at them. I'm guilty of that when I was feeding into the dogma before I got smart. But you know what, that's the mental games they play with us. They convinced us to be a pack full of dogs that would eat each other if the Master said so.

Part of this climate is the toleration of violence among players, as long as it is in the privacy of the "locker room." Daniel Barber told us, "It's an open secret. Everyone who's played, knows. . . . People fought. I mean, there were definitely fights in the locker room that never got punished. That [teammate], my freshman year, he would break people's doors. Like, if you're trying to sleep, he'd kick the shit out of your door. And other people would do that too. But he ended up getting [in] a fight in a classroom, that's where we crossed the line, because we fought in front of the normal people." In some cases, coaches not only tolerated but actively encouraged violence among players:

> TERRY DAVIS: You get to the NFL and there's guys that ask you, "Do you think I was good enough to play in the SEC?" And you got to ask yourself, "No you're not," but I know how you can be successful in the NFL and I know why, because nobody's actually trying to kill you out here. Everybody is happy that everybody's making money and they want to keep the money flowing. Nobody is actually what we know the SEC is. Year in and year out, there's a reason why. And I'm telling you, it may not be your superstars, it may not be your starters, but it's a guy just trying to get on the field that's third string that will fucking end your life out there, play after play. They got a young guy coming off the bench that will end your life. And that's what makes the SEC the SEC, because it's so dangerous of an environment to play in. You literally have to fight your teammates during the week to say that you had a good practice. And coaches don't let you out of practice until you fight.
>
> NKL: You mean literally fight?
>
> DAVIS: Literal fight. They'll keep running goal line or inside drills until y'all get chippy.
>
> NKL: You're saying across the SEC, a weekly occurrence, the coaches are trying to produce fights among players?
>
> DAVIS: Yes, they are.

The most extreme form of this tendency was when coaches literally *gambled* on players' violent interactions during practice:

> DAVIS: Let's just say if your offensive coordinator, defensive coordinator are getting into arguments going back and forth in the scrimmage leading up to a big game, they probably got a little money on the performance during the practice. Your O- and D-line coach who has one-on-one drills, they can say twenty dollars a rep. If my guy beats your guy, that's twenty dollars. Then when you end up having premier talent on your O-line, the prices go up. What I'll tell you is, at [school's] football practices, nobody's fucking watching seven on seven, everybody is over there at the pass rush. You've got these people that drive million-dollar motor coaches onto the practice fields standing there by us. You've got all these other assistant

coaches want to see the violence and stuff. This is the heavyweight boxing match of practice today. This is what we do.

Kane Holden recounts a particularly traumatic experience where coaches implicitly endorsed and enabled teammate-on-teammate violence:

It's called "jumping in" in a way where it's like you get jumped in to the gang. My former school, there was a big culture and tradition surrounding getting jumped by your teammates and things like that. And this was done on the last day of fall camp for the freshmen. And all the seniors would go into your dorm rooms and essentially jump you, beat you down to the ground. And that right there was my moment of, oh, this is violent, this is manipulative. I['m] just here to play football and then now I'm getting beat down by ten dudes in the dorm room. And that's something that the coaches said they didn't know about because it came out eventually my junior year that someone told. And they said they didn't know about it. But my position coach was there for twenty-five years . . . [the coaches] absolutely knew.

Given the fact that football is a sport predicated on violence and that coaching methodologies encourage and foster violent impulses, it is no surprise that one of the most problematic dimensions of college football culture is the misogyny and sexual violence associated with it and the fact that coaches all too often are complicit in the toleration of that violence. As Varda Burstyn explains, coercive entitlement is a feature of hegemonic masculinity conditioned by sporting cultures like football.[10] Ryan Leonard witnessed this firsthand:

Players that aren't, especially at offense line, aren't aggressive, aren't tough, they get called out. One of the most popular ones that one of my coaches would say is we'd be watching film and he'd look at it and he goes, "Do you think this is masculine or do you think this is feminine, and does this look soft or does this look tough," and so he would make you say, "This is soft. This is me not being a man to some extent." So yes, but to the outsider, I believe that would be seen as abusive. Now there is something about being in a locker room, there's something about being around alphas and about being around so much masculinity that it's almost a par for the course, I believe.

The imperative to dominate through violence and aggression conditioned through such practices cannot simply be switched off, which makes the sport a fundamentally antisocial institution. Daniel Barber explains how he saw this play out during his time in college football:

> Not to perpetuate the "football players are rapists," but there is a certain issue with the culture. . . . We had people on the team. . . . Friends that I had, that were girls, I would not leave them around them. . . . I was talking to someone that I met around here who played at [rival team], he's like, "Oh yeah, [a teammate would] bring his own Patrón [tequila] that was just spiked, and would give it to people, and the coaches knew." People went to the coaches and said, "Hey, he wrecked a good girl, like one of my friends now, and it's a problem." And the [head coach of rival team] was like, "Handle it." So they jumped him on the field and just beat his ass. Like I said, players do what the coaches say. They say, "Hey, handle that," or "Oh, he needs [to be] taken care of," or "Oh, handle it in the locker room. Bring gloves in the locker room. Fight each other in the locker room." Boxing gloves were brought into the locker room. The thing at [school] was "handle it on the [team logo]" kind of deal.

These dynamics are at their worst during recruiting, where the coercive entitlement fostered by the sport intersects with the commodification and objectification of women on campus whose bodies are deployed by university representatives to entice prospective players. Barber explains that many players will ask recruits they are hosting, "You want a girl?" But often it is the athletic department itself that is responsible for these practices, as young women on campus are specifically tasked with taking football recruits around. As Barber puts it, "It's just baked in. It's just the thing." Ryan Leonard tells his own horrific story of the pressure placed on young athletes to lead morally dubious recruiting visits:

> I was doing rehab on my knee and I was also some guy that the coaches had learned liked to go out and party, liked to go out on the night scenes. So I was able to show these athletes a side of college that some other players might not. . . . We would go to dinner, me, the position coach, oftentimes the O-line coach and our offensive coordinator and our head coach. And we would all go to a nice steakhouse. And then after that steakhouse, they would hand me forty dollars, I would sign a piece of paper, and I was to host that recruit for the night. And keep in mind, this is oftentimes sixteen-, seventeen-, sometimes eighteen-

year-old kids. And I was never told explicitly what to do. I was only ever told, show them a good time and what [the campus town] is all about. And what the city has to offer. Well it's kind of a[n] unwritten rule, but it's assumed that that includes going out to the club. That includes providing alcohol. That includes providing sometimes drugs if that player was into drugs and providing them a good time. So there was one example that I have that ended my time of recruiting. This was the last time I ever recruited somebody because it called into question my own morality. So I had a kid, we went out to our steakhouse, had a dinner, and afterwards the player had told me, he goes, "Well, do you have any weed or any Xanax?" I go, "Well, yeah, I can get you some of that." So I go out and I get this guy weed and Xanax and he rolls it into what we call a blunt and he smokes it and I take them out to one of the clubs. And while we were at the club, I knew a bunch of different girls that wanted to help the team, wanted to help show athletes a good time so that we might have a better team. And at the club, this girl comes up to me and I go up to this girl that I know, and I go, "Hey, can you go dance with this athlete?" And this is one of those dance clubs. So you can imagine the provocative dancing that goes on. And this kid was under the age on a variety of substances and that I had provided to him. And while they were out on the dance club, I wasn't keeping an eye on them, I wasn't looking at them. And a few moments later, this girl that I had asked to go dance with this athlete comes up to me and goes, "Hey, he's trying to finger people on the dance floor. He tried to finger me while I was dancing." And so I didn't know what to do. I was speechless. I hadn't been in this situation before. So I wanted to look out, not only for this girl, but for this athlete, for this institution, for myself. So I asked this girl, "Please don't say anything. I'll take care of it. I'm taking him home. I promise you won't ever have to see this guy again." So the next morning, that night I take him to this hotel, drop him off, and the next morning I walk into the coach's office, I go, "Never ask me to recruit again. And by no means would I allow this guy on my team." And they didn't ask any questions.

Conclusion

Toxic coaching saturates college football, from the coercion on which the sport is predicated to the egregious abuse that abounds across the nation's campuses and is so normalized that it often is not perceived as abusive. Ryan Leonard explains:

> I got plenty of friends in the military, and they talk about the same thing, about how the outside person might look at it as a verbal abuse, as degradation, as somebody degrading another human being, but oftentimes, it's just a coaching style and it's a coaching style that's been developed for decades of being in a not-PC culture, of decades of being behind the wall that is college athletics. Of feeling so secluded from outside criticism that it becomes a part of the culture. . . . I know guys that went into a severe depression, guys that became severely secluded, that hated going up to the facility because they knew they were going to be singled out and called feminine, called soft, called Charmin, called a Tampax.

The prevalence of coercion and harm makes any movement to simply reform college football likely to fail. The culture of violence and abuse is self-reproducing. Those socialized in this world have been conditioned to operate according to its norms and imperatives. This is something that Daniel Barber can clearly see after his time in the sport: "The abused become the abusers? Yeah. I mean, I say anyone, especially if you do a lot of contact, if you're in a position with a lot of contact, you've gotta be a little bit crazy. I like hitting people, like I'm into that. Not abusive, or anything like that. But it's fun for me. I'm a boy's boy. And that's something I miss, and that's something I crave. And football is the only legal outlet for that, except boxing and stuff. But yeah, I mean, it's just the kind of people that excel [in] football."

The testimony in this chapter offers a direct and explicit rebuttal to one of the most common rhetorical defenses for the creation and maintenance of contemporary big-time college football: that athletes "sign up" to play and therefore consent to its conditions. Certainly, the question of consent is a complex one, and the experiences of the college athletes we interviewed highlight the nuanced and multiple (often overlapping) ways they might consent to features of their sport. But at the same time, it is also apparent that there are myriad ways athletic workers *do not* consent to the system and many of the practices, tactics, and institutional logics within it. In confronting the question of consent, we have tried to unpack, both theoretically and empirically, how coercion flourishes at the heart of big-time college football. Consent, we argue, should only be understood in contemporary college football in the most tenuous and superficial sense. While players might sign official documentation acknowledging their willingness to participate, this act must be considered within an environment marred by structural restrictions set forth by the very college football apparatus they are said to be consenting to. In reading the testimony of college football players, it is difficult not to see how the many power brokers in big-time college football condition the possibility of consent, raising the question of whether true agency can exist in this context at all.

This chapter engages with structural and status coercion to understand how they work together to constrain the agency of players and submit them to the exploitation and harm inherent in college football.[11] College football is defined by status coercion, which is clearly exemplified when one considers the power coaches possess to determine access to the limited resources available. However, status coercion only exists in this context in relation to structural coercion. Informed consent in college football must be understood within the broader power dynamics that influence an athlete's capacity to consent to participation.[12] The power monopoly held by coaches over much-desired forms of social and economic capital compels players to yield to exploitative conditions they might otherwise reject. The inaccessibility of higher education, the ideological desire to play elite football, and the dream of socioeconomic mobility in the context of racial capitalism provide the motivation necessary to submit to coaches' harsh authority. And, if coercion is a defining feature of the sport, then we must seriously consider the possibility that there is no such thing as freedom in college football.

CHAPTER SIX

The Normalization of College Football during a Global Pandemic

In the spring and summer of 2020, as the global economy came to an almost immediate stop to prevent the spread of the deadly COVID-19 virus, universities across the United States shut their doors, sent (most) students home, and moved classes and other activities online. College football players, however, were a notable exception and were expected to remain on campus to prepare for the fall 2020 season.[1] The subjection of college football players to the dangers of a pandemic is a perfect microcosm for the general reality that they are treated as workers essential to the political economy of higher education and yet simultaneously disposable as human beings. Recounting his experiences during the pandemic season, Wallace Bell said he initially became concerned because his coach told players and parents that the campus was the safest place to be and that no one had tested positive. Yet Bell discovered his own roommate had tested positive and was instructed to keep the results quiet, leading Bell to check into a hotel. He joined a group chat with players across the conference having similar experiences:

> We [were] hearing so many unethical and just wrongful stories in order to get us to play and have a season that we honestly shouldn't have had. But at the same time, that was the player's decision. We Want to Play movement and We Are United and so many other movements, but I understood both sides. A lot of players who were draft eligible and wanted to be able to showcase their last year to be able to get that spot and make money for their family and for themselves, and things like that. But we shouldn't value money over laws, and that's what the pandemic definitely taught us. We definitely still ended up playing and valuing players playing instead of the health and safety of their lives. . . . We all get [exposed to] a virus that we have the option not to. But for athletes, we really didn't. . . . It's not about education. These are universities built on the money of athletes. What it showed me for sure that you would tell all regulars, all traditional students to leave campus and bring back the athletes. So that debunks the whole term of placing student in front of athlete. If you only had us on campus, if we're that valuable, why not pay us? Why not simply

give us health and safety protections or life insurance or things like that? That's sad. We still haven't got life insurance. Even after playing during the pandemic, you really see what the NCAA cares about, and it's really not us, but only their money.

The pandemic compounded conditions discussed earlier, both laying bare the brute exploitation of US college football and exacerbating its worst forms of harm. In this chapter, we trace how university presidents and athletic department figures, including prominent coaches like Dabo Swinney, Mike Gundy, Jim Harbaugh, Dan Mullen, Ed Orgeron, and others, justified playing college football during the pandemic and the harm to players that ensued. Above all, the pandemic reveals how central college football is to the political economy of US higher education, and the lengths to which universities will go—indeed, the degree of exploitation to which they will resort—to ensure the flow of revenue does not stop.

In late July 2020, as the Power Five conferences prepared for an unprecedented college football season during a pandemic, a Southeastern Conference (SEC) official told player representatives on a private call, "We're going to have cases on every single team in the SEC. That's a given. And we can't prevent it."[2] A couple days later, an anonymous player was quoted in the *Guardian* addressing the plight he and his colleagues faced on campuses across the country: "We need help."[3] Given the systematic extraction of value from uncompensated players asked to put their bodies on the line, Power Five college football is clearly a fundamentally exploitative and inherently harmful institution. But never has this been more apparent than during the 2020 season. Never has the question of consent been more central to the narratives constructed around the sport. In 2020, players were directly confronted with a choice: opt in or opt out of the season. Yet that apparently simple question concealed layers of structural coercion that made the decision anything but free, fair, or consensual. Unpacking the possibility of consent during the 2020 pandemic season allows us to understand more broadly how fundamental coercion is to the project of Power Five college football and offers insights into the nature of how racial capitalism continues to shape American life.

One benefit of the 2020 season was that coaches have never been more mask-off in their articulation of where their priorities lie. Sometimes the rhetoric was just ridiculous, for instance, when Clemson coach Dabo Swinney said in April, "I think that God is bigger than [the pandemic]. I think he's gonna be glorified and shine through this in a mighty way. I think he has the ability to stamp this thing out as quick as it rose up."[4] More often, the logic was more straightforward. At Oklahoma State University, Coach Mike Gundy defended the season on purely economic grounds: "In my opinion, we need to bring our players back. They are eighteen, nineteen, twenty, twenty-one, and twenty-two years old and they are healthy and they have the ability to fight this virus off. If that is true, then we sequester them, and continue because we need to run money through the state of Oklahoma."[5] In effect, he was arguing that the bodies of young, significantly racialized (50 percent of the team was Black in 2019) players belong to the university and the state as revenue machines, regardless of the personal cost. Louisiana State University (LSU) coach Ed Orgeron, coming off a national championship title, echoed Gundy: "We need to play. This state needs [football]. This country needs it. . . . This [coronavirus] can be handled."[6] But the virus could not be handled, and by September he was telling reporters, "I think, not all of our players, but most of our players have caught it." Notably, at LSU, 76.19 percent of players in 2019 were Black. University of Florida coach Dan Mullen declared he wanted "to pack the Swamp and have 90,000 in the Swamp to give us the home-field advantage."[7] Perhaps he should be lauded for demonstrating an equal willingness to sacrifice the safety of both fans and players.

Consent and Coercion during a Pandemic

The popular justification for a pandemic season was that players *wanted* to play. SEC commissioner Greg Sankey marshaled this logic, arguing in September, just before the season started, "This is their time. They love the games. There's hope associated with the games. Last year was Joe Burrow's time. This year it will be someone else's time. What if they don't get that chance? That's part of the responsibility I feel to provide the opportunity to play."[8] Coaches agreed. Alabama's Nick Saban suggested that "everybody acts like we want to play for the money. We want to play for the players. I want to play for the players." At the University of North Carolina (UNC), where thirty-seven football players, coaches, and staff members tested positive for the virus during summer training, Coach Mack Brown declared, "These young people are dying to play. Our young people would be crushed if they were told they couldn't play."[9] Indeed, a poll of forty-five players in May found that 80 percent did want to play despite the risks.[10] The assumption that players wanted to play became so ubiquitous it was reified as common sense in headlines from the *Los Angeles Times* ("Fate of College Football in the Air as Athletes and Coaches Express Desire to Play," August 10, 2020) and *Fox News* ("College Football Players Want to Play," August 10, 2020) to the *Knoxville News-Sentinel* ("The '#WeWantToPlay' Movement, Championed by College Football Players and Coaches, Has Become a Nationwide Phenomenon on Twitter," August 10, 2020).

The public testimony of the #WeWantToPlay movement's leaders is useful for exploring the question of consent during the pandemic. On August 9, 2020, Trevor Lawrence said, "People are at just as much, if not more risk, if we don't play. Players will all be sent home to their own communities where social distancing is highly unlikely and medical care and expenses will be placed on the families if they were to contract COVID-19. Not to mention the players coming from situations that are not good for them/their future and having to go back to that. Football is a safe haven for so many people."[11]

The #WeWantToPlay movement thus aimed to position players as actively consenting to and advocating for participation in a college football season, but a closer reading indicates that structural coercion also motivated some of their thinking. Structural coercion refers to how social and economic distribution of resources shape and constrain access to opportunity. Lawrence suggests "medical care and expenses" are an onerous burden that "will be placed on the families if they were to contract COVID-19." Choosing to play for this reason is not a function of desire, but rather a need to prevent devastating expenses. Furthermore, Lawrence alludes to "players coming from situations that are not good for them/their future." College is a safe space and site of opportunity, allowing many to escape a "situation" or, less euphemistically, conditions of privation and insecurity. If these dynamics were different, so too might be the motivation to play. A similar logic underpinned one of the most prominent attestations of the players' desire to move forward with a season. After the Atlantic Coast Conference (ACC), SEC, and Big 12 decided to conduct their seasons, agitation to play shifted to the Big Ten, which initially decided to postpone its season. In response, the league's most prominent player, Ohio State quarterback Justin Fields, organized a petition ultimately signed by 300,000 people demanding players be given the right to a season. The petition concluded, "We believe that we should have the right to make decisions about what is best for our health and our future. Don't let our hard work and sacrifice be in vain."[12] While the purpose of Fields's rhetoric is persuasion premised on the principle that players deserve the opportunity to exercise agency, or *choose*, it inadvertently reveals the structural factors constraining that choice. First, the claim that players deserve "the right to make decisions" about "our future" suggests it is not only a desire to play motivating this campaign. In a vacuum, the decision to play would come down to the question of whether the pleasure of the season outweighed the risk of health-related harm. Yet, by introducing the specter of the future, Fields invites us to consider how the choice to play *now* is inflected by that choice's implications for *later*. Unsaid but implied are the material repercussions of this choice—the future professional opportunities that may or may not exist. Future wages are a structural constraint on the choice, underlined by the sentence "Don't let our hard work and sacrifice be in vain." The football season is less about play than it is about work, including the work and harm already invested. Given the investments of players and families in building football players capable of earning economic and social capital through the sport, the idea of them *not* playing when so close to the finish line—the actual remuneration offered by professional football—is almost unfathomable. This has little to do with the desire to play football. It is a function of structural conditions that produce a *need* to labor at college football, including through the literal "sacrifice" of the body. Families and players have already tacitly accepted (via structural coercion, not pure consent) the risk of profound bodily harm through the sport as a precondition of entry. How much more extreme, really, was the risk of the virus?

Fields was one of the most outspoken advocates of #WeWantToPlay.[13] While his argument was couched in the crowd-pleasing rhetoric of his "love" for the game—Erin Hatton has shown that in hegemonic discourse, "being a college athlete is . . . construed as a labor of love, not work"—when asked about the risks of the virus, he replied, "I think COVID-19 brings a risk to everybody, but the question I would like to ask you is would we be more safe on campus playing football or off campus doing whatever. COVID, people could contract it anywhere. But, for me personally, I feel safer at the facility and around my teammates, knowing my teammates will be tested twice a week. That is the safest environment for me and my teammates, I think."[14] Campus safety became a central talking point of this campaign. Yet even if we leave aside this argument's flawed premise (players were essentially subjected to an experiment in herd immunity on many campuses), on its face it says more about structural coercion than individual choice. The fantasy of relative security in a context of frequent exposure to the virus during a pandemic is only intelligible in a situation where that virus has been allowed to rampage unimpeded through the broader community. This was the reality of life during the Trumpist era of the pandemic in the United States. Yet such a eugenicist approach to public health was far from an inevitability. Public policy produced a set of structural conditions individuals had to navigate to survive. In that context it was perhaps rational to imagine campuses offered greater security, much as it is rational to view college sport as a stepping-stone to access greater social, cultural, and economic capital, despite its exploitative character.

In the same vein, many parents in the Big Ten conference weighed in when the league was considering postponing the season. Dianne Freiermuth, mother of a Penn State tight end and leader of the Penn State Football Parents Association, released a statement on the organization's behalf.[15] The statement also inadvertently highlighted the structural conditions informing the parents' advocacy for their children to play: "I truly believe that these young men are being cared for both physically and mentally in a manner that could not be replicated in their own homes." Similarly, eleven University of Nebraska families represented by a law firm sent a letter to the league making the same case: "We strongly believe that the football environment at the University of Nebraska is the safest place for them to be."[16] Given that the care for players on campus included both exposure to the virus and repeated head impacts, asserting campus was relatively safer, if taken at face value, suggests the profound insecurity experienced in homes across the country during the pandemic from both economic and health standpoints. That this insecurity militated in favor of participation in college football during a pandemic is further evidence of coercion rather than consent.

Explicit status coercion and concomitant fear were persistent factors in many college football players' decision to participate in the 2020 season. One Power Five player explained, "When everything first was shut down and cancelled, we were actually going to have like a team workout. And they told us we were going to try and have a spring ball practice that day even though we weren't supposed to practice for like I think a week after that." He did say teammates were informed if they chose not to practice, "it's not going to be held against you," but "people kind of didn't really trust that." Another Power Five player explained that in the face of the imminent threat of the virus, he and his teammates "feel like our protocols are inadequate, and that they don't properly protect us. . . . We are in communication with athletes at schools in our conference as well as in other Power Five conferences, and every university seems to be following different guidelines. One specific problem that we have with current policies, is the apparent scarcity of testing. We have not been tested since first arriving on campus. It's been almost two months since then. . . . This is all alarming given the rate of asymptomatic carriers being as high as 40 percent as reported by some studies. We are not happy."[17]

At least one Power Five player found that coaches violated "a bunch of the protocols and testing standards we expected when we came."[18] After having his concerns ignored and downplayed, he elected to "boycott" workouts and planned to opt out of the season. Another Power Five player said he and his teammates weren't told about the most serious risks, like potential heart damage, when given the choice to opt out. "We don't really feel safe," he said.[19] Still another Power Five player added, "It's laughable to many of us that anyone could expect a lack of backlash if you were to sit out . . . if a coach wants to, they can find ways to push players out of the program. Even if you were planning to transfer afterwards, you have to ask yourself how coaches at other universities might view you. You risk being blackballed as a player."[20] And no wonder, given that at Utah State, Coach Gary Anderson told players, "At least in our program, we don't have an opt out. And it's not an option. If you opt out, you're not with us."[21] This is what Wallace Bell experienced at his Power Five school when he decided to opt out: "You get ostracized from your team; you have to get removed. Group chats, that's what happened to me. You get told to remove yourself from the locker room. I was told to remove all my equipment from the locker room. So yes, they may not say we cut the player, but they can put you in every action that makes you dismissed from the team and to be cut." When he attempted to transfer, "They ostracized me from my team and they stripped me of my film, which is what I couldn't even use. I couldn't even post about."

Players articulated a desire to resist, but it was tempered by a fear of the repercussions: lost opportunity and access to both higher education and a platform for building a potential NFL career. One Power Five player said, "There have been talks of boycotting or striking. I don't think anyone else will actually do anything, though, because of the power dynamics inherent in college football as we know it today. We don't feel safe actually doing anything, because at the end of the day who is going to support us or protect us? It seems that everyone in charge of us is in the process of circling the wagons, and the priority of coaches and administration has been set on protecting the program, not student-athletes."[22] Yet athletes were left afraid of what would happen to them if they did continue with the season. Brigham Young University linebacker Zayne Anderson told the *Salt Lake Tribune*, "If someone were to get tested, you kind of know the guys that have had it and stay away from some of the guys that might be out and about all the time, but they're pretty discreet in keeping their privacy of who has it and who doesn't. Really, you're out there on your own."[23] Another Power Five player said, "Why are people having this power over us, and why aren't they being checked? I'm honestly the most stressed out that I've been in my life. I have a teammate [near] me who has tested positive and has complained to me about how much his lungs hurt. This is coming from an incredibly fit, athletic guy with six-pack abs. He told me verbatim, that 'there is no way I could go through a whole practice much less a game within three weeks.' This shit breaks down your body. We need help."[24]

Harms of Pandemic Football

If coercion and consent are one side of the equation in considering the participation of college football players in the 2020 COVID season, the other side is the harm universities exposed athletes to in order to ensure a season was played. This raises the questions of both the nature and scope of that harm experienced by athletes and the ways universities actually facilitated and abetted it.

When universities began inviting players back on campus to participate in training activities before the season, they sometimes furnished athletes with waivers absolving the institution of responsibility for harm resulting from the virus. One *USA Today* report quoted an anonymous player who said his school "required him to sign a document before he could begin voluntary workouts. . . . It states in part that the signee understands he may be at higher risk for exposure to COVID-19 because playing football involves close contact with others."[25] A different Power Five player shared a waiver that began "with the statement that the university in question is unable to ensure that team members will not be infected with COVID-19 during football activities." The waiver then stated that participation in football activities is "voluntary," before suggesting that it would "potentially" expose players to COVID-19. After this, the waiver asks players to "'release from fault' any employees or agents of the university for injury and illness including death that occurs as a consequence of contracting the virus from football activities."[26] These waivers represent an admission by these institutions that they were subjecting players to an exceptional level of danger.

University complicity extended beyond athletic departments deciding to endanger athletes in training and eventually the season. The academic side also exposed campus athletic workers to potentially extreme harm. One Power Five player recounted a coercive dynamic where he was required to participate in a COVID-related research study in order to take part in team activities. Around May, a coach told him if he didn't "consent to be a participant in an ongoing study" that "we would be set back as individuals for what could be weeks, a setback which they directly said could affect our playing time." Teammates were also instructed to sign "a waiver that freed the university of any liability from a wide variety of things, including the loss of our own life. . . . [We] were told things were voluntary, but things were framed in a way that felt manipulative. They specifically asked us if we wanted to play football, as well as other things in the same vein. Throughout the process my teammates and I have joked about how false this whole voluntary pretense feels."[27]

When the Big Ten ultimately decided to move ahead with a season in October, Dr. Jim Borchers, head team medical official at Ohio State and cochair of the medical subcommittee of the conference's return to competition task force, explained that all players in the conference would be enrolled in a mass research project on COVID: "Everyone associated with the Big Ten should be very proud of the groundbreaking steps that are now being taken to better protect the health and safety of the student-athletes and surrounding communities. The data we are going to collect from testing and the cardiac registry will provide major contributions for all 14 Big Ten institutions as they study COVID-19 and attempt to mitigate the spread of the disease among wider communities."[28] What remained unsaid was how exactly informed consent would be procured from these players without the coercion present in the May example.

It became clear that university officials in conferences like the SEC were under no illusion they could keep players safe from the virus when they asked them to "consent" to participate.[29] Consequently, medical officials across the Power Five rhetorically minimized the threat posed by COVID, normalizing the virus long before vaccines existed. Cameron Wolfe, ACC medical advisory chair, said, "You have to feel some level of comfortable playing in a non-zero risk environment. You can't tell me that running onto a football field is supposed to be a zero-risk environment. . . . Now the reality is we have to accept a little bit of COVID risk to be a part of that."[30] And risk there certainly was. At Clemson, after twenty-three players contracted the virus, the team continued to practice (only infected players were asked to isolate for ten days), leading to *fourteen* more players subsequently testing positive.[31] The University of North Carolina (UNC) temporarily shut down the program when thirty-seven players got COVID.[32] At Vanderbilt, a game against Missouri was canceled because the team could not field the fifty-three scholarship players required by SEC conference rules.[33] At Baylor, twenty-eight players and fourteen staff tested positive.[34]

Players experienced the same hardships as others who endured COVID in the prevaccine era. Clemson's Xavier Thomas struggled with long COVID symptoms for over five months: "I was at a really good point after spring ball, and then dealing with COVID and stuff, it just set me back a lot. My symptoms were really bad. A really bad fever and my body was really bad. I felt really weak and stuff like that. With the breathing and stuff, it was pretty tough to get over." He also said his "chest would be tight" when climbing stairs. Thomas added, "Coming back in the summer I was really winded. My breathing wasn't really good coming back, returning from COVID. It was really affecting me. Then I started to make a little bit of progress and I got strep, which put me back even more. Before fall camp I realized it would get real tight in my chest and everything would tighten down. I would really be struggling to breathe. So I really just had to talk to my coaches and things like that and tell them what I was going through. They had a protocol for me."[35]

Player Resistance during the Pandemic

If the 2020 pandemic season served as a condensed form of the myriad harms of college football, it was also a locus for resistance. Across the country, players flexed their power both individually and collectively, realizing their capacity to withhold athletic labor as a valuable instrument for achieving justice. At Mississippi State, running back Kylin Hill refused to play until the state flag, which included the confederate flag, was changed.[36] He tweeted (@H_Kylin, June 22, 2020), "Either change the flag or I won't be representing this State anymore 100 & I meant that . . . I'm tired. . . . Unlike rest I was born in this state and 100 and I know [sic] what the flag mean." He was ultimately successful, and the flag was changed.

Likewise, University of Texas players refused to stand for the playing of "The Eyes of Texas" because of the song's links to racist minstrel shows.[37] But the outcome at Texas was different, owing to the plantation dynamics so fundamental to the sport. Wealthy donors, angered by the protests, threatened to withhold funding if the song did not continue. One email sent by donor Larry Wilkinson stated that "less than 6 percent of our current study body is Black . . . the tail cannot be allowed to wag the dog. . . . The dog must instead stand up for what is right. Nothing forces those students to attend UT Austin. Encourage them to select an alternate school . . . NOW!"[38] Such letters were effective, leading to players being told that continued protest might lead to fewer job opportunities after college.[39]

At Oklahoma State, running back Chuba Hubbard took issue with Coach Mike Gundy wearing a T-shirt promoting far-right broadcaster One America News, tweeting (@Hubbard_RMN, June 15, 2020), "I will not stand for this. . . . This is completely insensitive to everything going on in society, and it's unacceptable. I will not be doing anything with Oklahoma State until things CHANGE." His statement ultimately prompted Gundy to perform some level of contrition: "[I was] made aware of some things that players feel like can make our organization, our culture even better than it is here at Oklahoma State. I'm looking forward to making some changes, and it starts at the top with me."[40] He also apologized more directly to players: "I want to apologize to all members of our team, former players and their families for the pain and discomfort that has been caused over the last two days. Black lives matter to me. Our players matter to me."[41] Similarly, at Kansas State, football players threatened to boycott all team activities if the university did not put a social media policy in place for students prohibiting racist speech after student Jaden McNeil tweeted, "Congratulations to George Floyd on being drug free for an entire month!"[42]

While racial justice was a clear impetus for athlete organizing and resistance in the summer of 2020, given the explosion of activism across the United States following the murder of George Floyd by police in Minneapolis, significant organizing also focused on the working conditions caused by the pandemic. In June 2020, thirty football players at UCLA (University of California, Los Angeles) sent a letter to the university in which they chafed at how, from "neglected and mismanaged injury cases, to a now mismanaged Covid-19 pandemic, our voices have been continuously muffled. . . . We as a football community assert our right to protect, preserve, and make decisions with regard to our own personal health and safety and now demand that we are able to do so without consequence in terms of reduction, or cancellation of scholarship benefits, or retaliation from coaches and faculty in any shape or form." To enforce these freedoms, players demanded "third-party health officials in charge of overseeing and enforcing health and safety guidelines," "whistleblower protections provided for athletes and staff," and the "ability to make decisions with regard to personal health without consequences."[43] Likewise, at Michigan State, offensive lineman Jordan Reid tweeted (@jordanreid58, July 24, 2020), "Guys are testing positive across the country left and right . . . why is there still discussion on a season? Why is it taking so long to make a logical decision? Hmm let me guess REVENUE." Ramogi Huma, founder and president of the National College Players Association, told *USA Today* what he heard from "more than two dozen football players upset about how Covid-19 testing is being handled by their respective schools." Huma said, "These players I'm talking to are really angry. They are truly, genuinely angry. They're realizing, from their mouth, they're saying, 'Our program doesn't care about us.'" An anonymous player confirmed this, telling *USA Today* that he "is one of 20 to 25 players at his school who are talking about refusing to play this season because of Covid-19 concerns. I'm not out here just acting like everything's normal when it's not."[44]

All this unrest coalesced in large-scale organizing projects such as #WeAreUnited in the Pac-12, College Athlete Unity in the Big Ten, and Mountain West United in the Mountain West. #WeAreUnited published a series of strong demands in *The Players' Tribune*, including allowing players to opt out of the season without punishment, the prohibition of all waivers limiting institutional liability for harm caused by COVID, the imposition of health and safety protocols approved of by players and administered by a third party, medical insurance for players for six years after the end of eligibility, six-year scholarships to improve educational experiences, and a 50 percent share of revenue, among others.[45] #WeAreUnited secured a meeting with Pac-12 commissioner Larry Scott to discuss their concerns, but its members were frustrated when they were not taken seriously. Although they pushed the commissioner to implement more COVID testing and eligibility protections for players who opted out, they made little progress. The commissioner reportedly called their public statement a "misguided P.R. stunt."[46] UCLA's Otito Ogbonnia, a junior at the time and a member of the #WeAreUnited group that spoke with Scott, said of the meeting, "I don't think he thought of us as people who were making a legitimate case." The Pac-12 initially canceled the season after the meeting, but ultimately went ahead with an abridged season, joining the other Power Five conferences in ensuring revenue would not be conceded in the name of health and safety.

Athlete mobilizations like #WeAreUnited and #WeWantToPlay were not immune from the broader power relations already discussed. Wallace Bell recalled being cut from his football team because he participated in #WeAreUnited:

> During the pandemic, colleges were closed, so therefore I couldn't meet with my coach in person. So I set up a phone call [with my coach], just let them know I'll be opting out and I'm thinking that I would be able to work out with the team, even though I'm choosing to opt out. Because that's what other teams are doing across the nation. So I'm not thinking that I'm going to be cut or anything. . . . Also I

did record the conversation. It was just for my parents to have a full understanding of what was said on my end and what was said on his end. And little did I know that it went the way it did. I didn't think it was going to go that way. So was basically just my evidence for myself, because we know the power dynamic when it comes to coaches and players. They can do whatever they want to do to us, because it constantly renews itself. Like the system constantly renews the athletes. So we're easily replaceable.

The school further retaliated against Bell by refusing to release any of his game footage to him, compromising his ability to transfer to another Football Bowl Subdivision (FBS) roster. Still, he said, "I'm not trying to bash the university at all, because that's not me. I try to move through love with everything, but it was just an unfortunate circumstance and it ended up playing the way it did. But at the same time, I feel like I am an example of how gruesome the system can be. And my story, I just want to empower college athletes to be able to think for themselves within a system that psychologically oppresses them." Bell shared the recorded audio with us, and it is clear he was being punished for his participation in #WeAreUnited, highlighting the power dynamics at play between athletic workers and coaches, which were amplified during the season of pandemic football.

Experiencing the Pandemic Season

Some players we interviewed participated in the 2020 COVID season. Their experiences testify to how universities do and do not value the well-being of the athletes under their care and authority. Matt Jensen walked us through some of the strange dynamics of that season: "They had to basically do two practices back to back, because it couldn't have a whole group of 120 guys. They had to break it up into 60 and 60. So we could only practice for an hour and a half, as opposed to letting it drag on for like two and a half, three hours. . . . In that respect it was nice because it forced them to let us go at a reasonable time so we could get back and like do other stuff." The emphasis on efficiency is notable partly because it shows that the structural constraints on educational experiences produced by endless football responsibilities are not even necessary. If teams were authentically concerned with offering a robust student-athlete experience, they could do so. Jensen goes on to explain how the chaos produced by

COVID made the educational side of college football even more untenable than usual:

> When we got quarantined up in [another state], that sucked. . . . We thought we were going to take our finals up there. . . . I didn't bring any of my study materials because like, "Oh it's a one-day trip . . . no big deal." But then when I heard that, I went to my buddy, and I was like, "Hey, if you want to go fifty-fifty on a rental car, we can get the hell out of here so we can go back and take our finals in person. Or, not in person but, like, at our houses, so we don't fucking fail." And he's like, "Dude, yes." [Laughs] But, thankfully, they were able to send us back home.

Aaron Peters was frustrated by the double standard of coaches, who waived protocols for team functions but then strictly enforced them for players' leisure time: "They told us we couldn't have parties, we couldn't do this, we couldn't do that. Okay, so it sounds like y'all are just complying, because at the same time, we'll go to lunch and nobody would have a mask on. We won't be six feet apart." One benefit to the COVID season was more spontaneity with scheduling, restoring some of the fun of the game, as Jensen explains:

> We canceled and planned a new game within like twenty-four hours. We were supposed to play [conference team A]. But then [they] got COVID. Coincidentally [conference team B] got COVID and they were supposed to play [conference team C]. So, we just hopped on [conference team B's] private charter, and their hotel reservation, and we played a pickup game of football. . . . Which is probably, it was one of the funnest games I've ever had. Probably because it was one of the few games [that] I played [almost] the whole game. So there's experiences like that, where it's cool, one-in-a-million experiences . . . like playing in the [stadium] when there's nobody there.

Jensen also experienced #WeAreUnited from the inside, not as an organizer but as one of the hundreds of players being organized in real time as the possibility of the season unfolded:

> A lot of what they were talking about was paying the athletes. And I knew as a walk-on I wasn't going to see a lot of that money. But I was like, "You know, it's good for the future movements. Some future walk-on sixty years from now will thank me. I might as well do what

I can now." [Leader involved with #WeAreUnited] was a really big spearhead for the movement, and he was the same way, he's like, "I'm graduating this year but this will be good for the younger generations." I believe it was, they want longer than four years' health care after you graduate, and maybe some financial compensation, and that sort of thing. But it was definitely cool to be a part of, because we had this huge group chat full of 400 to 500 people from schools all over the country. It was cool to just like get everybody talking.

For Daniel Barber, #WeAreUnited's concerns about the implications of opting out of the COVID season were far from an abstraction: "When I opted out, I was basically told, 'Okay, well, you can forget about your fifth year.' I ended up entering the transfer portal because I was basically told, 'You're losing your scholarship.' I think we had eighteen people on my team enter into the transfer portal, maybe five of them landed at a comparable program. And so, that's a whole year of education, that's a whole year of play, that's what it really is. That's what a lot of people want, that people will miss out on. I mean, yeah, we were failed." Barber underlines that even if a formal rule or regulation exists about opting out, as with all dynamics in college sport, the actual practice is shaped and constrained by coercive conditions controlled by coaches. Whether one has an additional year of eligibility is largely academic if a coach determines not to offer that player playing time in that additional year. This was both a threat that compelled some players to participate in the COVID season and a concrete reality for those who chose to opt out. Brock Adler had a similar experience:

> When I opted out, my coach told me like, "Oh, because you didn't play during this COVID year, it's gonna be tough for you to get back out there, you're going to be third string and that stuff, but you're going to have to work hard for that," and I just said, "No, thank you." This was in 2020. And I live with my grandparents, and that's why I opted out, because I'm like, "I don't want to put them at risk for a dumb season that I probably won't play in." And I don't know if I would have played in it or not, but it wasn't worth it to me. And then the coaches held that against me.

One threat facing players during the COVID season was the possibility that coaches, like so many others, simply did not take the virus seriously. Brock Adler explains, "I'm gonna tell you this right now, [head coach] does not believe in COVID. He is against [city] Public Health. . . . He's expressed his anger with them, and the media has tried to cover it up. And in that regard, he is very negligent. Because my defensive line room has gotten—when I opted out—my room got infected twice with a COVID outbreak." Similarly, Daniel Barber describes the complete failure of a coaching staff to implement health and safety protocols commensurate with the threat posed by the virus. To begin with, most of the promises coaches made in the beginning proved empty: that players would have private dorm rooms (they were moved together after a few months), regular testing (that didn't start until an outbreak one month into training), or small practice groups (they were quickly doubled in size). Worse yet, when a player first tested positive, coaches didn't disclose that information and players had to find out by word of mouth. Once the cat was out of the bag, coaches asked players if they were comfortable practicing:

> They called us into meeting rooms. They had offense huddled up, I don't know what they did, I was on defense. I'm imagining they did a group meeting and they're like, "Do you want to practice? Like, we do not have this under control. We tried to contact trace. Are you okay to practice?" And they were like, "Yeah." No one sat out. Defense, they called us all in. Had us come to the meeting room during warm-ups, and they were like, "Hey, are you okay with practicing?" Like, you can walk out if you want, but no one on offense walked out. "So do you want to practice?" And everyone was like, [shrugs] "Fuck it." And it was, "You can stop. But, are you *going to stop?*"

Ultimately, for Barber, the coaching staff's failure to protect players and appropriately respond to the danger of the virus in advance of the season was simply too much to endure: "I ended up just snapping. I couldn't sleep the night before I opted out. [Shakes head] It was rough."

In the end, the COVID season was not so much exceptional as it was exemplary of the themes that define the college football experience. The coercion and harm experienced by players like Barber, Adler, and Jensen were a logical extension of the exploitative dynamics that define the sport. As Ryan Leonard explains,

> A pandemic hit America, and so many professionals . . . weren't allowed to go to work, but yet these amateurs that was college football, these amateurs that weren't being paid to be there, weren't getting hazard paid, weren't getting overtime, they were allowed to participate and they were allowed to make profits for the institution

and the individuals under that institution. They were considered essential workers of the institution, and they were allowed to perform. And, in an environment that is probably the least conducive environment in the pandemic you can imagine, sweating and spitting . . . everything was shut down except for college football. You were allowed to sweat on people. You were allowed to spit on people, you were allowed to exchange bodily fluids with another man, but so many other professions were shut down. It just highlights to me how much . . . not only the institution is dependent upon that revenue, but how much the cities that surround the institution are depending on it. One of the greatest examples I have is actually this pancake house, and I went up and asked them, I was like, "Well, why do you guys do this? Why do you give athletes free pancakes?" And they answered as, "Well, we would go out of business if it weren't for football season. We wouldn't be able to pay our employees if it wasn't for you guys, so this is our way of paying you back."

Wallace Bell adds of the pandemic experience, "And we really honestly should not be playing, when it's something that continually affects our heart and things like that and it's an airborne disease, but they're not going to tell us to not play 'cause of the entertainment industry and monetary value it holds and things like that, then how can you say that they truly care for us?" Confronted with the choice of whether to prioritize the health, safety, and well-being of college athletes or the copious revenue those athletes produced, the sport's decision makers kept the cash flowing. After all, if college football as we know it is predicated on the systematic subjection of athletes to brain trauma, what difference does the odd viral outbreak make?

Conclusion: The Normalization of Pandemic Football

Normal. That is what we called the eerily dystopian push to go on with a college football season in 2020.[47] While the world entered into lockdown, college football players were expected to show up to practice as if it were business as usual. During a time that was nothing short of abnormal—even chaotic—sport was a cultural vestige we clung to for some sense of normality. When it comes to professional sport—wherein athletic workers are remunerated according to agreed-on contracts that include labor and health and safety protections—powering on through a pandemic, while still rather insidious, might fairly be viewed as justified, certainly more so than in the context of college football, where athletic workers are *not* compensated and *not* subject to labor laws that protect their health and safety. In this case, playing through pandemic conditions is not only morally unjustifiable, it is reprehensible.

Perhaps no other case study can show the reality that college football does not care about athletes, so long as the revenue wheels keep churning, more clearly than pushing through a season during a global pandemic. As universities shut their campuses down to avoid the spread of the deadly virus, college football players were among the *only* students asked to remain on campus—and asked to subject themselves to a contagion with consequences yet unknown.

Yet how many times were college athletes praised as "essential workers"? While other "essential workers" were applauded for risking their health in service of humanity, college football players were told to be grateful for the opportunity to play. The harm associated with playing college football during the pandemic must be centered in our broader analysis of the lived reality of college football. As a clear case study in harm and exploitation, above all, the pandemic revealed the economic centrality of college football to higher education, and the lengths to which universities will go to ensure the cash flow does not stop.

Conclusion

Cancel College Football

This book has attempted to illuminate the myriad axes of exploitation and harm that are fundamental to contemporary big-time college football. By focusing on the voices and experiences of the campus athletic workers who have endured the injustices of a system built to systematically extract wealth from them through intense and corporeal violence, we have brought the reader face to face with the human cost of this exploitation. We have documented how college football operates as a modality of racial capitalism that is and always has been characterized by economic exploitation, harm, abuse, educational inequality, gender inequity, and plantation dynamics.

There is an academic fetish for solutions, as if any treatise articulating a problem must also solve it—a sort of spoonful of sugar to help the medicine go down. We aren't interested in that. We are, however, genuinely concerned about where things go from here, particularly because this is a moment of seemingly seismic change in US college athletics. For many college athletics activists and reformers, changes like liberalized name, image, and likeness (NIL) policies and less punitive transfer rules signify an end of exploitation. But let us be very clear: while these changes are necessary and beneficial to campus athletic workers, they are also in no way sufficient to the magnitude of injustice, inequity, and harm that define the college football system and have defined it for decades.

We have two entirely distinct answers to the question of what should be done to ameliorate the harm and exploitation that suffuse college football. One states what we consider to be an ultimate ethical vanishing point. The other is a pragmatic path forward to address some of the harm and injustice done to college athletes. The latter has the most realistic policy implications, but the former should loom as a specter over all thought and action in the sphere of college football.

Let us begin with the question of what *should* be done. College football, like so many sites of socially reproductive high-performance spectator sport, is morally unsustainable. It is impossible to reconcile the pedagogical mission of universities with the inherent harm caused by the sport itself and its inextricable imbrication in a radically stratified system of US racial capitalism. The only ethical solution to the problem of college football is abolition. The sport cannot continue to exist if we are serious about universities as places where students are nurtured, developed, and protected from harm.

College football is premised on economic exploitation as a—if not the—fundamental characteristic of its operation. The tremendous value produced by athletes is distributed to university athletic departments and their staff instead of the athletes who produce lucrative commodity spectacle through their labor. In return for this work, athletes are promised an unorthodox wage: an educational experience. Yet due to structural constraints on their time, energy, and capacity to follow their academic aspirations and inclinations, college football players do not receive the education they are promised. Recall the story shared by Derek in the preface about his students being expected to attend early-morning classes after playing out of state well past midnight. Campus athletic workers *cannot* receive the education they are promised precisely because of their participation in athletics. This failure to educate is an egregious form of wage theft that cannot be reconciled so long as college football exists as commodity spectacle to be sold in stadiums and via broadcast for the explicit gain of predominantly white institutions (PWIs), media conglomerates, and those in the college sports/media industrial complex.

If in the exchange between college football player and college sports/media complex the *value* principally accrues to those who do not labor on the gridiron, this is not true of the *harms* generated in the transaction. Regardless of the doubt manufactured at concussion research institutions conveniently embedded in and funded by the very college football system they study, tackle football inherently requires physical trauma, particularly to the brains of participants. As Thomas Rycliff puts it in reflecting on his time in the sport, "I would've rather had student debt and been a regular student and not carry the physical and mental baggage, really lifelong baggage things. I want to be there for my kids physically and mentally, so there's guilt in that as you get older, that these fleeting moments of glory aren't always worth it in the long run." This life-altering and sometimes life-ending trauma is inextricable from the sport as it is now played, which means that college football is built on a form of human sacrifice. For this reason, above all, the sport is ethically indefensible, particularly from the standpoint of institutions of higher education and development.

It is also morally repugnant given that all of the value reaped by coaches, administrators, and even media figures is predicated on that sacrifice. This makes the sport one of the most unjust forms of work currently being performed in the United States today. Terry Davis puts it best:

> I don't think the game should exist. There's no real reason for it outside of benefiting the people who benefit the most currently, and the violent nature of the game and the things that we are learning about it. You can't consider yourself an advanced society while having this continue to be so pervasive. . . . You care for your child so much and you want them to be successful and chase their dreams, that you will cheer for them walking to their deaths with real killers who seen real shit happen in their lives. That's why the game shouldn't exist. You cannot guarantee you can keep these kids safe from that game, in that game, during that game. Your rules and your whistle does not keep them safe. I don't think you can make the game equitable enough in college for the game to exist, because it would have to. . . . You need that level of advancement in life-changing money to exist in college level to justify high school.

Yet, remarkably, this is only part of the explanation for the necessity of abolition of the sport. The unjust distribution of benefit and harm in college football must also be understood within the context of the structural racism that shapes US society. Put differently, college football is a principal site in which the plantation dynamics of US history are reproduced because those who bear the costs of producing the commodity spectacle are disproportionately racialized, while those who reap the benefits are disproportionately white. This system of value exploitation premised on physical sacrifice is also a mechanism for the further racial transfer of wealth from Black Americans to white Americans. These plantation dynamics cannot be understood as a function of choice or consent. Rather, they are the direct product of the broader plantation dynamics that have shaped US history, from chattel slavery and Jim Crow to the putative postracial civil rights era. Participation in college football is a product of structural coercion that feeds into a system that empowers coaches via the status coercion they wield over unpaid workers to inflict harm and abuse almost indiscriminately in the relentless attempt to maximize the extraction of performance that yields value. At no point have these dynamics been more evident than during the COVID season of 2020, in which the administrators charged with decision-making powers over the sport decreed that players would "play" despite the presence of a mortal virus that could not be meaningfully mitigated or protected against. For all of the above reasons we declare the sport morally unsustainable and illegitimate in the context of higher education. College football should be abolished.

Institutions of supposed "higher education" have been lamentably culpable in the violent exploitation of a predominantly racialized group of athletic laborers to explicitly transfer wealth from them to a largely white class of coaches, athletic directors, and other campus administrators. Following this, we contend that collegiate athletics is perhaps one of the best points of departure for a revolution in higher education writ large because it is the most tangible and conspicuous site of the exploitation that extends through the capillaries of academia today. Our interviews made clear that the current neoliberal structure of higher education commodified is fueled by the sacrifice of a disproportionately racialized group of athletic laborers even as it exploits students en masse through increased tuition, residential costs, and other features of university spectacle.[1] In fact, the existence of big-time college football within interuniversity sport is in so many ways antithetical to the mission of higher education—which often purports to provide students with the tools necessary to build things like "character," "integrity," and "leadership," to promote the "betterment of global society," and to "enrich lives" and "advance the intellectual and social condition of the people."[2] Wallace Bell perhaps articulated the hypocrisy of such claims best when he said, "Your true identity is not with football. I'm getting taught that. Not a lot of my peers are getting taught that. It's so sad because we value what we do on the field more than the people that we are. And it's sad that we're conditioned and programmed to think like that and then we accept it as such. I would say it's a psychologically depressive system because it doesn't teach us to really be stable outside of football or be human outside."

We have witnessed a shift in higher education to focus on the delivery of an enhanced "student experience" intimately connected to college athletics.[3] To redress the exploitation of campus athletic workers we must first reimagine what higher education as a whole would look like without the harm addressed in this book. We thus conclude with a plea to revolutionize higher education in all respects. We demand an end to the violent exploitation of campus athletic workers to provide other students (and nonstudents) with forms of entertainment clearly branded by universities as integral to their experience; to completely revolutionize the funding model for both institutions and students so that *all* students have the means and ability to access higher education; and to fundamentally change admissions criteria to ensure that any person who wants a university education can access it. These are but some of the changes that must happen before we begin to reimagine sport.

While college sport enthusiasts and apologists would have you believe reform can come with liberalized transfer and NIL rules, we are firm in our stance that the only way to redress the harms inherent in college football is to fundamentally reshape *both* college athletics and the higher education system that is increasingly subordinate to it.

Yet to abolish college football is in turn to introduce a range of additional challenges. Across the United States, an astounding number of people participate in tackle football. In 2021, 677,872 children aged six to twelve and 976,886 students in high school participated in tackle football.[4] As of 2018–19, the NCAA reported a total of 73,712 participants in college football.[5] All these young people have invested time, labor, and, tragically, physical harm in the sport. To abolish college football (and, logically extending the point, professional football, which, although not as exploitative in terms of degree, is still ultimately morally unsustainable and thus deserving of abolition) means eliminating some of the value that is to potentially be recouped by participants, particularly those who do so in the hopes of achieving opportunities otherwise denied. In a society stratified by extreme forms of inequality, the removal of one lever of opportunity and improved life chances can understandably be construed as compounding the harm that already exists. This is a legitimate rejoinder to the question of abolishing college football that must be addressed in any serious treatment of the subject. While we do not purport to have all of the answers to this question, we present some possible horizons for the future of tackle football—both radical and pragmatist.

The only just mechanism for abolishing college football is, in our view, one that centers reparations. In *Reconsidering Reparations*, Olúfẹ́mi O. Táíwò writes, "The just world we are trying to build is a better distribution system, by apportioning rights, advantages, and burdens in a better manner than the one we've inherited from the global racial empire. It is also a view that looks to justly distribute the benefits and burdens of that transitional process of rebuilding."[6] By connecting and building on various critiques of the merits of reparations, Táíwò offers a nuanced theorization of slavery and colonialism's interwoven life course within a racial capitalist political economy.[7] In so doing, Táíwò ambitiously suggests unraveling racial capitalism by grappling with its interconnected history of colonialism, and the robust set of strategies, practices, processes, and actions that comprise the tangible performance of that world order. In this way, Táíwò's theory moves the needle beyond historical materialist and decolonial propositions insofar as it presents a road map for reparations that focuses not only on correcting harms of the past, but on building new futures within a radically different social structure.[8] This is part of what he refers to as a "constructivist" vision of reparations, a vision we share. Building on his generative work, we argue for the abolition of college football in conjunction with a system of reparations, not only to both current and former participants, but also to those already enrolled in youth football who aspire to access higher education through the sport. Like it or not, US higher education is fundamentally complicit in the enterprise of football at every level, relying as it does on youth and high school ranks to train its labor force and serving as the de facto minor league for the professional levels. US college football and its attendant sports/media complex have a profound debt to pay, particularly to Black Americans. The dismantling of the system means that restitution must be made and that the harm must cease. In the most literal possible sense, institutions of higher education, the NCAA, the NFL, broadcasters like ESPN, CBS, and Fox, and so many others, collectively owe a remarkable debt to all of those playing tackle football in the United States and elsewhere for the harm *they have already suffered* at the hands of the sport and those who benefit from it. Any just process of abolition and reparations requires actual redistribution from these entities to those who have played and are currently playing the sport.

But, as Táíwò reveals, the most productive approaches to reparations are constructivist *as well as* compensatory.[9] We must ultimately imagine sport as a site of play, aesthetics, and pleasure, and that requires imagining a society beyond racial capitalism, wherein participation is predicated on enthusiastic consent. In that sense, justly abolishing college football requires radical and material forms of structural decolonization, antiracism, and anticapitalism in society at large. Football serves as an avenue of opportunity in a society that otherwise denies it. To genuinely benefit those who turn to football as a life raft for themselves and their families, the sport must be replaced by alternatives that offer better material conditions without the personal cost.

The first and perhaps most obvious form of constructivist reparation involves improved access to higher education.[10] Higher education should be a right enjoyed by all Americans (everyone, actually). Were higher education made genuinely accessible—that is, free—a principal incentive for participation in football would disappear. Moreover, the experience of attending college without the obligation of football activities would be all the richer. We already know that all groups have not equally benefited from the expansion of higher education admissions over the past several decades.[11] This fact is not lost on us, and we would be remiss not to acknowledge that any structural changes to college admissions must be part of broader shifts in the racial capitalist system—the shifts called for by W. E. B. Du Bois in his powerful exposé of the interwoven nature of race, class, neighborhood, and higher education.[12]

The second, and equally imperative, form of constructivist reparation is well-resourced and freely available public health care. If the moral unsustainability of football is a product above all of its inherent physical harm, one of the most reprehensible by-products of the sport is the fact that those who participate and experience harm are also saddled with all the attendant medical expenses. To abolish football in the context of the current system of US health care is to leave all those young people currently participating in the sport holding the bag for their long-term health costs, which is ethically unacceptable. The construction of a genuine public health care system would provide the care needed for those who participate and would remove one form of structural coercion—the need to ward off the possibility of future medical debt, a reality for a considerable proportion of the nation's population.

These are only the most concrete and direct partial solutions. In truth, a constructivist approach to reparations that will fully justify the abolition of college football is connected to a renovation (which is to say teardown) of the global political economy of racial capitalism. As long as the world system relies on the systematic hyperexploitation of racialized groups, even forms of potential opportunity as inherently harmful as college football will always appear to be a lesser evil. The vanishing point of abolition and constructivist reparations, then, must be anticapitalist and antiracist to the core, from the social structures' very foundation. But, while this is not the absolute end goal, building robust systems of freely available public higher education and health care, in conjunction with direct material redistribution from the entities that benefit from the sport, would be the necessary prerequisites to abolishing college football through a process of reparations. Without the reimagining of public education and public health care as a right—rather than a commodity—it is impossible to imagine a world free from the harms produced by tackle football.

This book should also be viewed as a challenge to at least three of the central arguments that most often work to produce, sustain, and protect the mass exploitation of predominantly Black young men in college football: 1) the compensation argument that athletes are indeed fairly compensated for their labor; 2) the education argument that athletes are students first and athletes second; and 3) the opportunity argument that athletes choose to participate in order to benefit from innumerable opportunities that can only be afforded by the NCAA.

The first theme we took on was the ubiquitous question of compensation. Rather than parsing the budgets of NCAA institutions or speculating on how we might more equitably distribute the revenue produced by the labor of college football players—which is indeed where much of the sociological, economic, legal, and sport management discourse resides—we focused explicitly on the human cost of the exploitation.

A second goal was to distill and critique the putative compensation college athletic workers receive: their education. We argued that the failure of NCAA member institutions to deliver on this most basic tenet of the so-called student-athlete experience is a function of a structural failure to produce conditions conducive to learning. The fundamental barrier to an enriching academic experience for college football players is the burden of simultaneously having to endure a full-time and exceptionally strenuous form of unpaid labor.

A third objective of our book was to counter the tired justification of consent in college football, which typically takes the form of this statement: "Athletes signed up for it and play voluntarily." Indeed, this is often the refrain of college football apologists, who contend that players consent to participate in the NCAA system and thus have no recourse to either contest the conditions they are subjected to or demand better ones. It's also an insidious misappraisal of the ways in which US histories of racialized labor exploitation, capital accumulation, and the neoliberalization of higher education intersect to produce radically differential positions from which potential students confront the prospect of university attendance. It's only by situating college football within the context of a deeply stratified society that the full measure of its injustice can be appraised.

We are firm in the determination that abolition and reparations are the only just resolution to the system of college football that currently exists. Nevertheless, we are not oblivious to the fact that football is among the most popular cultural forms in the United States today. It is an understatement to refer to our position as heretical. Understanding that we are not on the precipice of such a change, we hold that there is only one reformist option that meaningfully addresses the myriad forms of harm and exploitation that comprise big-time college football: unionization.[13] College football players *are* university employees, whether or not they have that status.[14] General Counsel of the National Labor Relations Board (NLRB) Jennifer Abruzzo has argued in a memorandum that "misclassifying [college athletes] as mere 'student-athletes,' and leading them to believe that they do not have statutory protections is a violation of [the National Labor Relations] Act."[15] Above all, recategorizing college football players as employees matters because it means they should be afforded the right to organize and engage in collective bargaining. Again, Abruzzo agrees: "Those football players, and other similarly situated Players at Academic Institutions, should be protected . . . when they act concertedly to speak out about their terms and conditions of employment, or to self-organize."[16] And, as we write, change is already afoot. At Dartmouth College, men's basketball players voted 13-2 to unionize with SEIU; at the University of Southern California, Ramogi Huma's NCPA has filed a complaint with the NLRB that players have been misclassified as amateurs rather than employees.[17] While the legal road ahead is long, these are substantive developments to be sure.

It must be acknowledged that unionization does not ultimately address the fundamental reasons why the sport should no longer exist. But if it *must* exist, at least in the near term, unionization is the single best reformist palliative for its most egregious problems because it allows players to leverage their collective power to demand better wages and working conditions. This is no mere hypothetical. In fact, there is a rich history of Black athlete labor action and protest, including the Wyoming 14 who wore black armbands in a 1969 game protesting opponent BYU's racist policies.[18] More recently, in 2015, the University of Missouri football team threatened to strike from all its games if the university's president, Tim Wolfe, refused to address racism on campus. As a consequence of that *threatened* labor action, without the players actually having to miss a game, Wolfe and the chancellor of the university system both resigned.[19] It is evident from the Missouri example that Power Five college football players are at minimum among the most powerful figures on American university campuses with the leverage to impose almost any conceivable demand. But, as former player and *Slate* columnist Joel Anderson has written, that power only exists if players use it: "Going back to work accomplishes little but returning the power to the institution. The games need not go on, if the players don't want them to."[20] Wallace Bell agrees, "If we don't play, what would they do?" It thus seems plausible to imagine that by flexing their power, players could negotiate for a 50 percent revenue share (commensurate with most revenue-sharing agreements negotiated by professional players' associations in men's sports), educational protections like lifetime scholarships that could be used after careers end to fulfill the promise of a full educational experience, and, perhaps most importantly, occupational health and safety protections and long-term health insurance. As one Pac-12 football player told us in a piece published in the *Guardian* to coincide with the introduction of federal legislation to authorize college athlete unionization, "A union would be powerful for us. There are so many issues across all of our sports that a union could help resolve ranging from coaches that habitually cross the line or being able to put our foot down and ask for health benefits and ultimately being able to profit off our talents. As of right now there isn't an entity that is able to hold the schools accountable and act in our best interest."[21] Players we interviewed agreed with this appraisal. Terry Davis explained, "I want the game to end, but if the game isn't going to end or the game is going to have a long bloody death, I am advising players to say, 'Hey quarterback, take your $4 million and you start your own NIL collective yourself,' similar to an independent music label. And you sign all the athletes, you take all the athletes off the table, you guys have your own organization, you come in together." Likewise, Ryan Leonard argued that collective bargaining is the best path forward for players: "The only way things will change is if the players leverage their value to implement their interests. The only way this changes is the creation of a college football players' association." Through unionization and employee status, players can recoup at least some of the forms of compensation they deserve:

> The injuries that you can directly or indirectly relate to football should be paid for by the institution that profited the most from that exposure, from that risk that you took. I believe that athletes should be considered employees and receive workman's comp when injuries occur that debilitate or limit the opportunities that they can have in the future. For me, for example, for the longest time I wanted to be a college coach. But one of the reasons why I no longer pursue that dream is because I know being on my feet every day for the next thirty, forty years will not only be excruciatingly painful, but will limit how long I will even be able to walk. So the opportunities that I no longer can pursue because of the price that I paid with my body to play college football, I do believe should be compensated for. . . . In terms of long-term health insurance, if you have long-term problems, yes. It's no-brainer in my mind that the institution in some ways should subsidize or provide completely health insurance for the athletes that paid a heavy price on their health to play that sport.

It is ultimately impossible to redress the exploitative dynamics of college sports without first acknowledging the salience of racial justice in this project, particularly in the Power Five conferences wherein Black athletes are disproportionately providing the revenue-generating labor.[22] The only meaningful counterforce to this exploitation is, in our view, unionization. Unionization offers the promise of empowerment of athletes to defend their rights and interests as a collective unit rather than a disjointed assortment of similarly vested interests as we saw in 2020 with the #WeAreUnited and #WeWantToPlay movements.[23] Indeed, collective action is perhaps the most potent step toward an end goal of pay for play, which is terrifying to the NCAA and its member institutions.

Ultimately, pay for play is the only way to remedy the mass system of exploitation that the NCAA has successfully erected over the past several decades. The NCAA knows this, and views pay for play as an existential threat because its entire structure is predicated on the exploitation of its laborers. How else would the NCAA and member institutions compensate their university presidents, senior administrators, athletic directors, coaches, and so on? The only way this business model works is if the NCAA can ensure a monopsony on the labor force and thus keep wages low for member institutions. Not only does this explain the NCAA's willingness to move on NIL rights—because it has effectively allowed others to pay its workers—it also explains why Mark Emmert and the rest of the NCAA brass shook in their boots any time pay for play was uttered.[24] Emmert was correct; pay for play likely does present an existential threat to the NCAA. But that doesn't mean we can ignore workers' rights.

As we mentioned in the introduction, in the 1960s, Walter Byers, the first executive director of the NCAA, famously coined the term "student-athlete" to counter the threat of athletes seeking out workers' compensation for injuries sustained while representing their universities. At the same time, Byers was working to get universities collaborating in both their pursuit of athletic laborers and the commercialization of NCAA sport by negotiating lucrative TV deals. In so doing, Byers was laying the foundation for a system of mass racialized exploitation that even he would later call "a nationwide money-laundering scheme."[25]

While we have seen a number of reformist changes made to modern-day college sports, none have addressed the fundamental issue of exploitation. This is precisely because the NCAA was founded on the basis of that exploitation, and unless that foundation is demolished, there is no way to escape it. College sport existed before the NCAA, and it will exist long after it is gone. We can undo and reconcile the harms done against a racialized class of workers over decades just as easily as Byers was able to enshrine them into college athletics. It just requires us all to accept the uncomfortable truth that the NCAA is built on the same system of racial capitalism as the rest of society.

In a white supremacist capitalist society, 'solutions' to plantation dynamics are most often tokenistic diversity initiatives devoid of tangible action. The actual substantive solution, however, is reparations broadly conceived and the abolition of racial capitalism itself. In this way, abolition is not merely a metaphor, but requires tangible and long-lasting change to a system of harm that has, for far too long, exploited a racialized group of workers to benefit predominantly white coaches, administrators, and institutions. Genuine, constructive abolition also requires reparations in the form of both financial remuneration to those who have been harmed for decades and radical structural change to ensure that the current system is not replicated.

To be clear, the reformist logic that permeates the minds of even the most critical observer of the NCAA is not enough to redress the long-standing inequalities and harm done over decades of racialized exploitation. That may mean that the college sport of tomorrow is unrecognizable—undoing an athletic system predicated on racial capitalism requires genuinely transformative radical change. But, indeed, perhaps it is time to make college sport unrecognizable.

Likewise, unionization ensures that if compromises must be made, they will be made not by people like us operating in what could fairly be perceived as a paternalistic mode, but by the actual participants and stakeholders: college football players. The ugly beauty of collective bargaining is that it forces compromises on labor and capital both. If college football players are required to work under exploitative and harmful conditions, then those conditions should be the ones they choose to live with. A Pac-12 football player put it this way: "I just don't want to be used anymore. A union would give us a legitimate voice by being represented and having a seat at the table so we can protect ourselves from continuously being taken advantage of."[26] Wallace Bell says, "I hope athletes . . . realize that if we don't come together in this time, nobody's going to see anything and they're going to perfect the system." Collective bargaining, via debate, struggle, and compromise, affords college football players a genuine form of agency, albeit a form, as always, constrained and circumscribed by capital.

It is, of course, precisely those constraints we would ultimately seek to abolish in an ideal world. Falling short of that, let's start with canceling college football.

Methodological Appendix

Here we provide more details about the campus athletic workers interviewed for this study, the methods of data collection and analysis, and the justifications for the analytic decisions made to bring this project to fruition. In a project like this—part sociology of Power Five college football part polemical call to action against a system of violent and racialized exploitation—using interview data permits a much more nuanced analysis of the reality that folks enduring the system live on an everyday basis.

This book draws on twenty-five semistructured interviews with former NCAA players who experienced the lived realities of big-time college football. These interviews were conducted between 2019 and 2023, in person and via Zoom or other online communications programs. Interviews ranged from thirty-five minutes to over three hours, and sometimes multiple interviews were conducted. The book also draws in part on qualitative field observations made by both authors over the past decade of working within a variety of institutions of higher education as well as working closely with college football players and other campus athletic workers who want to change the system for the better. While these observations do not make up a large portion of the book, they nonetheless informed our reading of the testimony.

To identify interview participants, we used snowball sampling, wherein we identified a few members of a relatively rare and difficult-to-access population and asked them to identify other members of the same group.[1] Through our scholarship and public work detailing the realities of big-time college football, we fostered a small group of campus athletic worker confidants who were willing and able to connect us with other football players within their networks. This form of convenience sampling alleviated many of the pressures of accessing traditionally hard-to-reach populations.[2] We consider college football players difficult to reach given the structural and symbolic constraints placed on them by virtue of their participation in college football, which we detailed in this book. The bulk of snowball sampling work was done through social media, through e-mail, or during interviews, where we asked each participant if he would connect us with colleagues for the study.[3] Given the purposive snowball sampling techniques used, this study is not generalizable or reflective of all college football players who have played in Division I of the NCAA.

We hope after reading the stories in this book that the reader takes seriously the very real material constraints acting on former college football players who might consider speaking out against the sport. There are myriad ways that college football continues to shape and inform the lives of former players long after they retire. To this end, we must express our gratitude to the twenty-five campus athletic workers who spoke to us and shared their often painful personal experiences.

Sociological and academic norms dictate that we must call this intervention "small-n" research, acknowledge its nonrepresentativeness and lack of generalizability, and highlight its limitations vis-á-vis scientific methods.[4] We acknowledge and invite those critiques. We view this intervention as a point of departure for the wide-scale analysis of the political economy of big-time college football and its entanglement with higher education. Some may view our findings as illegitimate given the relatively low sample size. To this we challenge our social scientific research communities to gain more insight, conduct more research, do more analysis of the conditions that characterize big-time college sport, and report those findings. If this book provides the impetus for deeper, more "representative" interrogation of this egregious site of harm, exploitation, and wage theft, we ecstatically accept a reference to this book as rudimentary.

All participants were given pseudonyms and identifying information was deleted from their responses. When we refer to the Power Five conferences, we mean the five dominant revenue-generating football conferences that existed in the Football Bowl Subdivision (FBS) at the time this research was being conducted—Southeastern Conference (SEC), Atlantic Coast Conference (ACC), Big Ten, Big 12, and Pac-12. We withheld all participants' conference affiliations due to the possibility that their identity may be triangulated through a review of their testimony. Interview respondents were asked questions from our semistructured interview guide that covered demographic details; history in college football; injury; relationships with coaches, fans, media, and others; thoughts on compensation, NIL (name, image, and likeness), racial politics, racism, and recruiting; and experiences of violence and abuse. Questions particular to each respondent emerged during our interviews, and we asked relevant probing questions when necessary. Descriptive and biographical information for all interview participants can be found in table 3.

We took a grounded theoretical approach to axial coding and met numerous times to reflexively engage with the data before inputting them into NVivo qualitative data management software, Google Docs, and Microsoft Word to code based on a number of important themes, which were then examined through the principles of critical discourse analysis (CDA). The research was conducted on the basis of CDA, which has a long-standing history of use within the field of sociology and enables researchers to explore how power relations are reflected in text vis-à-vis transcribed interviews.[5] Proponents of CDA posit that one can study the ways in which discourses in the form of textual interview data are structured and situated in such a way as to reflect certain organizing and structuring forces in social life. Close interview analysis through resulting transcribed text, then, can be conducted to highlight how language works to structure social realities. To accomplish these objectives, the authors coded central themes and noted the discursive and sociolinguistic strategies used by participants to give meaning to those themes. The resulting coding schema highlights not only the themes that are most centrally discussed among news media, but also how the environments of those themes are approached through the text. We then analyzed the patterned text associated with each theme on the basis of understanding the cultural messages being adopted by readers through the tenets of CDA and grounded theory.

The authors input all interviews into either Microsoft Word, Google Docs, or NVivo (at times with aid from research assistants) and coded line by line based on principles of open coding and grounded theory.[6] Each interview transcript was read in detail by the authors, and several themes emerged, which we operationalized as

TABLE 3 Campus athletic workers: Quick reference guide

Pseudonym	Demographic characteristics	Biographical information
Galen North	White, 25–30 years old	Offensive lineman who played four years at a Power Five institution in the last fifteen years. College was the end of his football career. He described himself as having a "good" role on the team that was undermined by injury. He was on scholarship.
Michael Thomas	Black, 30–35	Running back who played four years at a Power Five institution in the last decade. He went on to play professionally, and he described himself as a team leader during his time in college. He was on scholarship.
Dallas Adams	White, 30–35	Offensive lineman who played four years at a Power Five institution in the last decade. He went on to play professionally and described himself as a "good contributor" on his college team. He was on scholarship.
Chris Andrews	White, 40–45	Offensive lineman who played four years at a Power Five institution in the early 2000s. He went on to play professionally and described himself as having "a leadership role" on his college team. He was on scholarship.
C. J. White	Black, 25–30	Wide receiver who played four years at a Power Five institution in the last decade. He went on to play professionally. He described himself as having a significant role on his college team. He was on scholarship.
Kevin Brown	White, 30–35	Offensive lineman who played four years at a Power Five institution between 2009 and 2013. College was the end of his football career. He described himself as a gritty backup player during his time in college. He was on scholarship.
Jalen Rice	Black, 25–30	Running back who played four years at a Power Five institution in the last decade. He went on to play professionally and was a team leader during his time in college. He was on scholarship.

(continued)

TABLE 3 *(continued)*

Pseudonym	Demographic characteristics	Biographical information
Brock Adler	Black, 25–30	Defensive lineman who played four years at a Power Five institution in the last decade. College football was the end of his football career, and he described himself as a player with a lot of potential who was undermined by a change in coaching staff during his time in college. He was on scholarship.
Daniel Barber	Black, 25–30	Linebacker who played four years at a Power Five institution in the last five years. College football was the end of his football career, and he described himself as a player in college who was perceived as a "star" and also someone who fell out of favor with coaches. He was on scholarship.
Ross Nielsen	White, 25–30	Linebacker who played one year at a Power Five institution in the last five years. College football was the end of his football career, and he described himself as a practice squad player. He was a walk-on.
Steven Summers	White, 25–30	Fullback who played at a Power Five institution and then transferred to a lower-tier school in the last five years. He was unclear if college football was the end of his football career, and he saw himself as someone who became a team leader by the end of his career. He was on scholarship.
Charlie Rogers	Black, 30–35	Defensive lineman who played two years at a Power Five institution in the last decade. College football was the end of his football career, and he described himself as "a live practice dummy" during his time in college. He was on scholarship.
Josh Hansen	Black, 35–40	Cornerback who played multiple years at a Power Five institution and transferred to a lower-tier school to finish his career during the last fifteen years. College football was the end of his football career. He described himself as a team leader. He was both a walk-on and on scholarship.

TABLE 3 *(continued)*

Pseudonym	Demographic characteristics	Biographical information
Matt Jensen	White, 25–30	Offensive lineman who played four years at a Power Five institution in the last decade. College football was the end of his football career, and he described himself as a player who tried to work his way up the team hierarchy from the bottom. He was a walk-on.
Jeremy Jones	Black, 25–29	Defensive lineman who played for four years at a Power Five institution in the last decade. College football was not the end of his football career, and he described himself as a team leader, a star lineman, and a potential NFL prospect. He continued to play professionally. He was on scholarship.
Kurt Weiss	White, 30–35	Linebacker who played four years at a Power Five institution in the last decade. He went on to play professionally and was a star and team leader during his time in college. He was on scholarship.
Thomas Rycliff	White, 50–55	Defensive lineman who played four years at a Power Five institution in the last twenty-five years. College was the end of his football career. He was largely a scout team player in college because he fell out of favor with a new coaching staff hired shortly after his time in college began. He was on scholarship.
Terry Davis	Black, 45–50	Offensive lineman who played four years at a Power Five institution in the last twenty years. He had a brief professional career. He played a significant role on the team and was on scholarship.
Landry West	Black, 30–35	Running back who played four years at a Power Five institution in the last ten years. College was the end of his football career. His role in college was largely on special teams. He was on scholarship.
Ryan Leonard	White, 30–35	Offensive lineman who played at multiple Power Five institutions. College was the end of his football career. He became a starter and a leader on the teams he played on. He was on scholarship.

(continued)

TABLE 3 *(continued)*

Pseudonym	Demographic characteristics	Biographical information
Nick Turner	White, 30–35	Offensive lineman who played four seasons at a Power Five school. College was the end of his football career, and he was largely a backup in college. He was on scholarship.
Ronnie Exeter	Black, 25–30	Linebacker who played four seasons at a Power Five school. College was the end of his football career, and he was largely a special teams player. He was on scholarship.
Wallace Bell	Black, 25–30	Wide receiver who played at a Power Five school before transferring to a lower division school. He was on scholarship.
Aaron Peters	Black, 25–30	Defensive lineman who played at a Power Five school, before transferring to a lower-level institution. He was on scholarship.
Kane Holden	White, 25–30	Offensive lineman who played five seasons at two different Football Championship Subdivision (FCS) schools. College was the end of his football career. He was on scholarship.

codes. Since our main focus was to amplify the lived experiences of athletes who endured the realities of big-time college football, our grounded theoretical approach in consultation with our initial semistructured interview guide resulted in the emergence of a coding scheme that closely resembles the structure of the book. Our coding scheme included, but was certainly not limited to, demographic information, football career, recruiting, 'play' vs. 'work,' experiences with injury, university life, college experience, higher education, compensation and remuneration, racial capitalism, racism, racial politics, discrimination, and relationships to fans and media. Given that the research was impacted by the emergence of the COVID-19 pandemic, a subsequent code of all pandemic-related discussion was added to the interview guide prior to any analysis taking place. The text from interviews were then coded on the basis of this open-coding process, whereby the most emergent set of concepts and their properties informed and integrated with the theoretical imperatives discussed in the book.[7]

Though these demographic data are important, we acknowledge that we cannot generalize our findings to all campus athletic workers or adequately address complex in-group differences. Given the relatively small sample size, this book is explicit in its goal of amplifying a group of athletic workers who have, for decades, been almost entirely silenced or ignored. This book is unrepentant in its objective as a polemical call to action against a system built to extract wealth from young, predominantly racialized, communities. We therefore urge scholars working in this area to speak with college football players who have endured this system and report their own findings. Based on our experience, we are confident that the experiences shared here are not particular to this group of athletes.

To be sure, race, geographic location, age, scholarship status, and position have profoundly shaped the lives and experiences of the campus athletic workers in this study. There are likely vast differences in how athletes experience their participation in college football, their institutions, and the broader society in which they live. As producers of unapologetic "small-n research," we do not seek to convince the reader that these are generalized findings that exist at the population level.[8] That said, as this book is an explicitly polemical intervention and, given the difficulties associated with accessing college athletes who have the desire and ability to report their experiences within a repressive and coercive system, we suggest readers take the testimony in this book as an invitation to think critically about the lived realities of 'playing' college football in a context of racial capitalism. This book therefore provides a point of departure for the development of critical theory in the context of US interuniversity sport and higher education—a useful entry point to explore and interrogate what has become one of the most egregious sites of wage theft in contemporary society. We hope future research will continue to build on our findings in service of the athletic workers who courageously came forward against this system.

Notes

Preface

1. See Carrington and McDonald, *Marxism, Cultural Studies, and Sport*.
2. Smith, *Women's Experience*, 21, 23.
3. Haraway, *Companion Species Manifesto*.

Introduction

1. Italicized quotations are dramatizations based on player testimony. Quotations with quotation marks are verbatim testimony from players.

2. The "Power Five" refers to the five major NCAA Division I conferences—the ACC (Atlantic Coast Conference), Big Ten, Big 12, Pac-12, and SEC (Southeastern Conference)—of the Football Bowl Subdivision (FBS) wherein the most significant revenue in college football is derived. These conferences include some sixty-nine, mostly public research-intensive universities. Note that a reorganization of college football has recently occurred with the collapse of the Pac-12 and consolidation of the other conferences into a new 'Power Four' that largely includes the same institutions.

3. Branch, *Cartel*; Schwarz and Trahan, "Mythology Playbook"; Silva and Kennedy, *Power Played*.

4. Branch, *Cartel*; Byers, *Unsportsmanlike Conduct*.

5. Byers, *Unsportsmanlike Conduct*, 73.

6. See Hatton, *Coerced*; King-White, *Sport and the Neoliberal University*; McCormick and McCormick, "Trail of Tears"; Murphy and Pace, "Plan for Compensating Student-Athletes"; Nocera and Strauss, *Indentured*; Overly, "Exploitation of African-American Men"; Sack and Staurowsky, *College Athletes for Hire*; R. Smith, *Pay for Play*; Southall and Staurowsky, "Cheering on the Collegiate Model"; Staurowsky, "Analysis of Northwestern University's Denial of Rights"; Van Rheenen, "Exploitation in College Sports."

7. Branch, *Cartel*; Leonard, *Sports Experience*; Purdy, Eitzen, and Hufnagel, "Are Athletes also Students?"; Southall et al., "Athletic Success"; Van Rheenen, "Exploitation in College Sports"; White, *Blood, Sweat, and Tears*.

8. Van Rheenen, "Exploitation in College Sports," 553.

9. Kalman-Lamb, "Athletic Labor and Social Reproduction"; Kalman-Lamb, *Game Misconduct*.

10. See Marx, *Capital*; Marx, "18th Brumaire of Louis Bonaparte"; Marx, "Poverty of Philosophy."

11. Hatton, *Coerced*.

12. Fisher, "Expanding the Frame of 'Voluntariness.'"

13. See Southall and Staurowsky, "Cheering on the Collegiate Model"; Southall et al., *NCAA*.

14. Ventresca and King, "'Anesthetized Gladiators.'"

15. Kalman-Lamb, "Defamiliarizing Concussions: Sports Fandom, Injury, and Potential Attitudinal Shifts."

16. Robinson, *Black Marxism*.

17. Du Bois, *Black Reconstruction*; Hall et al., *Policing the Crisis*; Hawkins, *New Plantation*, 14.

18. Burden-Stelly, "Modern U.S. Racial Capitalism."

19. Bhattacharyya, *Rethinking Racial Capitalism*; Kundnani, "What Is Racial Capitalism?"; McMillan Cottom, "Where Platform Capitalism"; Melamed, "Racial Capitalism"; Mills, *Racial Contract*; Patterson, *Slavery and Social Death*; Ralph and Singhal, "Racial Capitalism"; Carrington and McDonald, *Marxism, Cultural Studies, and Sport*.

20. Du Bois, *Black Reconstruction*; Hall et al., *Policing the Crisis*.

21. See Abdel-Shehid, *Who Da Man?*; Allison, Davis, and Barranco, "Comparison"; Beamon, "'I'ma Baller'"; Beamon, "Racism and Stereotyping"; Beamon, "'Used Goods'"; Benson, "Big Football"; Carrington, *Race, Sport, and Politics*; Dufur and Feinberg, "Race and the NFL Draft"; Grano, "Football after Fragmentation"; Guridy, *The Sports Revolution*; Jones and Black, "Basketball's Black Tax?," Keaton and Cooper, "Racial Reckoning"; Leonard and King, *Commodified and Criminalized*; Montez de Oca, "White Domestic Goddess"; Montez de Oca, "Marketing Politics and Resistance"; Moore, *We Will Win the Day*; Oates and Durham, "Mismeasure of Masculinity"; Ray, "Theory of Racialized Organizations"; Rhoden, *Forty Million Dollar Slaves*; Smith, *Race, Sport and the American Dream*; Trimbur, *Come Out Swinging*; Trimbur and Braun, "The NFL's Reversal on 'Race Norming'"; Ventresca and King, "'Anesthetized Gladiators.'"

22. See also Hextrum, *Special Admission*.

23. Of course, it is important to note that the domestic racial transfer of wealth is subsidized by a global transfer of wealth maintained by US financial and military coercion (e.g., imperialism). While this is not necessarily the focus of this book, we must also recognize the existence of international students in Division I football who are *unable* to benefit from NIL due to their precarious visa status as "students" in the United States (see Newell and Sethi, "Exploring the Perception") and the pattern of racialized exploitation that remains at the core of US racial capitalism.

24. Hawkins, *New Plantation*.

25. See also Cooper, Nwadike, and Macaulay, "Critical Race Theory"; Dancy, Edwards, and Earl Davis, "Historically White Universities"; Montez de Oca, "White Domestic Goddess"; Runstedtler, "More Than Just Play."

26. For the relevance of this question to men's *and* women's tackle football, see De La Cretaz, "The Complicated Case for Gender Equality in Football."

27. Bachynski, *No Game*; Bachynski and Goldberg, "Youth Sports and Public Health"; Binney and Bachynski, "Estimating the Prevalence of Death."

28. Mez et al., "Clinicopathological Evaluation."

29. D. Smith, *Women's Experience*, 25.

30. Chakrabarty, *Habitations of Modernity*, 105.

31. Chakrabarty, *Habitations of Modernity*, 113.

32. Jhally, "Spectacle of Accumulation."

33. Canada, *Tackling the Everyday*; Canada, "Spectacle of Black Family Trauma"; Canada, "Black Mothers."

34. Burstyn, *Rites of Men*.

Chapter One

1. Van Rheenen, "Exploitation in College Sports," 553.

2. Marx, *Capital*.

3. Burden-Stelly, "Modern U.S. Racial Capitalism"; Hawkins, *New Plantation*; Robinson, *Black Marxism*.

4. Kalman-Lamb, "Sleep Pods"; Van Rheenen, "Exploitation in College Sports."

5. Berri, "Paying NCAA Athletes"; Schwarz and Volante, "Ninth Circuit Decision."

6. This is not to suggest that these are the *only* beneficiaries of such wealth extraction. Indeed, the primary beneficiaries of the labor exchange in this case are, of course, the universities that house big-time college football programs, but also include those corporations that benefit from media coverage of college football, and the multitude of brands and advertisers extracting revenue from the commodity spectacle (see Kalman-Lamb and Silva, "'Play'ing College Football").

7. Quoted in Prisbell, "OU's Joe Castiglione."

8. NCAA, *NCAA Financial Dashboard*.

9. "College Sports Finances Database."

10. Vitale, "Highest Paid Head Coaches."

11. Lavigne and Schlabach, "FBS Schools Spent."

12. Wittry, "Power 5 Football Buyouts."

13. Sterling, "Record $77 Million Buyout."

14. Kalman-Lamb and Silva, "This is the Only Way to End College Sports Exploitation."

15. It should be noted that even this distinction is in question given recent reports that Florida State University is soliciting investment from private equity to raise capital for its athletic department. Novy-Williams, Badenhausen, and Soschnick, "Florida State Taps JPMorgan."

16. Athletic Director U, *Compensation Survey*.

17. Data generously provided by Anthony Crudup via a Freedom of Information Act request.

18. Brown, "Texas A&M Athletics Lays Off More than a Dozen Staff Members."

19. Kalman-Lamb, Silva, and Mellis, "'This is a Job.'"

20. Berri, "Paying NCAA Athletes."

21. Russo, "Explainer;" Myerberg, "College Football Playoff's New Six-Year Contract Starting in 2026 Opens the Door to Expansion."

22. There is much more that could be said about the wide range of beneficiaries in the world of college sports media at the national and local levels whose employment, like that of athletic department officials, is inextricably predicated on the

work performed by athletes, albeit not contingent on the unpaid nature of that work. This is mostly clearly personified by Kirk Herbstreit, who reportedly earns $6 million per year for his college football work from ESPN. Marchand, "Amazon Eyeing ESPN's Kirk Herbstreit." Also see Brown, "Do NFL Player Earnings Compensate"; Gaul, *Billion-Dollar Ball*; Grant, "African American College Football Players"; Oriard, *Bowled Over*; Siegfried and Burba, "College Football Association"; Singer, "Benefits and Detriments"; Van Rheenen, "Exploitation in the American Academy."

23. Marx, *Capital*.

24. Bogost, "America Will Sacrifice Anything."

25. Duke University Department of Athletics, "Unrivaled Ambition," 11.

26. Marx, *Capital*.

27. NCAA Research, "Five Themes."

28. Libit and Akabas, "67% of Americans."

Chapter Two

1. Beamon, "I'ma Baller"; Beamon, "Racism and Stereotyping"; Beamon, "Used Goods." On racism on college campuses, see also Costello, "Noose on Campus"; Strausbaugh, *Black like You*; Southern Poverty Law Center, "Hate in the News"; Van Kerckhove, "University of Arizona Students." On targeting campus athletic workers, see also Edwards, "Crisis of Black Athletes"; Eitzen, "Racism in Big-Time College Sport"; Harper, Williams, and Blackmon, *Black Male Student-Athletes*; Marcus et al., "Perceptions of Racism"; Sailes, "Investigation of Campus Stereotypes"; Sailes, "Betting against the Odds"; Sellers, "African American Student-Athletes"; Singer, "Understanding Racism"; E. Smith, "African American Student Athlete."

2. Duke University Financial Services Bursar, *Undergraduate Tuition & Fees*.

3. Smith and Willingham, *Cheated*.

4. Casper, Smith, and Kalman-Lamb, "Big Threat."

5. Western Association of Schools and Colleges, 2013 *Handbook of Accreditation*.

6. Casper, Smith, and Kalman-Lamb, "Big Threat."

7. Southall, Nagel, and Wallace, 2019 *Adjusted Graduation Gap Report*.

8. Kalman-Lamb, Silva, and Mellis, "'I Signed My Life.'"

9. Byers, *Unsportsmanlike Conduct*.

10. Calhoun, *Division I Student Athletes*.

11. Bourdieu, "Forms of Capital."

12. See Bowen and Levin, *Reclaiming the Game*; Cooper, "Excellence beyond Athletics"; French, *Ethics and College Sports*; Gould and Whitley, "Sources and Consequences"; Lanter and Hawkins, "Economic Model"; Leonard, "Sports Experience"; Orleans, "Effects of the Economic Model"; Shulman and Bowen, *Game of Life*.

13. Fisher, "Expanding the Frame of 'Voluntariness'"; Hatton, *Coerced*; Robinson, *Black Marxism*.

14. Kalman-Lamb, Silva, and Mellis, "Race, Money, and Exploitation."

15. Jackson, "How to Take the Scandal Out of Big-Time College Football and Basketball."

Chapter Three

1. Bachynski, *No Game*.
2. Archie, Brannan, and Bright, *Brain Damaged*; Bachynski, *No Game*; Harrison, "First Concussion Crisis"; Oates and Furness, *NFL*; Oates, "Erotic Gaze"; Oates, *Football and Manliness*; Van Rheenen, "Exploitation in College Sports."
3. Brown, "CTE Risk More than Doubles"; Mez et al., "Clinicopathological Evaluation"; Viswanathan, "Playing Football May Increase Risk."
4. Barnett, "NCAA Withheld Safety Info."
5. Building on analysis in Kalman-Lamb, *Game Misconduct*.
6. Kalman-Lamb, "Athletic Labor and Social Reproduction"; Kalman-Lamb, "Imagined Communities."
7. Crawford, "Healthism."
8. For more on conflict of interest in college football see Kalman-Lamb and Silva, "'The Coaches Always Make the Health Decisions.'"
9. See Cottler et al., "Injury"; Ekhtiari et al., "Opioid Use in Athletes"; Ford et al., "Sports Involvement"; Tricker, "Painkilling Drugs"; Tricker and Connolly, "Drug Education."
10. See Simonetto and Tucsok, "Former Athletes' Illness Stories of Brain Injuries."
11. See Ivarsson et al., "Negative Psychological Responses"; Koren et al., "Increased PTSD Risk"; Masten et al., "Psychological Response"; Moore, Vann, and Blake, "Learning from the Experiences"; Sanders and Stevinson, "Associations between Retirement Reasons"; Sheinbein, "Psychological Effect of Injury."
12. Bennett and Zirin, *Things that Make*, 20, 22.
13. See Casper, "Punch-Drunk Slugnuts."
14. See Boden et al., "Catastrophic Head Injuries"; Gavett, Stern, and McKee, "Chronic Traumatic Encephalopathy"; Jacks, Tereshko, and Moore, "Diagnosed Concussion"; Oliver et al., "Fluctuations"; Shurley and Todd, "Boxing Lessons"; Calhoun, *Division I Student Athletes*.
15. Weaver, "If College Athletes Return."
16. See Anderson, "Openly Gay Athletes"; Anderson and Kian, "Examining Media Contestation"; Foote, Butterworth, and Sanderson, "Adrian Peterson"; Oates and Durham, "Mismeasure of Masculinity"; Oates, *Football and Manliness*; Steinfeldt et al., "Masculinity Socialization"; Steinfeldt and Steinfeldt, "Athletic Identity."

Chapter Four

1. Robinson, *Black Marxism*; Mills, *Racial Contract*.
2. Hamilton and Darity, Jr., "Can 'Baby Bonds' Eliminate the Racial Wealth Gap in Putative 'Post-Racial' America?"
3. Kelley, "Foreword," xv.
4. Hall et al., *Policing the Crisis*, 386.
5. Burden-Stelly, "Modern U.S. Racial Capitalism."
6. Ray, "Theory of Racialized Organizations," 29.
7. Ray, *On Critical Race Theory*.

8. See Kalman-Lamb, Silva, and Mellis, "'I Signed My Life.'"

9. See also Bennett and Zirin, *Things that Make*.

10. Robinson, *Black Marxism*.

11. Eitzen, *Fair and Foul*; Hawkins, *New Plantation*, 13.

12. Ray, "Theory of Racialized Organizations"; Hawkins, *New Plantation*.

13. Kalman-Lamb, Silva, and Mellis, "'I Signed My Life.'"

14. Burden-Stelly, "Modern U.S. Racial Capitalism"; Tatos and Singer, "Antitrust Anachronism."

15. Kalman-Lamb, Silva, and Mellis, "'I Signed My Life.'"

16. Kalman-Lamb, Silva, and Mellis, "Race, Money, and Exploitation."

17. Kalman-Lamb, Silva, and Mellis, "Race, Money, and Exploitation."

18. In college football, the "Group of Five" are five athletic conferences whose members are part of NCAA Division I Football Bowl Subdivision (FBS). The five conferences are the American Athletic Conference (American or AAC), Conference USA (C-USA), Mid-American Conference (MAC), Mountain West Conference (MWC), and Sun Belt Conference (SBC). These are not to be confused with the "Power Five" conferences we speak of mostly throughout this book.

19. Bourdieu, "Forms of Capital."

20. Du Bois, *Black Reconstruction*; Hall et al., *Policing the Crisis*.

21. Broughton, "Power Five."

22. Kalman-Lamb, Silva, and Mellis, "'I Signed My Life.'"

23. McGee, "U-T Austin Football Players."

24. Associated Press, "Creighton Players Speak Out."

25. Khan, "Student-Athletes Kneeling."

26. Markus, Brown, and Reynolds, "Former NU Players."

Chapter Five

1. Hatton, *Coerced*.

2. Hatton, *Coerced*, 11–12.

3. Hatton, *Coerced*, 14.

4. Fisher, "Expanding the Frame of 'Voluntariness,'" 360.

5. Runstedtler, "More Than Just Play," 160.

6. Rittenberg, "Big 10 to Guarantee Scholarships."

7. Kersey, "How the NCAA Allows."

8. Markus, Brown, Reynolds, and Bhardwaj, "Former NU Football Player."

9. Perez, "Former Players."

10. Burstyn, *Rites of Men*.

11. Hatton, *Coerced*; Fisher, "Expanding the Frame of 'Voluntariness.'"

12. Fisher, "Expanding the Frame of 'Voluntariness.'"

Chapter Six

1. Kalman-Lamb, Silva, and Mellis, "'We Are Being Gaslit'"; Kalman-Lamb, Silva, and Mellis, "The Red Zone"; Mull, "College Football's Greatest Unraveling."

2. Klemko and Giambalvo, "On a Call."

3. Kalman-Lamb, Silva, and Mellis, "'We Are Being Gaslit.'"

4. "Dabo Swinney."

5. Kalman-Lamb, Silva, and Mellis, "College Football Feels."

6. Kalman-Lamb, Silva, and Mellis, "College Football Feels."

7. Bianchi, "UF Thankfully Rejects."

8. Forde, "After a Contentious Summer."

9. Pequeño, "UNC Athletics"; Forde, "After a Contentious Summer."

10. Chiari, "CFB Players' Comfort."

11. Kercheval and Sallee, "Trevor Lawrence."

12. Fields, "#WeWantToPlay Petition."

13. Gulick, "Justin Fields."

14. Hatton, *Coerced*, 52.

15. Kosko, "Penn State Football Parents."

16. Washut, "Husker Parents."

17. Kalman-Lamb, Silva, and Mellis, "'We Are Being Gaslit.'"

18. Kalman-Lamb, Silva, and Mellis, "'We Are Being Gaslit.'"

19. Kalman-Lamb, Silva, and Mellis, "College Football Feels All Too Normal."

20. Kalman-Lamb, Silva, and Mellis, "'We Are Being Gaslit.'"

21. Jag, "Opting Out."

22. Kalman-Lamb, Silva, and Mellis, "'We Are Being Gaslit.'"

23. Gonzalez, "BYU Quarterback Zach Wilson."

24. Kalman-Lamb, Silva, and Mellis, "'We Are Being Gaslit.'"

25. Peter, "Are College Football Players."

26. Kalman-Lamb, Silva, and Mellis, "'We Are Being Gaslit.'"

27. Kalman-Lamb, Silva, and Mellis, "'We Are Being Gaslit.'"

28. Rittenberg and Dinich, "Big Ten Football."

29. Klemko and Giambalvo, "On a Call."

30. Smith, "Top ACC Medical Advisor."

31. Kalman-Lamb, Silva, and Mellis, "Red Zone."

32. Cobb, "UNC Football Pauses Workouts."

33. Sallee, "Vanderbilt's Road Game."

34. Kalman-Lamb, Silva, and Mellis, "Red Zone."

35. Connolly, "Xavier Thomas."

36. Horka, "Mississippi State RB Kylin Hill."

37. Vertuno, "Conflict Raging."

38. Kalman-Lamb, Silva, and Mellis, "'I Signed My Life.'"

39. McGee, "'U-T Needs Rich Donors.'"

40. Adelson, "Oklahoma State's Chuba Hubbard."

41. Adelson, "Oklahoma State's Mike Gundy."

42. "K-State Players Announce Boycott."

43. Mellor, "Read the UCLA Football Players."

44. Peter, "Are College Football Players."

45. "#WeAreUnited."

46. Witz, "Pac-12 Players."

47. Kalman-Lamb, Silva, and Mellis, "College Football Feels."

Conclusion

1. See Breslin, "Disneyfication of American Education"; Brownlee, "Academic, Inc."; Kennedy, "Disneyfication of a University"; Mitchell, "Crimson Tide of Debt."

2. Duke University, "Mission Statement"; Oklahoma State University, "Mission"; University of Alabama, "Our Mission & Vision"; University of California, Los Angeles, "Our Mission"; University of Michigan, "Mission"; University of Texas, "Mission & Values."

3. Nadelson et al., "Why Did They Come Here?"; Tobolowsky and Lowery, "Selling College."

4. Aspen Institute, *Participation Trends*; Gilligan, "Declines in Youth Football."

5. NCAA, "Football."

6. Táíwò, *Reconsidering Reparations*, 74.

7. See Balfour, "Reparations after Identity Politics"; Boxill, "Lockean Argument"; Brophy, "Reparations Talk"; Butt, "Repairing Historical Wrongs"; Coates, "Case for Reparations"; Coates and Hughes, "Should America Pay Reparations; Corlett, "Race, Racism, and Reparations"; Darity and Mullen, *From Here to Equality*; wa Ngugi, "Pitfalls of Symbolic Decolonization"; Sriprakash, "Reparations"; Taylor and Reed, "Reparations Debate."

8. See also Táíwò, *Reconsidering Reparations*.

9. Táíwò, *Reconsidering Reparations*.

10. See Charron-Chénier et al., "Pathway to Racial Equity"; Hextrum, *Special Admission*; Seamster and Aja, "Regressive Student Loan System."

11. Ryan and Bauman, *Educational Attainment*.

12. Du Bois, *Black Reconstruction*.

13. It is important to note the College Football Players Association, founded in 2021 by Jason Stahl, as a genuine and tangible effort toward unionization in college football (https://www.cfbpa.org/). We do not downplay or disagree with this organization. Rather, we simply acknowledge that a wide-reaching unionization movement remains in its infancy.

14. Gilbert, "Not (Just) About the Money."

15. Abruzzo, "Memorandum GC 21–08," 1.

16. Abruzzo, "Memorandum GC 21–08," 4.

17. Kalman-Lamb and Silva, "Dartmouth's Vote to Unionize Could Help End College Sport's Plantation Dynamics"; Kalman-Lamb and Silva, "A New Day for College Athlete Unions Could Be on the Horizon."

18. Davis, "Black College Athletes are Rising Up Against the Exploitative System they Labor in."

19. Svrluga, "U. Missouri President, Chancellor Resign."

20. Anderson, "No Justice, No Football."

21. Kalman-Lamb, Silva, Mellis, "There's Never Been a Better Time."

22. Kalman-Lamb, Silva, and Mellis, "'I Signed My Life'"; Kalman-Lamb, Silva, and Mellis, "There's Never Been a Better Time"; Kalman-Lamb, Silva, and Mellis, "Race, Money, and Exploitation."

23. See also Black, Ofoegbu, and Foster, "#TheyAreUnited."

24. Benbow, "NCAA President Mark Emmert."

25. Byers, *Unsportsmanlike Conduct*.

26. Kalman-Lamb, Silva, and Mellis, "There's Never Been a Better Time."

Methodological Appendix

1. Coleman, "Relational Analysis"; Handcock and Gile, "Comment"; Merton, "Patterns of Influence"; Thompson, "On Sampling and Experiments"; Trow, *Right-Wing Radicalism*.

2. See Atkinson and Flint, "Accessing Hidden"; Audemard, "Objectifying Contextual Effects"; Dosek, "Snowball Sampling"; Salganik and Heckathorn, "Sampling and Estimation"; TenHouten, "Site Sampling."

3. Dosek, "Snowball Sampling."

4. See Blatter and Haverland, *Designing Case Studies*; Gobo, "Sampling"; Mahoney, "Strategies of Causal Inference"; Steinmetz, "Odious Comparisons."

5. Fairclough, "Discourse and Text"; Fairclough, *Critical Discourse Analysis*.

6. Charmaz, *Constructing Grounded Theory*; Glaser, "Future of Grounded Theory"; Glaser and Strauss, *Discovery of Grounded Theory*; Strauss and Corbin, *Grounded Theory in Practice*.

7. Glaser, "Future of Grounded Theory"; Glaser, "Open Coding Descriptions."

8. Hatton, *Coerced*.

Bibliography

Abdel-Shehid, Gamal. *Who Da Man? Black Masculinities and Sporting Cultures.* Toronto: Canadian Scholars' Press, 2005.

Abruzzo, Jennifer A. "Memorandum GC 21–08." Office of the National Labor Relations Board General Counsel, September 29, 2021. https://apps.nlrb.gov/link /document.aspx/09031d458356ec26.

Adelson, Andrea. "Oklahoma State's Chuba Hubbard Says He Had to Hold Coach Mike Gundy Accountable." *ESPN*, June 16, 2020. www.espn.com/college-football /story/_/id/29318461/oklahoma-state-chuba-hubbard-says-had-hold-coach-mike -gundy-accountable.

———. "Oklahoma State's Mike Gundy Apologizes for 'Pain, Discomfort Caused.'" *ESPN*, June 16, 2020. https://www.espn.com/college-football/story/_/id/29319943 /oklahoma-state-mike-gundy-apologizes-pain-discomfort-caused.

Allison, Rachel, Adriene Davis, and Raymond Barranco. "A Comparison of Hometown Socioeconomics and Demographics for Black and White Elite Football Players in the US." *International Review for the Sociology of Sport* 53, no. 5 (2018): 615–29. https://doi.org/10.1177/1012690216674936.

Anderson, Eric. "Openly Gay Athletes: Contesting Hegemonic Masculinity in a Homophobic Environment." *Gender & Society* 16, no. 6 (2002): 860–77. https://doi .org/10.1177/089124302237892.

Anderson, Eric, and Edward M. Kian. "Examining Media Contestation of Masculinity and Head Trauma in the National Football League." *Men and Masculinities* 15, no. 2 (2012): 152–73. https://doi.org/10.1177/1097184X11430127.

Anderson, Joel. "No Justice, No Football." *Slate*, June 18, 2020. https://slate.com /culture/2020/06/mike-gundy-chuba-hubbard-oklahoma-state-college-football -protests.html.

Archie, Kimberly, Solomon Brannan, and Tiffani Bright. *Brain Damaged: Two-Minute Warning for Parents.* Westlake Village, CA: USA Sport Safety Publishing, 2019.

Aspen Institute. *Participation Trends.* Washington, DC: Project Play, Aspen Institute, 2022. https://projectplay.org/state-of-play-2022/participation-trends.

Associated Press. "Creighton Players Speak Out for First Time on McDermott's Comments in Pregame Video." *Sports Illustrated*, March 6, 2021. www.si.com /college/2021/03/07/creighton-players-speak-greg-mcdermott-plantation -comments?fbclid=IwAR2NG8FhaEjcZE2Gz7_MLHPFvyLGL9pVaJCGZjsejCw LHC9uzDiwPXWJ6hs.

Athletic Director U. *2020–21 FBS Athletic Directors' Compensation Survey.* Athletic Director U, 2021. https://athleticdirectoru.com/2021-ad-compensation-survey/.

Atkinson, Rowland, and John Flint. "Accessing Hidden and Hard-to-Reach Populations: Snowball Research Strategies." *Social Research Update* 33, no. 1 (2001): 1–4.

Audemard, Julien. "Objectifying Contextual Effects. The Use of Snowball Sampling in Political Sociology." *Bulletin of Sociological Methodology/Bulletin de Méthodologie Sociologique* 145, no. 1 (2020): 30–60.

Bachynski, Kathleen. *No Game for Boys to Play: The History of Youth Football and the Origins of a Public Health Crisis.* Chapel Hill: University of North Carolina Press, 2019.

Bachynski, Kathleen E., and Daniel S. Goldberg. "Youth Sports & Public Health: Framing Risks of Mild Traumatic Brain Injury in American Football and Ice Hockey." *Journal of Law, Medicine & Ethics* 42, no. 3 (2014): 323–33. https://doi.org /10.1111/jlme.12149.

Balfour, Lawrie. "Reparations after Identity Politics." *Political Theory* 33, no. 6 (2005): 786–811. https://doi.org/10.1177/0090591705279067.

Barnett, Sophia. "NCAA Withheld Safety Info that Would 'Destroy Football'—And It Killed My Husband, Widow Says." *New York Post*, August 12, 2023. https://nypost .com/2023/08/12/ncaa-had-brain-damage-information-that-would-destroy -football-docs/.

Beamon, Krystal K. "'I'ma Baller': Athletic Identity Foreclosure among African-American Former Student-Athletes." *Journal of African American Studies* 16 (2012): 195–208. https://doi.org/10.1007/s12111-012-9211-8.

———. "Racism and Stereotyping on Campus: Experiences of African American Male Student-Athletes." *Journal of Negro Education* 83, no. 2 (2014): 121–34. https://doi.org/10.7709/jnegroeducation.83.2.0121.

———. "'Used Goods': Former African American College Student-Athletes' Perception of Exploitation by Division I Universities." *Journal of Negro Education* 7, no. 4 (2008): 352–64. www.jstor.org/stable/25608704.

Benbow, Dana Hunsinger. "NCAA President Mark Emmert Says Fair Play to Pay Act Turns Student-Athletes into Employees." *IndyStar*, October 3, 2019. www .indystar.com/story/sports/college/2019/10/03/ncaa-president-mark-emmert -responds-california-fair-play-pay-act/3850522002/.

Bennett, Michael, and Dave Zirin. *Things that Make White People Uncomfortable.* Chicago: Haymarket Books, 2018.

Benson, Peter. "Big Football: Corporate Social Responsibility and the Culture and Color of Injury in America's Most Popular Sport." *Journal of Sport and Social Issues* 41, no. 4 (2017): 307–34. https://doi.org/10.1177/0193723517707699.

Berri, David J. "Paying NCAA Athletes." *Marquette Sports Law Review* 26, no. 2 (2016): 479–91.

Bhattacharyya, Gargi. *Rethinking Racial Capitalism: Questions of Reproduction and Survival.* Lanham, MD: Rowman & Littlefield International, 2018.

Bianchi, Mike. "UF Thankfully Rejects Dan Mullen Plea to Pack Swamp after Texas A&M Loss." *Orlando Sentinel*, October 10, 2020. www.orlandosentinel.com/2020 /10/10/uf-thankfully-rejects-dan-mullen-plea-to-pack-swamp-after-texas-am -loss-commentary/.

Binney, Zachary O., and Kathleen E. Bachynski. "Estimating the Prevalence at Death of CTE Neuropathology among Professional Football Players." *Neurology* 92, no. 1 (2019): 43–45. https://doi.org/10.1212/WNL.0000000000006699.

Black, Wayne L., Ezinne Ofoegbu, and Sayvon L. Foster. "#TheyareUnited and #TheyWantToPlay: A Critical Discourse Analysis of College Football Player Social Media Activism." *Sociology of Sport Journal* 39, no. 4 (2022): 352–61. https://doi.org /10.1123/ssj.2021-0045.

Blatter, Joachim, and Markus Haverland. *Designing Case Studies: Explanatory Approaches in Small-n Research*. London: Springer, 2012.

Boden, Barry P., Robin L. Tacchetti, Robert C. Cantu, Sarah B. Knowles, and Frederick O. Mueller. "Catastrophic Head Injuries in High School and College Football Players." *American Journal of Sports Medicine* 35, no. 7 (2007): 1075–81. https://doi.org/10.1177/0363546507299239.

Bogost, Ian. "America Will Sacrifice Anything for the College Experience." *Atlantic*, October 20, 2020. www.theatlantic.com/technology/archive/2020/10/college-was -never-about-education/616777/.

Bourdieu, Pierre. "The Forms of Capital." In *Handbook of Theory and Research for the Sociology of Education*, edited by John G. Richardson, 241–58. Westport, CT: Greenwood Press, 1986.

Bowen, William G., and Sarah A. Levin. *Reclaiming the Game: College Sports and Educational Values*. Princeton, NJ: Princeton University Press, 2003.

Boxill, Bernard R. "A Lockean Argument for Black Reparations." *Journal of Ethics* 7, no. 1 (2003): 63–91. https://doi.org/10.1023/A:1022826929393.

Branch, Taylor. *The Cartel: Inside the Rise and Imminent Fall of the NCAA*. San Francisco: Byliner, 2011.

Breslin, Frank. "The Disneyfication of American Education," *HuffPost*, September 24, 2014, www.huffpost.com/entry/disneyfication-of-education_b_5872570.

Brophy, Alfred L. "Reparations Talk: Reparations for Slavery and the Tort Law Analogy." *Boston College Third World Law Journal* 24, no. 1 (2004): 81–138.

Broughton, David. "Power Five: An $8.3 Billion Revenue Powerhouse." *Sports Business Journal*, August 17, 2020. www.sportsbusinessjournal.com/Journal /Issues/2020/08/17/Colleges/Revenue.aspx.

Brown, Lisa. "CTE Risk More than Doubles after Just Three Years of Playing Football." *The Brink*, October 7, 2019. www.bu.edu/articles/2019/cte-football/.

Brown, Robert. "Do NFL Player Earnings Compensate for Monopsony Exploitation in College?" *Journal of Sports Economics* 13, no. 4 (2012): 393–405. https://doi.org /10.1177/1527002512450266.

Brown, Travis L. "Texas A&M Athletics Lays Off More than a Dozen Staff Members." *The Eagle*, April 23, 2024. https://theeagle.com/sports/college/aggiesports/tamu -athletic-department-lays-off-more-than-a-dozen-staffers/article_6c31326a-01b5 -11ef-9358-bfe78f95f213.html?utm_medium=social&utm_source=twitter&utm _campaign=user-share.

Brownlee, Jamie. *Academia Inc.: How Corporatization Is Transforming Canadian Universities*. Halifax, NS: Fernwood Publishing, 2015.

Burden-Stelly, Charisse. "Modern U.S. Racial Capitalism: Some Theoretical Insights." *Monthly Review* 72, no. 3 (2020). https://doi.org/10.14452/MR-072-03-2020-07_2.

Burstyn, Varda. *The Rites of Men: Manhood, Politics, and the Culture of Sport*. Toronto: University of Toronto Press, 1999.

Butt, Daniel. "Repairing Historical Wrongs and the End of Empire." *Social & Legal Studies* 21, no. 2 (2012): 227–42. https://doi.org/10.1177/0964663911435932.

Byers, Walter. *Unsportsmanlike Conduct: Exploiting College Athletes*. Ann Arbor: University of Michigan Press, 1995.

Calhoun, Vaughn A. *Division I Student Athletes and the Experience of Academic Clustering*. PhD diss., Northeastern University, 2012. https://eric.ed.gov/?id=ED546114.

Canada, Tracie. "Black Mothers and NFL Moms Safety Clinics: An Ethnography of Care in American Football." *Journal of Sport & Social Issues* 47, no. 2 (2023): 103–25. https://doi.org/10.1177/01937235221144431.

———. "The Spectacle of Black Family Trauma through the NFL Draft." *First and Pen*, May 4, 2022. https://firstandpen.com/the-spectacle-of-black-family-trauma-through-the-nfl-draft/.

———. *Tackling the Everyday: Race, Family, and Nation in Big-Time College Football*. Berkeley: University of California Press, forthcoming.

Carrington, Ben. *Race, Sport and Politics: The Sporting Black Diaspora*. Thousand Oaks, CA: Sage, 2010.

Carrington, Ben, and Ian McDonald, eds. *Marxism, Cultural Studies, and Sport*. London: Routledge, 2009.

Casper, Stephen T. "Punch-Drunk Slugnuts: Violence and the Vernacular History of Disease." *Isis* 113, no. 2 (2022): 266–88. https://www.journals.uchicago.edu/doi/full/10.1086/719720.

Casper, Stephen T., Jay M. Smith, and Nathan Kalman-Lamb. "The Big Threat to Academic Freedom No One's Talking About." *Inside Higher Ed*, January 19, 2022. www.insidehighered.com/views/2022/01/20/college-athletes-lack-academic-freedom-other-students-have-opinion.

Chakrabarty, Dipesh. *Habitations of Modernity: Essays in the Wake of Subaltern Studies*. Chicago: University of Chicago Press, 2002.

Charmaz, Kathy. *Constructing Grounded Theory: A Practical Guide through Qualitative Analysis*. Thousand Oaks, CA: Sage, 2006.

Charron-Chénier, Raphaël, Louise Seamster, Thomas M. Shapiro, and Laura Sullivan. "A Pathway to Racial Equity: Student Debt Cancellation Policy Designs." *Social Currents* 9, no. 1 (2022): 4–24. https://doi.org/10.1177/23294965211024671.

Chiari, Mike. "CFB Players' Comfort with Playing amid Pandemic Gauged in Anonymous Survey." *Bleacher Report*, May 22, 2020. https://bleacherreport.com/articles/2892963-cfb-players-comfort-with-playing-amid-pandemic-gauged-in-anonymous-survey.

Coates, Ta-Nehisi. "The Case for Reparations." *Atlantic*, June 2014. https://www.theatlantic.com/magazine/archive/2014/06/the-case-for-reparations/361631/.

Coates, Ta-Nehisi, and Coleman Hughes. "Should America Pay Reparations for Slavery?" *Guardian* (Manchester), June 19, 2019. www.theguardian.com/commentisfree/2019/jun/19/reparations-slavery-ta-nehisi-coates-v-coleman-hughes.

Cobb, David. "UNC Football Pauses Workouts after High Number of Positive COVID-19 Tests among Athletic Teams." *CBS Sports*, July 8, 2020. www.cbssports

.com/college-football/news/unc-football-pauses-workouts-after-high-number-of -positive-covid-19-tests-among-athletic-teams/.

Coleman, James S. "Relational Analysis: The Study of Social Organizations with Survey Methods." *Human Organization* 17, no. 4 (1958): 28–36. https://doi.org/10 .17730/humo.17.4.q5604m676260q8n7.

"College Sports Finances Database." *Sportico*. www.sportico.com/business /commerce/2023/college-sports-finances-database-intercollegiate-1234646029/.

Connolly, Matt. "Xavier Thomas Details Tough Journey with COVID-19: 'My Symptoms Were Really Bad.'" *The State* (Columbia, South Carolina), November 2, 2020. www .thestate.com/sports/college/acc/clemson-university/article246895089.html.

Cooper, Joseph N. "Excellence beyond Athletics: Best Practices for Enhancing Black Male Student Athletes' Educational Experiences and Outcomes." *Equity & Excellence in Education* 49, no. 3 (2016): 267–83. https://doi.org/10.1080/10665684.2016.1194097.

Cooper, Joseph N., Akuoma Nwadike, and Charles Macaulay. "A Critical Race Theory Analysis of Big-Time College Sports: Implications for Culturally Responsive and Race-Conscious Sport Leadership." *Journal of Issues in Intercollegiate Athletics* 10 (2017): 204–333.

Corlett, J. Angelo. "Race, Racism, and Reparations." *Journal of Social Philosophy* 36, no. 4 (2005): 568–85. https://doi.org/10.1111/j.1467-9833.2005.00295.x.

Costello, Maureen. "Noose on Campus." Southern Poverty Law Center, Teaching Tolerance, March 1, 2010. www.tolerance.org/blog/noose-campus.

Cottler, Linda B., Arbi Ben Abdallah, Simone M. Cummings, John Barr, Rayna Banks, and Ronnie Forchheimer. "Injury, Pain, and Prescription Opioid Use among Former National Football League (NFL) Players." *Drug and Alcohol Dependence* 116, no. 1–3 (2011): 188–94. https://doi.org/10.1016/j.drugalcdep.2010.12.003.

Crawford, Robert. "Healthism and the Medicalization of Everyday Life." *International Journal of Health Services* 10, no. 3 (1980): 365–88. https://doi.org/10 .2190/3H2H-3XJN-3KAY-G9NY.

"Dabo Swinney on COVID-19 Pandemic: 'I Think that God Is Bigger than This.'" *Clemson Sports Talk*, April 9, 2020. https://clemsonsportstalk.com/s/5201/dabo -swinney-on-covid-19-pandemic-i-think-that-god-is-bigger-than-this.

Dancy, T. Elon, Kirsten T. Edwards, and James Earl Davis. "Historically White Universities and Plantation Politics: Anti-Blackness and Higher Education in the Black Lives Matter Era." *Urban Education* 53, no. 2 (2018): 176–95. https://doi.org /10.1177/0042085918754328.

Darity, William A., Jr., and A. Kirsten Mullen. *From Here to Equality: Reparations for Black Americans in the Twenty-First Century*. Chapel Hill: University of North Carolina Press, 2020.

Davis, Amira Rose, "Black College Athletes are Rising Up Against the Exploitative System they Labor in." *Washington Post*, August 11, 2020. https://www .washingtonpost.com/outlook/2020/08/11/black-college-athletes-are-rising-up -against-exploitative-system-they-labor/.

De La Cretaz, Frankie. "The Complicated Case for Gender Equality in Football." *In These Times*, May 1, 2023. https://inthesetimes.com/article/wfa-nfl-womens -football-gender-equality.

Dosek, Tomas. "Snowball Sampling and Facebook: How Social Media Can Help Access Hard-to-Reach Populations." *PS: Political Science & Politics* 54, no. 4 (2021): 651–55. https://doi.org/10.1017/S104909652100041X.

Du Bois, W. E. B. *Black Reconstruction: An Essay toward a History of the Part which Black Folk Played in the Attempt to Reconstruct Democracy in America, 1860–1880.* New York: Harcourt, Brace and Company, 1935.

Dufur, Mikaela J., and Seth L. Feinberg. "Race and the NFL Draft: Views from the Auction Block." *Qualitative Sociology* 32, no. 1 (2009): 53–73. https://doi.org/10.1007/s11133-008-9119-8.

Duke University. "Mission Statement." Duke University, 2024. https://admissions.duke.edu/mission-statement/.

Duke University Department of Athletics. "Unrivaled Ambition: A Strategic Plan for Duke Athletics." Duke University, 2008. https://goduke.com/documents/2008/5/10/127971.pdf.

Duke University Financial Services Bursar. *Undergraduate Tuition & Fees.* Accessed May 4, 2023. https://finance.duke.edu/bursar/TuitionFees/tuition.

Edwards, Harry. "Crisis of Black Athletes on the Eve of the 21st Century." *Society* 37, no. 3 (2000): 9–13. https://doi.org/10.1007/BF02686167.

Eitzen, D. Stanley. *Fair and Foul: Beyond the Myths and Paradoxes of Sport.* Lanham, MD: Rowman & Littlefield, 1999.

———. "Racism in Big-Time College Sport: Prospects for the Year 2020 and Proposal for Change." In *Racism in College Athletics: The African American Athlete's Experience*, edited by Dana D. Brooks and Ronald C. Althouse, 293–306. Morgantown, WV: Fitness Information Technology, Inc., 2000.

Ekhtiari, Seper, Ibrahim Yusuf, Yosra AlMakadma, Austin MacDonald, Timothy Leroux, and Moin Khan. "Opioid Use in Athletes: A Systematic Review." *Sports Health* 12, no. 6 (2020): 534–39. https://doi.org/10.1177/1941738120933542.

Fairclough, Norman. *Critical Discourse Analysis: The Critical Study of Language.* New York: Routledge, 2013.

———. "Discourse and Text: Linguistic and Intertextual Analysis within Discourse Analysis." *Discourse & Society* 3, no. 2 (1992): 193–217. https://doi.org/10.1177/0957926592003002004.

Fields, Justin. #WeWantToPlay [Petition]. *MoveOn.org*, 2020. https://sign.moveon.org/petitions/wewanttoplay.

Fisher, Jill A. "Expanding the Frame of 'Voluntariness' in Informed Consent: Structural Coercion and the Power of Social and Economic Context." *Kennedy Institute of Ethics Journal* 23, no. 4 (2013): 355–79. https://doi.org/10.1353/ken.2013.0018.

Foote, Justin Gus, Michael L. Butterworth, and Jimmy Sanderson. "Adrian Peterson and the 'Wussification of America': Football and Myths of Masculinity." *Communication Quarterly* 65, no. 3 (2017): 268–84. https://doi.org/10.1080/01463373.2016.1227347.

Ford, Jason A., Corey Pomykacz, Philip Veliz, Sean Esteban McCabe, and Carol J. Boyd. "Sports Involvement, Injury History, and Non-Medical Use of Prescription Opioids among College Students: An Analysis with a National Sample." *American Journal on Addictions* 27, no. 1 (2018): 15–22. https://doi.org/10.1111/ajad.12657.

Forde, Pat. "After a Contentious Summer, Football Plays On. Why? It's Complicated." *Sports Illustrated*, September 3, 2020. www.si.com/college/2020/09 /03/ncaa-football-2020-politics-big-ten-daily-cover.

French, Peter A. *Ethics and College Sports: Ethics, Sports, and the University*. Lanham, MD: Rowman & Littlefield, 2004.

Gaul, Gilbert M. *Billion-Dollar Ball: A Journey through the Big-Money Culture of College Football*. New York: Penguin, 2015.

Gavett, Brandon E., Robert A. Stern, and Ann C. McKee. "Chronic Traumatic Encephalopathy: A Potential Late Effect of Sport-Related Concussive and Subconcussive Head Trauma." *Clinics in Sports Medicine* 30, no. 1 (2011): 179–88. https://doi.org/10.1016/j.csm.2010.09.007.

Gilbert, Daniel A. "Not (Just) about the Money: Contextualizing the Labor Activism of College Football Players." *American Studies* 55, no. 3 (2016): 19–34. https://doi .org/10.1353/ams.2016.0103.

Gilligan, Chris. "Declines in Youth Football Predate Damar Hamlin's Collapse. Will They Continue?" *US News and World Report*, January 25, 2023. https://www .usnews.com/news/health-news/articles/2023-01-24/youth-football-participation -declining-amid-safety-concerns.

Glaser, Barney G. "The Future of Grounded Theory." *Qualitative Health Research* 9, no. 6 (1999): 836–45. https://doi.org/10.1177/104973299129122199.

———. "Open Coding Descriptions." *Grounded Theory Review* 15, no. 2 (2016): 108–10.

Glaser, Barney G., and Anselm L. Strauss. *The Discovery of Grounded Theory: Strategies for Qualitative Inquiry*. New York: Aldine, 1967.

Gobo, Giampietro. "Sampling, Representativeness and Generalizability." *Qualitative Research Practice* 405 (2004): 426. https://doi.org/10.4135/9781848608191.d34.

Gonzalez, Norma. "BYU Quarterback Zach Wilson Says He Had the Coronavirus over the Summer." *Salt Lake Tribune*, September 21, 2020. www.sltrib.com/sports /byu-cougars/2020/09/21/byu-quarterback-zach/.

Gould, Daniel, and Meredith A. Whitley. "Sources and Consequences of Athletic Burnout among College Athletes." *Journal of Intercollegiate Sport* 2, no. 1 (2009): 16–30. https://doi.org/10.1123/jis.2.1.16.

Grano, Daniel A. "Football after Fragmentation: Brain Banking, Chronic Traumatic Encephalopathy, and Racial Biosociality in the NFL." *Communication and Critical/ Cultural Studies* 17, no. 4 (2020): 339–59. https://doi.org/10.1080/14791420.2020 .1820058.

Grant, Otis B. "African American College Football Players and the Dilemma of Exploitation, Racism and Education: A Socio-Economic Analysis of Sports Law." *Whittier Law Review* 24 (2002): 645–62.

Gulick, Brendan. "Justin Fields: 'We Wanted People Who Are Making Decisions to Hear Our Voice.'" *Fan Nation*, August 17, 2020. www.si.com/college/ohiostate /football/justin-fields-we-want-to-play-movement.

Guridy, Frank. *The Sports Revolution: How Texas Changed the Culture of American Athletics*. Austin: University of Texas Press, 2021.

Hall, Stuart, Chas Critcher, Tony Jefferson, John Clarke, and Brian Roberts. *Policing the Crisis: Mugging, the State and Law and Order*. London: Red Globe Press, 2013.

Hamilton, Darrick and William Darity, Jr. "Can 'Baby Bonds' Eliminate the Racial Wealth Gap in Putative 'Post-Racial' America?" *The Review of Black Political Economy* 37, no. 3–4 (2010): 207–16.

Handcock, Mark S., and Krista J. Gile. "Comment: On the Concept of Snowball Sampling." *Sociological Methodology* 41, no. 1 (2011): 367–71. https://doi.org/10.1111/j.1467-9531.2011.01243.x.

Haraway, Donna J. *The Companion Species Manifesto: Dogs, People and Significant Otherness*. Chicago: Prickly Paradigm Press, 2003.

Harper, Shaun R., Collin D. Williams, and H. W. Blackmon. *Black Male Student-Athletes and Racial Inequalities in NCAA Division I College Sports*. Philadelphia: University of Pennsylvania, Center for the Study of Race and Equity in Education, 2013.

Harrison, Emily A. "The First Concussion Crisis: Head Injury and Evidence in Early American Football." *American Journal of Public Health* 104, no. 5 (2014): 822–33. https://doi.org/10.2105/AJPH.2013.301840.

Hatton, Erin. *Coerced: Work under Threat of Punishment*. Berkeley: University of California Press, 2020.

Hawkins, Billy. *The New Plantation: Black Athletes, College Sports, and Predominantly White Institutions*. New York: Palgrave Macmillan, 2010.

Hextrum, Kirsten. *Special Admission: How College Sports Recruitment Favors White Suburban Athletes*. New Brunswick, NJ: Rutgers University Press, 2021.

Horka, Tyler. "Mississippi State RB Kylin Hill Says He Won't Represent 'This State Anymore' if Flag Not Changed." *USA Today*, June 22, 2020. www.usatoday.com/story/sports/ncaaf/sec/2020/06/22/mississippi-state-football-bulldogs-kylin-hill-state-flag-change/3237379001/.

Ivarsson, Andreas, Ulrika Tranaeus, Urban Johnson, and Andrea Stenling. "Negative Psychological Responses of Injury and Rehabilitation Adherence Effects on Return to Play in Competitive Athletes: A Systematic Review and Meta-Analysis." *Open Access Journal of Sports Medicine* 8, no. 1 (2017): 27–32. https://doi.org/10.2147/OAJSM.S112688.

Jacks, Dean E., William D. Tereshko, and Justin B. Moore. "Diagnosed Concussion and Undiagnosed Head Trauma Is Associated with Long-Term Concussion-Related Symptoms in Former College Football Players." *American Journal of Physical Medicine & Rehabilitation* 101, no. 3 (2022): 250–54. https://doi.org/10.1097/PHM.0000000000001782.

Jackson, Victoria. "How to Take the Scandal Out of Big-Time College Football and Basketball." *Los Angeles Times*, January 4, 2019. https://www.latimes.com/opinion/op-ed/la-oe-jackson-ncaa-lifetime-scholarships-20190104-story.html.

Jag, Julie. "Opting Out This Season Is an Option for Most College Football Players, But Maybe Not at Utah State." *Salt Lake Tribune*, October 2, 2020. www.sltrib.com/sports/utah-state-sports/2020/10/02/opting-out-this-season-is/.

Jhally, Sut. "The Spectacle of Accumulation: Material and Cultural Factors in the Evolution of the Sports/Media Complex." *Critical Sociology* 12, no. 3 (1984): 41–57. https://doi.org/10.1177/089692058401200304.

Jones, Willis A., and Wayne L. Black, "Basketball's Black Tax? An Examination of Historically Black College and University Men's Basketball Guarantee Game Compensation." *Journal of Sport Management*, 36, no. 2 (2021): 159–70.

Kalman-Lamb, Nathan. "Athletic Labor and Social Reproduction." *Journal of Sport and Social Issues* 43, no. 6 (2019): 515–30. https://doi.org/10.1177/0193723519850879.

———. "Defamiliarizing Concussions: Sports Fandom, Injury, and Potential Attitudinal Shifts." Paper delivered at North American Society for the Sociology of Sport annual meeting, Virginia Beach, VA. November 7, 2019.

———. *Game Misconduct: Injury, Fandom, and the Business of Sport.* Black Point, NS: Fernwood Publishing, 2018.

———. "Imagined Communities of Fandom: Sport, Spectatorship, Meaning and Alienation in Late Capitalism." *Sport in Society* 24, no. 6 (2021): 922–36. https://doi.org/10.1080/17430437.2020.1720656.

———. "Sleep Pods, Plush Carpets, and the Dark Heart of the NCAA." *Chronicle of Higher Education*, August 6, 2019. www.chronicle.com/article/sleep-pods-plush-carpets-and-the-dark-heart-of-the-ncaa/.

Kalman-Lamb, Nathan, and Derek Silva. "'The Coaches Always Make the Health Decisions:' Conflict of Interest as Exploitation in Power Five College Football." *SSM-Qualitative Research in Health* 5 (2024): 1–9. https://www.sciencedirect.com/science/article/pii/S2667321524000143.

———. "Dartmouth's Vote to Unionize Could Help End College Sport's Plantation Dynamics." *The Guardian*, March 5, 2024. https://www.theguardian.com/sport/2024/mar/05/dartmouths-vote-to-unionize-could-help-end-college-sports-plantation-dynamics.

———. "A New Day for College Athlete Unions Could Be on the Horizon." *Jacobin*, March 14, 2024. https://jacobin.com/2024/03/usc-college-athletes-nlrb-unioniza.

———. "'Play'ing College Football: Campus Athletic Worker Experiences of Exploitation." *Critical Sociology* (2023). https://doi.org/10.1177/0896920523 1208036.

———. "This is the Only Way to End College Sports Exploitation." *The Daily Beast*, March 17, 2024. https://www.thedailybeast.com/pay-for-play-is-the-only-way-to-end-college-sports-exploitation.

Kalman-Lamb, Nathan, Derek Silva, and Johanna Mellis. "College Football Feels All Too Normal during the Pandemic." *TIME*, October 22, 2020. https://time.com/5901657/college-football-covid-19/.

———. "'I Signed My Life to Rich White Guys': Athletes on the Racial Dynamics of College Sports." *Guardian*, March 17, 2021. www.theguardian.com/sport/2021/mar/17/college-sports-racial-dynamics.

———. "Race, Money and Exploitation: Why College Sport is Still the 'New Plantation.'" *Guardian*, September 7, 2021. www.theguardian.com/sport/2021/sep/07/race-money-and-exploitation-why-college-sport-is-still-the-new-plantation.

———. "The Red Zone." *The Baffler*, October 19, 2020. https://thebaffler.com/latest/the-red-zone-kalman-lamb-mellis-silva.

———. "There's Never Been a Better Time for College Athletes to Unionize." *Guardian*, May 27, 2021. https://www.theguardian.com/sport/2021/may/27/college-sports-union-right-to-organize-act

———. "'This Is a Job': Why College Players Reject the Insidious Term 'Student Athlete.'" *Guardian*, December 8, 2021. www.theguardian.com/sport/2021/dec/08/this-is-a-job-why-college-players-reject-the-insidious-term-student-athlete.

———. "'We Are Being Gaslit': College Football and COVID-19 Are Imperiling Athletes." *Guardian*, August 2, 2020. www.theguardian.com/sport/2020/aug/03/college-football-coronavirus-athletes.

Keaton, Ajhanai C. I., and Joseph N. Cooper. "A Racial Reckoning in a Racialized Organization? Applying Racialized Organization Theory to the NCAA institutional Field." *Journal of Issues in Intercollegiate Athletics* 15 (2022): 189–218. https://scholarcommons.sc.edu/jiia/vol15/iss1/4/.

Kelley, Robin D. G. "Foreword." In *Black Marxism: The Making of the Black Radical Tradition*, by Cedric Robinson, xi–xxxiii. Chapel Hill: University of North Carolina Press, 2021.

Kennedy, Dane. "The Disneyfication of a University." *Chronicle of Higher Education*, February 9, 2020. www.chronicle.com/article/the-disneyfication-of-a-university/.

Kercheval, Ben, and Barrett Sallee. "Trevor Lawrence Sparks United #WeWantToPlay Movement, Players Association Goal as 2020 Season Hangs in Balance." *CBS Sports*, August 10, 2020. www.cbssports.com/college-football/news/trevor-lawrence-sparks-united-wewanttoplay-movement-players-association-goal-as-2020-season-hangs-in-balance/.

Kersey, Jason. "How the NCAA Allows Medical Exemptions." *Oklahoman*, July 21, 2012. www.oklahoman.com/story/sports/college/sooners/2012/07/31/how-the-ncaa-allows-medical-exemptions/61055460007/.

Khan, Yussuf. "Student-Athletes Kneeling Is the Latest GOP Suppression Target." *First and Pen*, February 25, 2021. https://firstandpen.com/student-athletes-kneeling-is-the-latest-gop-suppression-target/.

King-White, Ryan. *Sport and the Neoliberal University: Profit, Politics, and Pedagogy*. New Brunswick, NJ: Rutgers University Press, 2018.

Klemko, Robert, and Emily Giambalvo. "On a Call with SEC Leaders, Worried Football Players Pushed Back: 'Not Good Enough.'" *Washington Post*, August 1, 2020, www.washingtonpost.com/sports/2020/08/01/sec-football-players-safety-meeting/.

Koren, Danny, Doron Norman, Ayala Cohen, Jason Berman, and Ehud M. Klein. "Increased PTSD Risk with Combat-Related Injury: A Matched Comparison Study of Injured and Uninjured Soldiers Experiencing the Same Combat Events." *American Journal of Psychiatry* 162, no. 2 (2005): 276–82. https://doi.org/10.1176/appi.ajp.162.2.276.

Kosko, Nick. "Penn State Football Parents Release Season Supporting Statement." *247 Sports*, August 10, 2020. https://247sports.com/Article/Penn-State-football-parents-we-want-to-play-release-season-supporting-statement-Pat-Freiermuth-Dianne-COVID-19-pandemic-150073293/.

Kundnani, Arun. "What Is Racial Capitalism?" *Arun Kundnani on Race, Culture, and Empire* (blog), April 23, 2020. www.kundnani.org/what-is-racial-capitalism/.

"K-State Players Announce Boycott after Student's Floyd Tweet." *Associated Press News*, June 29, 2020. https://apnews.com/article/e6f4ca14d711b1633ff2f4951c63d6ec.

Lanter, Jason R., and Billy J. Hawkins. "The Economic Model of Intercollegiate Athletics and Its Effects on the College Athlete Educational Experience." *Journal of Intercollegiate Sport* 6, no. 1 (2013): 86–95. https://doi.org/10.1123/jis.6.1.86.

Lavigne, Paula, and Mark Schlabach. "FBS Schools Spent over $533.6 Million in Dead Money over 10+ Years." *ESPN*, November 5, 2021. www.espn.com/college-football/story/_/id/32552130/schools-spent-5336-million-dead-money.

Leonard, David J., and C. Richard King (Eds.), *Commodified and Criminalized: New Racism and African Americans in Contemporary Sports*. Lanham: Rowan and Littlefield, 2011.

Leonard, Wilbert Marcellus, II. "The Sports Experience of the Black College Athlete: Exploitation in the Academy." *International Review for the Sociology of Sport* 21, no. 1 (1986): 35–49. https://doi.org/10.1177/101269028602100103.

Libit, Daniel, and Lev Akabas. "67% of Americans Favor Paying College Athletes: Sportico/Harris Poll." *Sportico*, August 17, 2023. www.sportico.com/leagues/college-sports/2023/americans-favor-college-athletes-pay-harris-poll-1234734402/.

Luther, Jessica. *Unsportsmanlike Conduct: College Football and the Politics of Rape*. New York, NY: Akashic, 2016.

Mahoney, James. "Strategies of Causal Inference in Small-n Analysis." *Sociological Methods & Research* 28, no. 4 (2000): 387–424. https://doi.org/10.1177/0049124100028004001.

Marchand, Andrew. "Amazon Eyeing ESPN's Kirk Herbstreit as Its Top NFL Analyst." *New York Post*, February 27, 2022. https://nypost.com/2022/02/27/amazon-eyeing-espns-kirk-herbstreit-as-its-top-nfl-analyst/.

Marcus, Ann, Larry C. Mullins, Kimberly P. Brackett, Zongli Tang, Annette M. Allen, and Daniel W. Pruett. "Perceptions of Racism on Campus." *College Student Journal* 37, no. 4 (2003): 611–27.

Markus, Nicole, Alyce Brown, and Cole Reynolds. "Former NU Players Describe Racist Environment in Football Program." *Daily Northwestern*, July 10, 2023. https://dailynorthwestern.com/2023/07/10/sports/former-nu-players-describe-racist-environment-in-football-program/.

Markus, Nicole, Alyce Brown, Cole Reynolds, and Divya Bhardwaj. "Former NU Football Player Details Hazing Allegations after Coach Suspension." *Daily Northwestern*, July 8. 2023. https://dailynorthwestern.com/2023/07/08/sports/former-nu-football-player-details-hazing-allegations-after-coach-suspension/.

Marx, Karl. "Alienated Labor." In *Karl Marx: Selected Writings*, edited by L. H. Simon, 58–68. Indianapolis: Hackett, 1994.

———. *Capital*, Volume 1. Marx/Engels Internet Archive, 1995 (1867). www.marxists.org/archive/marx/works/1867-c1/.

———. "18th Brumaire of Louis Bonaparte." Marx/Engels Internet Archive, 1995 (1852). www.marxists.org/archive/marx/works/1852/18th-brumaire/.

———. *The Poverty of Philosophy*. Marx/Engels Internet Archive, 1999 (1847). www.marxists.org/archive/marx/works/1847/poverty-philosophy/.

Masten, Robert, Klemen Stražar, Iztok Žilavec, Matej Tušak, and Manca Kandare. "Psychological Response of Athletes to Injury." *Kinesiology* 46, no. 1 (2014): 127–34.

McCormick, Robert A., and Amy C. McCormick. "A Trail of Tears: The Exploitation of the College Athlete." *Florida Coastal Law Review* 11 (2009): 639–66.

McGee, Kate. "U-T Austin Football Players Say They Were Forced to Stay on Field for 'The Eyes of Texas' to Appease Angry Donors and Fans." *Texas Tribune*, March 3, 2021. www.texastribune.org/2021/03/03/ut-austin-eyes-of-texas-donors/?utm _campaign=trib-social&utm_content=1614809642&utm_medium=social&utm _source=twitter.

McMillan Cottom, Tressie. "Where Platform Capitalism and Racial Capitalism Meet: The Sociology of Race and Racism in the Digital Society." *Sociology of Race and Ethnicity* 6, no. 4 (2020): 441–49. https://doi.org/10.1177/2332649220949473.

Melamed, Jodi. "Racial Capitalism." *Critical Ethnic Studies* 1, no. 1 (2015): 76–85. https://doi.org/10.5749/jcritethnstud.1.1.0076.

Mellor, Cam. "Read the UCLA Football Players Full Letter." *Bruins Nation*, June 21, 2020. www.bruinsnation.com/2020/6/21/21298261/ucla-football-read-full-letter -coronavirus-protection-demanding-chip-kelly-dorian-thompson-robinson.

Merton, Robert K. "Patterns of Influence: A Study of Interpersonal Influence and Communications Behavior in a Local Community." In *Communications Research*, 1948-1949, edited by Paul L. Lazarfeld and Frank N. Stanton, 180–219. New York: Harper, 1949.

Mez, Jesse, Daniel H. Daneshvar, Patrick T. Kiernan, Bobak Abdolmohammadi, Victor E. Alvarez, Bertrand R. Huber, Michael L. Alosco et al. "Clinicopathological Evaluation of Chronic Traumatic Encephalopathy in Players of American Football." *JAMA* 318, no. 4 (2017): 360–70. https://doi.org/10.1001 /jama.2017.8334.

Mitchell, Josh. "A Crimson Tide of Debt." *Atlantic*, August 1, 2021. www.theatlantic .com/ideas/archive/2021/08/public-universities-debt/619546/.

Mills, Charles W. *The Racial Contract*. Ithaca, NY: Cornell University Press, 1997.

Montez de Oca, Jeffrey. "Marketing Politics and Resistance: Mobilizing Black Pain in National Football League Publicity." *Sociology of Sport Journal* 38, no. 2 (2021): 101–10. https://doi.org/10.1123/ssj.2021-0005.

———. "White Domestic Goddess on a Postmodern Plantation: Charity and Commodity Racism in *The Blind Side*." *Sociology of Sport Journal* 29, no. 2 (2012): 131–50. https://doi.org/10.1123/ssj.29.2.131.

Moore, Louis. *We Will Win the Day: The Civil Rights Movement, the Black Athlete, and the Quest for Equality*. Lexington: The University of Kentucky Press, 2021.

Moore, Matt A., Sasa Vann, and Allison Blake. "Learning from the Experiences of Collegiate Athletes Living through a Season- or Career-Ending Injury." *Journal of Amateur Sport* 7, no. 1 (2021). https://doi.org/10.17161/jas.v7i1.14501.

Mull, Amanda. "College Football's Greatest Unraveling." *Atlantic*, August 13, 2020. www.theatlantic.com/health/archive/2020/08/college-football-falling-apart /615277/.

Murphy, Steve, and Jonathan Pace. "A Plan for Compensating Student-Athletes." *Brigham Young University Education and Law Journal* (1994): 167–86.

Myerberg, Paul. "College Football Playoff's New Six-Year Contract Starting in 2026 Opens the Door to Expansion." *USA TODAY*, March 15, 2024. https://www .usatoday.com/story/sports/ncaaf/2024/03/15/college-football-playoff-contract -expansion-14-teams/72984984007/.

Nadelson, Louis S., Carrie Semmelroth, Gregory Martinez, Matthew Feather-stone, Casey Alex Fuhriman, and Andrew Sell. "Why Did They Come Here?— The Influences and Expectations of First-Year Students' College Experience." *Higher Education Studies* 3, no. 1 (2013): 50–62. https://doi.org/10.5539/hes .v3n1p50.

National Collegiate Athletic Association (NCAA). "Football: Probability of Competing beyond High School." National Collegiate Athletic Association, April 20, 2020. www.ncaa.org/sports/2015/2/27/football-probability-of -competing-beyond-high-school.aspx.

————. *NCAA Financial Dashboard* (Data visualization dashboard). National Collegiate Athletic Association, 2022. https://www.ncaa.org/sports/2019/11/12 /finances-of-intercollegiate-athletics-database.aspx.

National Collegiate Athletic Association Research. "Five Themes from the NCAA GOALS Study of the Student-Athlete Experience" (PowerPoint presentation). National Collegiate Athletic Association Research, 2020. https://ncaaorg.s3 .amazonaws.com/research/goals/2020D1RES_GOALS2020con.pdf.

Newell, Emily M., and Simran Kaur Sethi. "Exploring the Perception of Division I Coaches and Administrators about International Collegiate Athlete Exclusion from Name, Image, and Likeness Opportunities." *Journal of Sport Management* 37, no. 5 (2023): 345–58.

Ngugi, Mukoma wa. "The Pitfalls of Symbolic Decolonization." *Africa Is a Country*, January 17, 2020. https://africasacountry.com/2020/01/the-pitfalls-of-symbolic -decolonization.

Nocera, Joe, and Ben Strauss. *Indentured: The Battle to End the Exploitation of College Athletes*. New York: Penguin Publishing Group, 2018.

Novy-Williams, Eben, Kurt Badenhausen, and Scott Soschnick. "Florida State Taps JPMorgan for Equity Raise as ACC Decision Looms." *Sportico*, August 4, 2023. www.sportico.com/business/finance/2023/florida-state-athletics-jpmorgan -private-equity-funding-acc-1234733152/.

Oates, Thomas P. "The Erotic Gaze in the NFL Draft." *Communication and Critical/ Cultural Studies* 4, no. 1 (2007): 47–90. https://doi.org/10.1080/14791420601138351.

————. *Football and Manliness: An Unauthorized Feminist Account of the NFL*. Champaign: University of Illinois Press, 2017.

Oates, Thomas P., and Meenakshi Gigi Durham. "The Mismeasure of Masculinity: The Male Body, 'Race' and Power in the Enumerative Discourses of the NFL Draft." *Patterns of Prejudice* 38, no. 3 (2004): 301–20. https://doi.org/10.1080 /0031322042000250475.

Oates, Thomas P., and Zack Furness. *The NFL: Critical and Cultural Perspectives*. Philadelphia: Temple University Press, 2014.

Ohio State University. *Athletic Department Directory*. Accessed March 8, 2023. https://ohiostatebuckeyes.com/staff-directory/.

Oklahoma State University. "Mission." Oklahoma State University, 2023. https://go
.okstate.edu/about-osu/mission-landgrant.html.

Oliver, Jonathan M., Anthony J. Anzalone, Jason D. Stone, Stephanie M. Turner,
Damond Blueitt, J. Craig Garrison, Andrew T. Askow, Joel A. Luedke, and
Andrew R. Jagim. "Fluctuations in Blood Biomarkers of Head Trauma in NCAA
Football Athletes over the Course of a Season." *Journal of Neurosurgery* 130, no. 5
(2018): 1655–62. https://doi.org/10.3171/2017.12.JNS172035.

Oriard, Mike. *Bowled Over: Big-Time College Football from the Sixties to the BCS Era.*
Chapel Hill: University of North Carolina Press, 2009.

Orleans, Jeffrey H. "The Effects of the Economic Model of College Sport on Athlete
Educational Experience." *Journal of Intercollegiate Sport* 6, no. 1 (2013): 79–85.
https://doi.org/10.1123/jis.6.1.79.

Overly, Kathleen B. "The Exploitation of African-American Men in College Athletic
Programs." *Virginia Sports & Entertainment Law Journal* 5 (2005): 31–63.

Patterson, Orlando. *Slavery and Social Death.* Cambridge, MA: Harvard University
Press, 2018 (1982).

Pequeño, Sara. "UNC Athletics Just Had Thirty-Seven People Test Positive for
COVID-19." *Indy Week,* July 9, 2020. https://indyweek.com/news/orange/the-unc
-football-team-just-had-37-people-test-positive-for-c/.

Perez, A. J. "Former Players, Staff Reveal Troubling Allegations of Toxic Culture
under P. J. Fleck." *Front Office Sports,* July 26, 2023. https://frontofficesports.com
/former-gophers-players-staff-reveal-troubling-allegations-of-toxic-culture
-under-p-j-fleck/.

Peter, Josh. "Are College Football Players the 'Guinea Pig' for COVID-19 Protocol
Planning at Universities?" *USA Today,* July 17, 2020. www.usatoday.com/story
/sports/ncaaf/2020/07/17/college-football-players-guinea-pigs-schools-covid-19
-plans/5443267002/.

Prisbell, Eric. "OU's Joe Castiglione Says College Sports Reform Needs a Plan B
'and C and D and E.'" *On3,* July 14, 2023. www.on3.com/nil/news/oklahoma
-sooners-athletic-director-joe-castiglione-on-why-college-sports-needs-a-plan-b
-and-c-and-d-and-e/.

Purdy, Dean A., D. Stanley Eitzen, and Rick Hufnagel. "Are Athletes Also Students?
The Educational Attainment of College Athletes." *Social Problems* 29, no. 4 (1982):
439–48. https://doi.org/10.2307/800032.

Ralph, Michael, and Maya Singhal. "Racial Capitalism." *Theory and Society* 48 (2019):
851–81. https://doi.org/10.1007/s11186-019-09367-z.

Ray, Victor E. *On Critical Race Theory: Why it Matters and Why You Should Care.*
New York: Random House, 2022.

———. "A Theory of Racialized Organizations." *American Sociological Review* 84,
no. 1 (2019): 26–53. https://doi.org/10.1177/0003122418822335.

Rhoden, William C. *Forty Million Dollar Slaves: The Rise, Fall, and Redemption of the
Black Athlete.* New York: Crown, 2006.

Rittenberg, Adam. "Big 10 to Guarantee Scholarships." *ESPN,* October 8, 2014. www
.espn.com/college-sports/story/_/id/11666316/big-ten-guarantees-four-year
-scholarships-student-athletes.

Rittenberg, Adam, and Heather Dinich. "Big Ten Football to Resume Weekend of Oct. 24." *ESPN*, September 16, 2020. www.espn.com/college-football/story/_/id/29897305/sources-big-ten-announce-october-return.

Robinson, Cedric. *Black Marxism: The Making of the Black Radical Tradition*. Chapel Hill: University of North Carolina Press, 1983.

Runstedtler, Theresa. "More Than Just Play: Unmasking Black Child Labor in the Athletic Industrial Complex." *Journal of Sport and Social Issues* 42, no. 3 (2018): 152–69.

Russo, Ralph. "Explainer: How Will College Football Expansion Work?" *Associated Press*, December 2, 2022. https://apnews.com/article/college-football-entertainment-sports-802d4685eba648e5ba6c098c72a92e6f.

Ryan, Camille L., and Kurt Bauman. *Educational Attainment in the United States: 2015. Population Characteristics. Current Population Reports*. Washington, DC: United States Census Bureau, Department of Commerce, 2016.

Sack, Allen L., and Ellen J. Staurowsky. *College Athletes for Hire: The Evolution and Legacy of the NCAA's Amateur Myth*. Westport, CT: Praeger, 1998.

Sailes, Gary A. "Betting against the Odds: An Overview of Black Sports Participation." In *African Americans in Sports*, edited by Gary A. Sailes, 23–35. New Brunswick, NJ: Transaction, 1998.

———. "An Investigation of Campus Stereotypes: The Myth of Black Athletic Superiority and the Dumb Jock Stereotype." *Sociology of Sport Journal* 10, no. 1 (1993): 88–97. https://doi.org/10.1123/ssj.10.1.88.

Salganik, Matthew J., and Douglas D. Heckathorn. "Sampling and Estimation in Hidden Populations Using Respondent-Driven Sampling." *Sociological Methodology* 34, no. 1 (2004): 193–240. https://doi.org/10.1111/j.0081-1750.2004.00152.x.

Sallee, Barrett. "Vanderbilt's Road Game against Missouri Postponed Due to COVID-19 Concerns, Rescheduled for Dec. 12." *CBS Sports*, October 12, 2020. www.cbssports.com/college-football/news/vanderbilts-road-game-against-missouri-postponed-due-to-covid-19-concerns-rescheduled-for-dec-12/.

Sanders, George, and Clare Stevinson. "Associations between Retirement Reasons, Chronic Pain, Athletic Identity, and Depressive Symptoms among Former Professional Footballers." *European Journal of Sport Science* 17, no. 10 (2017): 1311–18. https://doi.org/10.1080/17461391.2017.1371795.

Schwarz, Andy, and Kevin Trahan. "The Mythology Playbook: Procompetitive Justifications for 'Amateurism,' Biases and Heuristics, and 'Believing What You Know Ain't So.'" *Antitrust Bulletin* 62, no. 1 (2017): 140–83. https://doi.org/10.1177/0003603X17691382.

Schwarz, Andy, and Richard J. Volante. "The Ninth Circuit Decision in *O'Bannon* and the Fallacy of Fragile Demand." *Marquette Sports Law Review* 26, no. 2 (2015): 391–410.

Seamster, Louise, and Alan Aja. "Regressive Student Loan System Results in Costly Racial Disparities." Brookings, January 24, 2022. www.brookings.edu/articles/aregressive-student-loan-system-results-in-costly-racial-disparities/.

Sellers, Robert M. "African American Student-Athletes: Opportunity or Exploitation?" In *Racism in College Athletics: The African American Athlete's Experience*, edited by Dana D. Brooks and Ronald C. Althouse, 133–54. Morgantown, WV: Fitness Information Technology, 2000.

Sheinbein, Shelly. "Psychological Effect of Injury on the Athlete: A Recommendation for Psychological Intervention." *Journal of the American Medical Athletic Association* 29, no. 3 (2016): 8–10.

Shulman, James L., and William G. Bowen. *The Game of Life: College Sports and Educational Values.* Princeton, NJ: Princeton University Press, 2001.

Shurley, Jason P., and Janice S. Todd. "Boxing Lessons: An Historical Review of Chronic Head Trauma in Boxing and Football." *Kinesiology Review* 1, no. 3 (2012): 170–84. https://doi.org/10.1123/krj.1.3.170.

Siegfried, John J., and Molly Gardner Burba. "The College Football Association Television Broadcast Cartel." *Antitrust Bulletin* 49, no. 3 (2004): 799–819. https://doi.org/10.1177/0003603X0404900309.

Silva, Derek, and Liam Kennedy. *Power Played: A Critical Criminology of Sport.* Vancouver, BC: University of British Columbia Press, 2022.

Simonetto, Deana, and Michelle Tucsok, "Former Athletes' Illness Stories of Brain Injuries: Suspected Chronic Traumatic Encephalopathy and the Entanglement of Never-Aging Masculinities." *Symbolic Interaction* 46, no. 2 (2023): 182–206. https://onlinelibrary.wiley.com/doi/full/10.1002/symb.646.

Singer, John N. "Benefits and Detriments of African American Male Athletes' Participation in a Big-Time College Football Program." *International Review for the Sociology of Sport* 43, no. 4 (2008): 399–408. https://doi.org/10.1177/1012690208099874.

———. "Understanding Racism through the Eyes of African American Male Student-Athletes." *Race, Ethnicity, and Education* 8, no. 4 (2005): 365–86. https://doi.org/10.1080/13613320500323963.

Smith, Dorothy. *Women's Experience as a Radical Critique of Sociology.* Toronto: University of Toronto Press, 1990.

Smith, Earl. "The African American Student-Athlete." In *Race and Sport: The Struggle for Equality On and Off the Field,* edited by Charles K. Ross, 121–45. Jackson: University of Mississippi Press, 2004.

———. *Race, Sport and the American Dream.* Durham: Carolina Academic Press, 2014.

Smith, Jay M., and Mary Willingham. *Cheated: The UNC Scandal, the Education of Athletes, and the Future of Big-Time College Sports.* Sterling, VA: Potomac Books, 2015.

Smith, Michael. "Top ACC Medical Advisor Says Football Can Be Played Safely." *Sports Business Journal,* August 11, 2020. www.sportsbusinessjournal.com/Daily/Issues/2020/08/11/Colleges/ACC.aspx.

Smith, Ronald A. *Pay for Play: A History of Big-Time College Athletic Reform.* Champaign: University of Illinois Press, 2011.

Southall, Richard M., E. Woodrow Eckard, Mark S. Nagel, and Morgan H. Randall. "Athletic Success and NCAA Profit-Athletes' Adjusted Graduation Gaps." *Sociology of Sport Journal* 32, no. 4 (2015): 395–414. https://doi.org/10.1123/ssj.2014-0156.

Southall, Richard M., Mark S. Nagel, Chris Core, and Allen Wallace. *2022–23 Adjusted Graduation Gap Report: NCAA FBS Football.* Columbia, SC: College Sport Research Institute, 2023.

Southall, Richard M., Mark S. Nagel, Ellen J. Staurowsky, Richard T. Karcher, and Joel G. Maxcy. *The NCAA and the Exploitation of College Profit-Athletes: An Amateurism that Never Was.* Columbia: University of South Carolina Press, 2023.

Southall, Richard M., Mark S. Nagel, and Allen Wallace. *2019 Adjusted Graduation Gap Report: NCAA FBS Football.* Columbia, SC: College Sport Research Institute, 2020.

Southall, Richard M., and Ellen J. Staurowsky. "Cheering on the Collegiate Model: Creating, Disseminating, and Imbedding the NCAA's Redefinition of Amateurism." *Journal of Sport and Social Issues* 37, no. 4 (2013): 403–29. https://doi .org/10.1177/0193723513498606.

Southern Poverty Law Center. "Hate in the News." Southern Poverty Law Center, Teaching Tolerance, 2002. Accessed May 12, 2023 from http://www.tolerance.org /news/ article_hate.jsp?id=403.

Sriprakash, Arathi. "Reparations: Theorising Just Futures of Education." *Discourse: Studies in the Cultural Politics of Education* 44, no. 5 (2023): 782–95. https://doi.org /10.1080/01596306.2022.2144141.

Staurowsky, Ellen J. "An Analysis of Northwestern University's Denial of Rights to and Recognition of College Football Labor." *Journal of Intercollegiate Sport* 7, no. 2 (2014): 134–42. https://doi.org/10.1123/jis.2014-0135.

Steinfeldt, Jesse A., Brad D. Foltz, Jessica Mungro, Quentin L. Speight, Y. Joel Wong, and Jake Blumberg, J. "Masculinity Socialization in Sports: Influence of College Football Coaches." *Psychology of Men & Masculinity* 12, no. 3 (2011): 247–59. https://doi.org/10.1037/a0020170.

Steinfeldt, Matthew, and Jesse A. Steinfeldt. "Athletic Identity and Conformity to Masculine Norms among College Football Players." *Journal of Applied Sport Psychology* 24, no. 2 (2012): 115–28. https://doi.org/10.1080/10413200.2011 .603405.

Steinmetz, George. "Odious Comparisons: Incommensurability, the Case Study, and 'Small N's' in Sociology." *Sociological Theory* 22, no. 3 (2004): 371–400. https://doi.org/10.1111/j.0735-2751.2004.00225.x.

Sterling, Wayne. "Jimbo Fisher to Reportedly Receive Record $77 Million Buyout After Being Relieved of Head Football Coach Duties." *CNN.com*, November 13, 2023. www.cnn.com/2023/11/13/sport/jimbo-fisher-record-buyout-texas-am-spt -intl/index.html.

Strausbaugh, John. *Black like You: Blackface, Whiteface, Insult and Imitation in American Popular Culture.* New York: Tarcher, 2006.

Strauss, Anselm L., and Juliet M. Corbin. *Grounded Theory in Practice.* Thousand Oaks, CA: Sage, 1997.

Svrluga, Susan. "U. Missouri President, Chancellor Resign over Handling of Racial Incidents." *Washington Post*, November 9, 2015. www.washingtonpost.com/news /grade-point/wp/2015/11/09/missouris-student-government-calls-for-university -presidents-removal/.

Táíwò, Olúfẹ́mi. *Reconsidering Reparations.* Oxford: University of Oxford Press, 2022.

Tatos, Ted, and Hal Singer. "Antitrust Anachronism: The Interracial Wealth Transfer in College Athletics under the Consumer Welfare Standard." *Antitrust Bulletin* 66, no. 3 (2021): 396–430. https://doi.org/10.1177/0003603X211029481.

Taylor, Keeanga Yamahtta, and Adolph Reed Jr. "The Reparations Debate." *Dissent*, June 24, 2019. www.dissentmagazine.org/online_articles/the-reparations -debate.

TenHouten, Warren D. "Site Sampling and Snowball Sampling—Methodology for Accessing Hard-to-Reach Populations." *Bulletin of Sociological Methodology/Bulletin de Méthodologie Sociologique* 134, no. 1 (2017): 58–61. https://doi.org/10.1177 /0759106317693790.

Thompson, Steven K. "On Sampling and Experiments." *Environmetrics: The Official Journal of the International Environmetrics Society* 13, no. 5–6 (2002): 429–36. https://doi.org/10.1002/env.532.

Tobolowsky, Barbara F., and John Wesley Lowery. "Selling College: A Longitudinal Study of American College Football Bowl Game Public Service Announcements." *Journal of Marketing for Higher Education* 24, no. 1 (2014): 75–98. https://doi.org/10 .1080/08841241.2014.911790.

Tricker, Ray. "Painkilling Drugs in Collegiate Athletics: Knowledge, Attitudes, and Use of Student Athletes." *Journal of Drug Education* 30, no. 3 (2000): 313–24. https://doi.org/10.2190/N1K3-V8BK-90GH-TTHU.

Tricker, Raymond, and Declan Connolly. "Drug Education and the College Athlete: Evaluation of a Decision-Making Model." *Journal of Drug Education* 26, no. 2 (1996): 159–81. https://doi.org/10.2190/11Q1-R721-QTWJ-R6A5.

Trimbur, Lucia. *Come Out Swinging: The Changing World of Boxing in Gleason's Gym.* Princeton, NJ: Princeton University Press, 2013.

Trimbur, Lucia, and Lundy Braun, "The NFL's Reversal on 'Race Norming' Reveals How Pervasive Medical Racism Remains." *NBC News THINK*, June 8, 2021. https://www.nbcnews.com/think/opinion/nfl-s-reversal-race-norming-reveals -how-pervasive-medical-racism-ncna1269992.

Trow, Martin A. *Right-Wing Radicalism and Political Intolerance.* New York: Arno Press, 1957.

University of Alabama. "Our Mission & Vision." University of Alabama, 2023. www .ua.edu/strategicplan/mission-vision#:~:text=The%20University%20of%20 Alabama%20will,of%20teaching%2C%20research%20and%20service.

University of California, Los Angeles. "Our Mission." University of California, Los Angeles, 2023. www.ucla.edu/about/mission-and-values.

University of Michigan. "Mission." University of Michigan, 2023. https://president .umich.edu/about/mission/#:~:text=The%20mission%20of%20the%20 University,present%20and%20enrich%20the%20future.

University of Texas. "Mission & Values." University of Texas, 2023. www.utexas.edu /about/mission-and-values.

Van Kerckhove, Carmen. "University of Arizona Students Celebrate MLK Day with Blackface Party." *Racialicious*, February 12, 2007. Accessed September 14, 2023. www.racialicious.com/2007/02/12/university-of-arizona-students-celebrate-mlk -day-with-Blackface-party/#disqus_thread.

Van Rheenen, Derek. "Exploitation in the American Academy: College Athletes and Self-Perceptions of Value." *International Journal of Sport & Society* 2, no. 4 (2011): 11–26. https://doi.org/10.18848/2152-7857/CGP/v02i04/53882.

———. "Exploitation in College Sports: Race, Revenue, and Educational Reward." *International Review for the Sociology of Sport* 48, no. 5 (2012): 550–71. https://doi.org/10.1177/1012690212450218.

Ventresca, Matt, and Samantha King. "'Anesthetized Gladiators': Painkilling and Racial Capitalism in the NFL." *Sociology of Sport Journal* 40, no. 1 (2023): 21–29. https://doi.org/10.1123/ssj.2021-0172.

Vertuno, Jim. "Conflict Raging over 'The Eyes of Texas' School Song." *Associated Press News*, October 23, 2020. https://apnews.com/article/eyes-of-texas-controversy-school-song-ced5a2c90f2f847fb58be59971d7a494.

Viswanathan, Giri. "Playing Football May Increase Risk of Parkinson's Disease, Study Suggests." *CNN*, August 11, 2023. www.cnn.com/2023/08/11/health/parkinsons-football-risk/index.html.

Vitale, Joe. "College Football's Highest Paid Head Coaches for 2022 Season." *UGA Wire*, July 26, 2022. https://ugawire.usatoday.com/lists/college-football-head-coach-salaries-2022-season-georgia-bulldogs-kirby-smart-contract-ranks-number-one/.

Wade, Lisa. "Race Themed Events at Colleges" (trigger warning). *The Society Pages*, September 23, 2011. Accessed June 12, 2023 http://thesocietypages.org/socimages/2011/09/23/individual-racism-alive-and-well/.

Washut, Robin. "Husker Parents Issue New Letter to Big Ten." *Inside Nebraska*, August 20, 2020. https://nebraska.rivals.com/news/husker-parents-issue-new-letter-to-big-ten.

"#WeAreUnited." *Players' Tribune*, August 2, 2020. www.theplayerstribune.com/articles/pac-12-players-covid-19-statement-football-season.

Weaver, Karen. "If College Athletes Return, Who Will Pay the Medical Bill?" *Forbes*, April 20, 2020. www.forbes.com/sites/karenweaver/2020/04/20/if-college-athletes-return-who-will-pay-the-medical-bills/?sh=2bb215a87752.

Western Association of Schools and Colleges. *2013 Handbook of Accreditation*. Western Association of Schools and Colleges, 2021. www.wscuc.org/handbook/#standard-1--defining-institutional-purposes-and-ensuring-educational-objectives.

White, Derrick E. *Blood, Sweat, and Tears: Jake Gaither, Florida A&M, and the History of Black College Football*. Chapel Hill: University of North Carolina Press, 2019.

Wittry, Andy. "Power 5 Football Buyouts Reached Second-Highest Total Ever in 2022." *On3*, May 8, 2023. www.on3.com/os/news/college-football-coaching-buyouts-ncaa-financial-reports-2021-2022-fiscal-year/.

Witz, Billy. "Pac-12 Players Say Commissioner Was Dismissive of Their Virus Concerns." *New York Times*, August 8, 2020.

Wrigley-Field, Elizabeth. "US Racial Inequality May Be as Deadly as COVID-19." *Proceedings of the National Academy of Sciences* 117, no. 36 (2020): 21854–56. https://doi.org/10.1073/pnas.2014750117.

Index

149–50; exclusion and bigotry and, 95; plantation dynamics and, 125–26; violence among players and, 171
Huma, Ramogi, 202

insurance malfeasance, 106–9

Jensen, Matt (pseudonym): abusive behavior by coaches and, 167–68; academic cheating and, 64; academic clustering and, 59; academics and, 51–52; athletic trainers and, 82–83; biographical information of, 211; coercive entitlement and, 15; COVID-19 player movements and, 189; COVID-19 season and, 188–89; head trauma and, 103; healthism and, 75; playing through injury and, 76, 103; racism and, 132–33; treatment of scout team players and, 109; walk-ons and, 39–40
Jones, Jeremy (pseudonym): academic clustering and, 61; biographical information of, 211; coercion and, 152; college football and, 13; exploitation and, 28–29; NIL and, 36–37; racial capitalism and, 118–19; racism and, 122

Kelley, Robin, 115
Knoxville News-Sentinel, 179

Lawrence, Trevor, 179
Leonard, Ryan (pseudonym): abusive behavior by coaches and, 174; academic cheating and, 65; academic clustering and, 62; academics, 49; biographical information of, 211; on coaches, 160; coaches' marijuana use and, 155; coercion and, 151–53; collective bargaining and, 203; compliance department complicity and, 80–81; consent and, 161; crime and, 32–33; drug and alcohol use and, 88–89, 155; drug testing and, 154–55;

exploitation and, 43; head trauma and, 101; long-term consequences of injury and, 112; money in college sports and, 17–18, 23; NIL and, 38; playing through injury and, 72, 105; preferential treatment of athletes and, 65–66; quality of care received and, 85; racism on campus and, 134; structural racism and, 122; student loans and, 31; unethical academic practices and, 65–66; voluntary workouts and, 153
Libit, Daniel, 36
Los Angeles Times, 178
Louisiana State University, 178
Luther, Jessica, 15

Mahoney, Denzel, 138
Mark, Karl, 24, 27–28
McDermott, Greg, 138
methodology. *See* research methodology
Mitchell, Shereef, 138
Mullen, Dan, 178

National Collegiate Athletics Association (NCAA): head injuries and, 70; NIL and, 2–3, 20, 22; pay for play and, 204; plantation dynamics and, 116; revenue and finances and, 17–19. *See also* athletic departments; NIL (name, image, likeness)
National College Players Association (NCPA), 2
National Football League (NFL): coercion and, 89; playing through injury and, 83; racial undertones in, 122
National Labor Relations Board (NLRB), 2, 201–2
Nielsen, Ross (pseudonym): abusive behavior by coaches and, 163, 165; academic clustering and, 58; biographical information of, 210; coercion and, 147, 152–53; college football as pyramid scheme and, 15;

Nielsen, Ross (pseudonym) (*continued*)
exploitation and, 35; head trauma
and, 103; on his father's experience,
71; post-career emotions and, 41;
racism amongst campus police and,
137; structural coercion of black
players and, 120–21; student loans
and, 31; treatment of scout team
players and, 109; voluntary workouts
and, 152–53; walk-ons and, 38–39
NIL (name, image, likeness), 2–3, 20,
21, 22, 36–38, 194
North, Galen (pseudonym): biographical information of, 209; coercion and,
149; drug and alcohol use and, 86;
exploitation and, 30; fans and, 40–41;
injury and emotional hardship and,
90–91; insurance and, 107; long-term
consequences of injuries and, 98;
playing through injury and, 72, 81,
91–92; post-career emotions and, 42;
stereotyping of athletes and, 55;
treatment of injured players and,
92–93
Northwestern University, 138–39, 159

Orgeron, Ed, 178

Parkinson's disease, 70
pay for play, 204
Penn State Football Parents Association,
181
Peters, Aaron (pseudonym): abusive
behavior by coaches and, 164; on
being pushed out, 140–41; biographical information of, 212; COVID-19
and, 189; family rhetoric and, 161–62;
locker room dynamics and, 131;
regret and, 112–13
posttraumatic stress disorder (PTSD),
99–100

race: blackness and, 115; capitalism
and, 6–8; racialized exploitation and,
4, 6; racialized political economy of

United States and, 9; wage theft and,
46. *See also* coercion; exploitation
racial capitalism: coercion and, 117–18;
college football and, 116–17, 119–20,
200; NCAA and, 205; structural
racism in college football and, 114.
See also coercion; exploitation
racism: academic clustering and,
136–37; athletic trainers and, 127–28;
boosters and, 128–29; BYU and, 202;
on campuses, 46, 123, 132–39, 202;
campus police and, 137; coaches and,
123–24, 126–27, 129–30; college
football and, 117; locker room
dynamics and, 130–31; NFL and,
122; plantation dynamics and, 8, 114,
116, 125–28, 133–39, 196, 205;
preferential treatment for white
players and, 127–28; structural,
119–20; systematic, 121; use of racist
imagery and, 144–45; white supremacy, 8, 117, 121–22. *See also* coercion;
exploitation
Ray, Victor, 115–16
Reconsidering Reparations (Táíwò),
198–99
Remember the Titans (film), 130
reparations, 198–201
research methodology: anonymity and,
11, 208; coding and, 208, 212; critical
discourse analysis (CDA), 208;
interview participants and, 207–12;
interviews and, 207; qualitative
research and, 11
revenue. *See* athletic departments
Rice, Jalen (pseudonym): academics
and, 54; biographical information
of, 209; exploitation and, 28, 31,
35–36; playing through injury in NFL
and, 83
The Rites of Men (Burstyn), 15
Robinson, Cedric, 6, 116
Rogers, Charlie (pseudonym): abolition
of football and, 151; abusive behavior
by coaches and, 163–65; academic

clustering and, 60; academic staff complicity and, 168–69; biographical information of, 210; coercion and, 148, 153, 157–58; college football and, 16; crime and, 32; CTE and, 100; drug and alcohol use and, 87–88; head trauma and, 101, 104; NIL and, 38; playing through injury and, 104; practice and, 1–2; racism on campus and, 134–36; racist dynamics and, 125; recruiting and, 159–60; selective drug testing and, 155; stereotyping of athletes and, 56; treatment of injured players and, 94; treatment of scout team players and, 109–10; voluntary workouts and, 153

Runstedtler, Theresa, 146

Rycliff, Thomas (pseudonym): academics and, 48–49; biographical information of, 211; coercion and, 147, 158; drug and alcohol use and, 87–88; head trauma and, 101, 104–5; long-term effects of college football and, 195; playing through injury and, 72–74, 77; PTSD and, 99–100

Saban, Nick, 178

Sankey, Greg, 178

Service Employees International Union (SEIU), 2, 202

Singer, Hal, 116

Smith, Dorothy, 9

social reproduction: college football and, 4–5, 194; player/fan relationship and, 40–41; in sport and, 115

Southeastern Conference (SEC), 138, 177–79, 184

student-athletes, 3–4, 47–48, 204. *See also* campus athletic workers

student loans, 31–32

suicide, 149–50

Summers, Steven (pseudonym): academics and, 49–50; anonymity and, 11; biographical information of, 210; coercion and, 152; expenses and,

31; fantasy sports and, 41; long-term consequences of injuries and, 96; NIL and, 37; playing through injury and, 73; play vs work, 22, 24; racism and, 133–34; stereotyping of athletes and, 55

Swinney, Dabo, 177–78

Táíwò, Olúfémi O., 198–99

Tatos, Ted, 116

Texas A&M University, 19–20, 138

Thomas, Michael (pseudonym): biographical information of, 209; injury and emotional hardship and, 90; playing through injury and, 71, 74; play vs work and, 24–25

Thomas, Xavier, 185

Turner, Nick (pseudonym): abusive behavior by coaches and, 164–65; biographical information of, 212; coercion and, 152; drug and alcohol use and, 88; expenses and, 32; head trauma and, 102, 104, 111–12; healthism and, 75; long-term consequences of injuries and, 97–98; playing through injury and, 72; punitive overtraining and, 78; regret and, 111

unions, 2

University of Alabama, 178

University of Florida, 178

University of Georgia, 138

University of Nebraska, 181

University of North Carolina, 178, 184

University of Southern California (USC), 2, 202

University of Texas, 138

University of Wyoming, 202

Unsportsmanlike Conduct (Luther), 15

USA Today, 183

Utah State, 182

Vanderbilt University, 184

Van Rheenen, Derek, 4

violence: as attraction to game of football, 14; in practice, 68–69; support of coaches for, 169–72

walk-ons, 38–40

We Are United movement. *See* COVID-19

Weiss, Kurt (pseudonym): abusive behavior by coaches and, 163; athletic trainers and, 82; biographical information of, 211; coercion and, 145–46, 149, 153; consent and, 160; drug and alcohol use and, 86–87, 130; expenses and, 31; exploitation and, 34–35; fights and, 68–69; financial costs of injuries and, 107; head trauma and, 102–3, 113; impermissible benefits and, 33; insurance and, 106; long-term consequences of injuries and, 99; pain vs injury and, 78–79; playing through injury and, 72–73, 76; quality of care received and, 83–84; sports media and, 11; voluntary workouts and, 153

West, Landry (pseudonym): abusive behavior by coaches and, 169; biographical information of, 211; coercion and, 148, 157; drug and alcohol use and, 88–89; healthism and, 75; punishments and, 64; selective drug testing and, 155

We Want to Play movement. *See* COVID-19

White, C. J. (pseudonym): academics and, 50, 53; athletic trainers and, 82; biographical information of, 209; exploitation and, 29; head trauma and, 100–101; indirect costs of injuries and, 108; playing through injury and, 79; racism and, 134; stereotyping of athletes and, 54–55

white supremacy. *See* racism

Williamson, Marcus, 144–45

Wilson, Donald, 70

Wolfe, Cameron, 184

Wolfe, Tim, 202

9 781469 683461